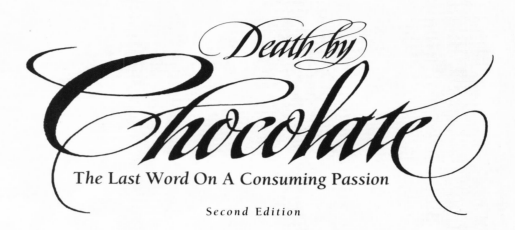

# Death by Chocolate

## The Last Word On A Consuming Passion

### Second Edition

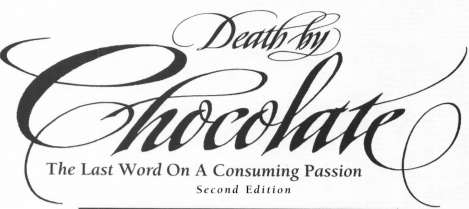

# Death by Chocolate

## The Last Word On A Consuming Passion

### Second Edition

# Marcel Desaulniers

### of the Trellis Restaurant

### Photography by Michael Grand

# RIZZOLI
NEW YORK

**A KENAN BOOK**

Published in the United States of America in 2003 by
Rizzoli International Publications, Inc.
300 Park Avenue South, New York, NY 10010
Original edition published in 1992

Library of Congress Cataloging-in-Publication Data

Desaulniers, Marcel.
    Death by chocolate / second edition: the last word~on a consuming passion!/ Marcel
Desaulniers; recipes with John Twichell; photographs by Michael Grand; additional
photographs by Ron Manville.
          p.      cm.
      Includes bibliographical references and index.
      ISBN  0-8478-2557-4
      1.  Cookery (Chocolate).   2.  Chocolate.   3.  Trellis Restaurant.
    I.  Twichell, John.   II.  Grand, Michael.   III.  Title.
    TX767.C5D47   1992
    641.6'374- - dc2O                                91-45878
                                                        CIP

*DEATH BY CHOCOLATE*
*The Last Word on a Consuming Passion*
was prepared and produced by
Kenan Books, Inc.
611 Broadway
New York, New York 10012

Second Edition produced by
Hudson Park Press
New York

Photography © Michael Grand 1992, 2003
Photography © Ron Manville 2003
Illustration © Cynthia Busch 1992

Typeset by Classic Type, Inc.
Color separations by United South Sea Graphic Art Co.
Printed in Singapore by KHL Printing Co. Pte. Ltd.

## DEDICATION

*Chocolate, the food of the gods*
*Connie, the food of my passion*

## ACKNOWLEDGMENTS

*A sincere thank you to the following folks for making this new edition of* Death by Chocolate *possible: My agent and friend Dan Green; the management at Rizzoli International Publications, Inc.; Brett Bailey, former test kitchen chef at Ganache Hill; Ron Manville for his photos of the new recipes; Michael Grand, the original photographer; business partner and friend John Curtis; Trellis pastry chef Kelly Bailey, assistant pastry chef Shelley Salko; Trellis head chef Michael Holdsworth, senior assistant chef Steve Francisco. Additionally, my mom, Mrs D.; my friend Penny Seu; and my alma mater, the Culinary Institute of America.*

*Preface by John Ballinger*

# A DEATH BY CHOCOLATE

....................................................................................

Brad Parker was sitting in his bookshop in Williamsburg, Virginia, examining a copy of the 1511 edition of Vitruvius *that* someone had offered to sell him, when he glanced up to see Antoine Rustermann standing in the doorway of Parker's Rare Books.

"Come quickly," he said to Brad and then ran across the small brick patio that separated the bookshop from Rustermann's restaurant. Brad had never seen Antoine so upset and quickly followed.

Brad found Antoine in the restaurant's garden room, next to a table where the eminent rare-book dealer, Antonio Raimo, sat slumped forward, his head on the table, the victim of an apparent heart attack.

Brad rushed over and felt in vain for a pulse. "Did the waiter present Mr. Raimo with the bill?" Brad asked.

"No, we were just having dessert," Jennifer Raimo, Tony's wife, answered.

"Death By Chocolate," said Antoine in a dazed monotone. It was the first time Brad noticed how suspiciously thin and fit Antoine was for a world-class chef.

"That was what Tony ordered," Jennifer explained. "He's not much around the kitchen, and he tried in vain for the last two months to make the dessert from a recipe in the Death By Chocolate cookbook. Seeing a slice of it perfectly prepared apparently was too much for his system."

"We'll have to rule out poison," Brad said, wrestling the fork from Raimo's clenched fist. "I'd better have a taste."

"I'll help," Jennifer replied.

Charles Cadbury, the homicide detective, came five minutes later.

"What happened here?" he asked.

"Death By Chocolate," Antoine replied.

But by then the evidence had disappeared.

JOHN BALLINGER, A RESIDENT OF WILLIAMSBURG, IS CO-OWNER OF THE BOOKPRESS, AN ANTIQUARIAN BOOKSTORE, LOCATED NEXT DOOR TO THE TRELLIS RESTAURANT. MR. BALLINGER IS THE AUTHOR OF THE WILLIAMSBURG FORGERIES, ST. MARTIN'S PRESS, NEW YORK, 1989.

# INTRODUCTION

*Oh how sweet! More than ten years after* Death by Chocolate *was first published, I am pleased to note that my demise by chocolate has been greatly exaggerated. In fact, my own love affair with chocolate (as well as that of the general public) has only intensified during this time. During the past decade, chocolate has received so many accolades for bringing people who love it together, that it won't be long before chocolate is awarded a Nobel Peace Prize.*

*Chocolate lovers have always known what medical research has recently confirmed: chocolate is good for your heart. Chocolate has made people happy for centuries. Of course, in ancient Incan civilization, eating chocolate was part of a deadly act: a "bittersweet" drink of chocolate was used to sanctify the souls of human sacrifices. Alas, many years passed before chocolate was available as a sweet treat to sanctify the souls of the living. Once brought to Europe, chocolate was greedily hoarded by royalty, who did not want their subjects to be distracted by the passion that chocolate unleashed. It is no wonder that princely heads would roll before the populace was able to indulge. Fortunately, chocolate is now available to everyone. The lucky ones know how it deliciously seduces the mouth and the soul. A few more know that it is good for you as well!*

*First extolled by hedonists, chocolate's health benefits have now been confirmed by a legion of researchers, doctors, and chemists. Chocolate contains anandamide, a substance that mimics the euphoria of marijuana. Chocolate also contains a class of chemicals (phenolics) that help lower cholesterol, and is loaded with powerful antioxidant properties that have proven beneficial in warding off a number of diseases.*

*If those extraordinary data are not enough to encourage your obsession, I have included information in this second edition of* Death by Chocolate *that makes chocolate preparation stress-free (see page 152 for the section on melting chocolate in the microwave) plus four new spectacular chocolate delectations that will tantalize your five senses as no other obsession has ever done.*

*The "Big Dig," named after Boston's seemingly endless public roads project, is a construction* tour de force *that provides a forklift of chocolate textures, flavors, and hues. You better buckle up for the chaotically chocolaty "Cowboy Syd's Sextuple Truffle Tart." And, prepare to forgo innocence for the tongue-tingling amalgam of chocolate and apples in the "Chocolate Applesauce Spice Cake." Finally, be forewarned that not only your dentist will be smiling when you bite down into the crackling bliss of "Chocolate Caramel Popcorn Crunch."*

*My friends, now is the time to be resurrected by chocolate.*

— **MARCEL DESAULNIERS**
Williamsburg, Virginia
www.dessertstodiefor.com

# CHOCOLATE CHIPS AND CHUNKS

## *BITS AND PIECES OF INFORMATION ABOUT CHOCOLATE*

### CHOCOLATE

Chocolate is indeed mysterious. Its ancient history is clouded by pagan rituals and human sacrifices. Cacao trees, bearing the cacao pods from which chocolate is manufactured, were cultivated by Central and South American Indians. The harvest was used for a bitter drink that was thought to have aphrodisiacal powers. And so it was that for hundreds of years chocolate was enjoyed solely as a beverage. Chocolate as we enjoy it today is a contemporary concoction. "Eating chocolate" was not discovered until the nineteenth century. Happily, for those who love chocolate, there has never been such variety and quality available. Just like the birds and monkeys of Central America who spread the seeds of their addiction to cacao pods, so have contemporary chocophiles traveled and learned and developed chocolate confections that deliver the most pleasurable sensual experiences known, some of which can be found in the pages of this book.

### CHOCOLATE AS A PANACEA

Chocolate is a perfect food, as wholesome as it is delicious, a beneficent restorer of exhausted power; but its quality must be good, and it must be carefully prepared. It is highly nourishing and easily digested, and it is fitted to repair wasted strength, preserve health, and prolong life. It agrees with dry temperaments and convalescents, with mothers who nurse their children, with those whose occupations oblige them to undergo severe mental strains, with public speakers, and with all those who give to work a portion of the time needed for sleep. It soothes both stomach and brain, and for this reason, as well as for others, it is the best friend of those engaged in literary pursuits.

Baron von Liebig
Renowned Know-It-All

There is conclusive evidence today of the alimentary value of chocolate. It contains calcium, phosphorous, potassium, thiamine, riboflavin, niacin, and vitamin A. Of course, it is not a cure-all; rather, it is a food that brings great pleasure to the palate along with its nutritive value.

At The Trellis, "great pleasure" means great big portions of chocolate desserts—"theme-park-size desserts," according to some. Our portions are large; however, we do encourage our guests to share (although few do). The suggested servings noted with each recipe in this book relate to the size of the portion we serve at the restaurant. Significantly more portions can be cut from our desserts; however, in the instance of confections such as Death By Chocolate, it becomes difficult to stand a slice if the cake is cut too thin. If you have no aesthetic objections to placing a piece of cake on its side, then many of our desserts can serve up to twice as many people as the serving yield specifies.

### QUALITY OF CHOCOLATE

If you purchase *real* chocolate, manufactured by companies such as Baker's, Hershey's, and Nestlé, you cannot go wrong with the recipes in this book. After extensive testing and 12 years of extremely successful chocolate dessert sales at The Trellis, I can unequivocally state that the chocolate I mentioned above will produce spectacular desserts.

I emphasize using real chocolate because most major American chocolate manufacturers also market chocolate-flavored products. I always take a second look at the label of ingredients when purchasing chocolate. Be certain that you are not purchasing an item with fat additives such as palm kernel oil, or extenders such as soy flour. Good chocolate will usually contain nothing more than chocolate, sugar, cocoa butter, lecithin (an emulsifier), and vanilla.

## STORING CHOCOLATE

According to the experts, the optimum storage condition for chocolate is a well-ventilated area, free of foreign odors. The temperature should range between 65 to 68 degrees Fahrenheit with 50 percent relative humidity (in short, keep it dry and cool). Contrary to what many experts suggest, I have stored well-wrapped chocolate in both the refrigerator and the freezer with no apparent deterioration in quality. My best advice on this subject is to purchase enough chocolate for short-term needs. There is no sense buying chocolate that will not be used within a few weeks. However, if you do plan on purchasing chocolate for long-term storage, I suggest keeping it in the freezer. Allow the frozen chocolate to come to room temperature before using it in a recipe.

## TYPES OF CHOCOLATE USED IN THIS RECIPE BOOK

**Unsweetened chocolate** is hardened, pure, chocolate liquor (also known as *bitter* or *baking* chocolate). Chocolate liquor contains about 45 percent cocoa solids and 50 percent cocoa butter. The brand we used for testing recipes in this book was Baker's. The brand used at The Trellis is Baker's as well. Other acceptable brands available in grocery stores are Hershey's and Nestlé.

**Semisweet chocolate** is chocolate liquor that contains varying amounts of sugar, vanilla, and emulsifiers. (Bittersweet chocolate is similar to semisweet chocolate and they are interchangeable in any of our recipes.) Semisweet chocolate contains a minimum of 35 percent chocolate liquor, although the highest-quality bittersweet usually contains more. The brand we used for testing recipes in this book was Baker's. The brand used at The Trellis is Baker's as well. Other acceptable brands available in grocery stores are Lindt, Hershey's, and Nestlé.

**White chocolate** is essentially milk chocolate without cocoa solids. In the United States, the term "white chocolate" is a misnomer. By law, a product labeled "chocolate" must contain cocoa solids. Good-quality white chocolate will contain appreciable amounts of cocoa butter, as well as sugar, milk, and vanillin. The brand we used for testing recipes in this book was Tobler. The brand used at The Trellis is Cacao Barry. Another acceptable brand available in grocery stores is Droste's.

**Cocoa** is a highly concentrated powder produced by hydraulically pressing finely ground unsweetened chocolate. This process removes most of the cocoa butter from the chocolate. Cocoa is relatively low in fat compared to chocolate, and it delivers an intensely rich flavor. The brands used for testing recipes in this book were Hershey's Unsweetened, Nestlé's Unsweetened and Baker's Unsweetened. The brand used at The Trellis is Hershey's Unsweetened. Another acceptable brand available in grocery stores is Droste's Dutch Processed.

**Chocolate chips** must have a high fat content—about 27 to 30 percent—if they are to retain their shape during baking. Look for chips that have cocoa butter listed as the fat additive rather than palm oil. If you are purchasing chips to eat out of hand or to add to ice cream, choose a chip with no added fat, such as Guittard.

The brand used for testing recipes in this book was Baker's Semisweet Real Chocolate Chips. The brand used at The Trellis is Ambrosia Bittersweet. Other acceptable brands available in grocery stores are Hershey's Real Semisweet, Nestlé Real Semisweet Morsels, and Guittard.

## INGREDIENTS USED FOR OUR RECIPES

With one or two exceptions (white chocolate being one, unsalted nuts being the other), all the ingredients used to prepare desserts at The Trellis on a daily basis are available in most grocery stores or supermarkets. In fact, in order to be certain that the ingredients we used for testing the recipes in this book would be authentic, we actually purchased most of them in a local grocery store in Williamsburg, Virginia. The point is that first-class desserts can be produced at home with ingredients that are readily available.

Note: All eggs used should be "large."

## RECIPE DEVELOPMENT AND TESTING

Almost all the recipes in this book are based on desserts produced at The Trellis. All of the recipes have been painstakingly tested and retested. First, pastry chef John Twichell translated our restaurant recipes into a consumer-size version and then tested them at The Trellis, using the same equipment one would find in a reasonably well-equipped home kitchen. The baking was done with a Maytag model LCNE20 electric range.

John and I tested the recipes again in my own home kitchen on a General Electric model JBP22 electric range, making any necessary adjustments.

Our recipes may not be foolproof; however, the quality and honesty of the testing, as well as our detailed and explicit instructions, make successful Trellis chocolate desserts probable for those inclined to spend the time and to display the love of *metier* (craft).

# CHAPTER ONE

# SINGULAR SENSATIONS

*ESSENTIAL INDULGENCES FOR THE SERIOUS CHOCOPHILE*

# BITTERSWEET CHOCOLATE SAUCE

YIELDS 3 CUPS

### THE CHEF'S TOUCH

*The silky texture and fine luster of our Bittersweet Chocolate Sauce makes it a star on its own merit. Now, I am not suggesting that you sit down to a bowl of Bittersweet Chocolate Sauce; rather I submit that pairing a sauce of this caliber with other confections comes easily.*

*One of my favorite dessert presentations using this sauce consists of 4 oval scoops of White Chocolate "Ice Cream" (see page 35) positioned in a cluster on a pool of Bittersweet Chocolate Sauce. In the center of the cluster, place a peeled, ineffably piquant clementine from Morocco. (Clementines are tiny mandarin oranges. They are available during December and January. Besides the fact that they are delicious, I also love clementines because they peel like tangerines and are practically seedless.)*

*Serve the Bittersweet Chocolate Sauce at room temperature or slightly warm.*

2 cups heavy cream
³/₄ cup granulated sugar
2 tablespoons unsalted butter
¹/₄ teaspoon salt

4 ounces unsweetened chocolate, broken into ¹/₂-ounce pieces
¹/₂ teaspoon pure vanilla extract

**EQUIPMENT**
*Measuring cup, measuring spoons, 2¹/₂-quart saucepan, 2 stainless steel bowls (1 large), whisk, instant-read test thermometer, plastic container with lid*

Heat the heavy cream, sugar, butter, and salt in a 2¹/₂-quart saucepan over medium-high heat, stirring to dissolve the sugar. Bring to a boil. Place the unsweetened chocolate in a stainless steel bowl. Pour the boiling cream mixture over the chocolate and allow to stand for 5 minutes. Whisk vigorously until smooth.

Cool the Bittersweet Chocolate Sauce in an ice-water bath (see page 150) to a temperature of 40 to 45 degrees Fahrenheit, about 15 minutes. When cold, stir in the vanilla. Transfer to a plastic container. Securely cover and refrigerate until ready to use. The Bittersweet Chocolate Sauce may be kept refrigerated up to 5 days.

# HOT "LIQUOR" SAUCE

YIELDS 3 CUPS

### THE CHEF'S TOUCH

*This all-purpose hot fudge sauce is just the sort of final touch we like to lavish onto our desserts at The Trellis. Serve this sauce with an oversized balloon glass filled with White Chocolate "Ice Cream" (see page 35); a slice of Chocolate Cashew Brownie Cake (see page 74); and, one of my favorite overindulgences, "Hot" Chocolate Cake (see page 30).*

*The Hot "Liquor" Sauce may be refrigerated after it cools to room temperature. Keep the sauce in a sealed plastic container with lid for several days. Slowly warm the sauce in a double boiler before serving.*

1¹/₂ cups heavy cream
9 tablespoons unsalted butter
1 cup granulated sugar

1 cup tightly packed dark brown sugar
1¹/₂ cups Hershey's unsweetened cocoa, sifted
¹/₄ teaspoon salt

**EQUIPMENT**
*Measuring cup, measuring spoons, sifter, 2¹/₂-quart saucepan, whisk, double boiler*

Heat the heavy cream and butter in a 2¹/₂-quart saucepan over medium heat. Bring to a boil. Add the granulated sugar and dark brown sugar, stirring until they have dissolved. Remove from the heat. Allow the cream to cool for 5 minutes before adding the sifted cocoa and the salt. Whisk until smooth.

Keep the Hot "Liquor" Sauce warm in a double boiler over low heat until ready to serve.

# Mocha Anglaise

YIELDS 3 CUPS

1  cup heavy cream
1  cup whole milk
1/2  cup granulated sugar
4  egg yolks
1  teaspoon cornstarch

2  ounces semisweet chocolate, broken into
    1/2-ounce pieces
1  ounce unsweetened chocolate, broken into
    1/2-ounce pieces
1/2  teaspoon instant espresso powder
1/2  teaspoon pure vanilla extract

**EQUIPMENT**

Measuring cup, measuring spoons, 2 1/2-quart saucepan, 2 stainless steel bowls (1 large), whisk, metal spoon, instant-read test thermometer, plastic container with lid

Heat the heavy cream, milk, and 1/4 cup of sugar in a 2 1/2-quart saucepan over medium-high heat and bring to a boil.

While the cream is heating, whisk the egg yolks, remaining sugar, and cornstarch in a stainless steel bowl for 3 minutes. Pour the boiling cream into this mixture and stir gently to combine. Return to the saucepan and heat over medium-high heat, stirring constantly. Bring to a temperature of 180 degrees Fahrenheit, 1 1/2 to 2 minutes. Place the semisweet and unsweetened chocolate and the espresso powder in a stainless steel bowl. Pour the hot cream and egg mixture over the chocolate. Stir gently until the chocolate is thoroughly dissolved and combined.

Cool the Mocha Anglaise in an ice-water bath (see page 150) to a temperature of 40 degrees Fahrenheit, about 15 minutes. When cold, stir in the vanilla extract. Transfer to a plastic container. Securely cover and refrigerate until ready to use. The Anglaise may be kept refrigerated for up to 3 days.

**THE CHEF'S TOUCH**

*This elegant sauce is part of our Phantasmagoria presentation (see page 128). It can be used with less complicated desserts, say 3 oval scoops of Dark Chocolate Mousse (see page 32) placed in a pool of Mocha Anglaise and finished with toasted almonds, or enjoyed with Dark Chocolate and Pumpkin Cheesecake (see page 90).*

# MOCHA RUM SAUCE

YIELDS 3 CUPS

*O*riginally developed by pastry chef Donald Mack to accompany Death By Chocolate (see page 135), this Mocha Rum Sauce is a synergy of cocoa, rum, and coffee. The total effect is, I believe, quite sensual. I love the way this sauce couples with so many desserts, and I am passionate about the way the taste of the sauce rolls over the palate in a surge of flavor.

The room temperature Mocha Rum Sauce may be transferred to a plastic container and stored in the refrigerator for several days. Bring the sauce to room temperature before serving.

| | |
|---|---|
| 6 ounces unsalted butter | 3 tablespoons Myers's Dark Rum |
| 1¹/₃ cups granulated sugar | ¹/₄ teaspoon salt |
| 1¹/₃ cups heavy cream | 4 teaspoons instant coffee |
| 8 tablespoons unsweetened cocoa, sifted | 1 teaspoon pure vanilla extract |

## EQUIPMENT
*Measuring cup, sifter, measuring spoons, 2¹/₂-quart saucepan, whisk*

Heat the butter in a 2¹/₂-quart saucepan over medium heat. When melted, add the sugar, heavy cream, sifted cocoa, 2 tablespoons rum, and salt. Stir with a whisk to combine. Bring to a boil, then adjust the heat and allow to simmer for 5 minutes, stirring occasionally. Remove the saucepan from the heat. Add the instant coffee, vanilla extract, and the remaining tablespoon of rum, and stir until smooth. Allow to cool to room temperature before serving.

# WHITE CHOCOLATE SAUCE

YIELDS 3 CUPS

*I* certainly could fill up this page with many amicable unions of this sauce, but I will limit myself to my favorite confluence: generously pour White Chocolate Sauce over several scoops of Chocolate Raspberry Toasted Hazelnut Ice Cream (see page 45).

| |
|---|
| 2 cups heavy cream |
| 8 ounces white chocolate, broken into |
| ¹/₂-ounce pieces |
| ¹/₂ teaspoon pure vanilla extract |

## EQUIPMENT
*Measuring cup, measuring spoons, 2¹/₂-quart saucepan, 2 stainless steel bowls (1 large), film wrap, whisk, instant-read test thermometer, plastic container with lid*

Heat the heavy cream in a 2¹/₂-quart saucepan over medium-high heat. Bring to a boil. Place the white chocolate in a stainless steel bowl and pour the boiling cream over the chocolate. Tightly cover the top with film wrap and allow to stand for 5 minutes. Remove the film wrap and whisk until smooth.

Cool the white chocolate sauce in an ice-water bath (see page 150) to a temperature of 40 to 45 degrees Fahrenheit, about 15 minutes. When cold, stir in the vanilla. Transfer to a plastic container. Securely cover and refrigerate until ready to use. The White Chocolate Sauce may be kept refrigerated for up to 5 days.

# Semisweet Chocolate Ganache

YIELDS 2 CUPS

1 *cup heavy cream*
2 *tablespoons unsalted butter*
2 *tablespoons granulated sugar*
12 *ounces semisweet chocolate, broken into $^1/_2$-ounce pieces*

**Equipment**
*Measuring cup, measuring spoons, $2^1/_2$-quart saucepan, whisk, stainless steel bowl*

Heat the heavy cream, butter, and sugar in a $2^1/_2$-quart saucepan over medium-high heat. When hot, stir to dissolve the sugar. Bring the mixture to a boil. Place the chocolate in a stainless steel bowl. Pour the boiling cream over the chocolate and allow to stand for 5 minutes. Stir until smooth. Allow to cool to room temperature.

**THE CHEF'S TOUCH**

*Our method for preparing ganache is simple and virtually guaranteed to produce a smooth and silky icing or filling.*

*This is the designated ganache in three of our dessert recipes in this book: Dark Chocolate and Pumpkin Cheesecake (see page 90); Chocolate Strawberry Mousse Cake (see page 80); and Caramel Rum Delirium Ice Cream Cake (see page 108).*

# The Ultimate Chocolate Ganache

YIELDS 1 QUART

2 *cups heavy cream*
4 *tablespoons unsalted butter*
4 *tablespoons granulated sugar*
12 *ounces semisweet chocolate, broken into $^1/_2$-ounce pieces*
6 *ounces unsweetened chocolate, broken into $^1/_2$-ounce pieces*
4 *ounces white chocolate, broken into $^1/_2$-ounce pieces*

**Equipment**
*Measuring cup, measuring spoons, $2^1/_2$-quart saucepan, whisk, stainless steel bowl, plastic container with lid*

Heat the heavy cream, butter, and sugar in a $2^1/_2$-quart saucepan over medium-high heat. Stir to dissolve the sugar. Bring the mixture to a boil. Place the semisweet, unsweetened, and white chocolates in a stainless steel bowl. Pour the boiling cream over the chocolates and allow to stand for 5 minutes. Stir until smooth. Allow to cool to room temperature.

**THE CHEF'S TOUCH**

*Why an ultimate ganache? Why drive an automobile capable of going 120 miles per hour when the speed limit does not exceed 65 miles per hour? The answer is that when you need it—it's there.*

*Quite simply, this is supernal food. Just imagine a mountain cabin, a mellow fire, chilled Iron Horse Blanc de Blancs, and great big California strawberries to dip into a bowl of slightly warm ultimate ganache.*

*The Ultimate Chocolate Ganache can be used slightly warm as a sauce, at room temperature to ice an endless array of confections, piped chilled from a pastry bag to garnish desserts, and ad infinitum with anything you like.*

# CHAPTER TWO

# SIMPLY CHOCOLATE

*RECIPES THAT ARE EASY TO PREPARE
AND EVEN EASIER TO CONSUME*

# Chocolate Honey Almond Crunch

YIELDS ABOUT 2 3/4 POUNDS

- 4 *cups sliced almonds*
- 6 *ounces unsalted butter*
- 1 1/2 *cups granulated sugar*
- 1/2 *cup water*
- 1/4 *cup Myers's Dark Rum*
- 1/4 *cup honey*
- 8 *ounces semisweet chocolate, chopped into 1/4-inch pieces*
- 4 *ounces unsweetened chocolate, chopped into 1/4-inch pieces*

**Equipment**

*Measuring cups, cook's knife, cutting board, 2 9- by 13-inch baking sheets with sides, 2 1/2-quart saucepan, metal spoon, candy thermometer, cake spatula, plastic container with lid*

Preheat the oven to 325 degrees Fahrenheit.

Toast 2 cups of almonds on a baking sheet in the preheated oven until golden brown, about 12 to 14 minutes. Remove the almonds from the oven and allow to cool to room temperature. Transfer the almonds to a large dish or other suitable container and set aside until needed.

Melt the butter in a 2 1/2-quart saucepan over low heat, stirring constantly as it melts so it does not simmer or boil. As soon as the butter is completely melted, add the sugar, water, rum, and honey. Increase the heat to medium high. Heat the mixture to a temperature of 220 degrees Fahrenheit, stirring constantly. Add the untoasted almonds and continue to heat and stir until the mixture reaches a temperature of 225 degrees Fahrenheit.

Evenly divide the honey-almond mixture between the 2 baking sheets. Place the baking sheets on the top and middle shelves of the preheated oven and bake until the mixture is evenly caramelized, about 24 to 26 minutes. Rotate the baking sheets from top to bottom about halfway through the baking time. Remove from the oven and allow to cool for 5 minutes.

Combine the semisweet and unsweetened chocolate pieces and evenly divide and sprinkle over the surface of the caramelized honey-almond mixture. Allow to stand for 5 minutes. Use a spatula to spread the chocolate throughout the mixture. Evenly divide and sprinkle the toasted almonds over the chocolate. Place both baking sheets in the freezer for 20 minutes.

Remove the Chocolate Honey Almond Crunch from the freezer and break into irregular pieces. Store in a sealed plastic container in the freezer or refrigerator.

**The Chef's Touch**

*This candy is quite delicious eaten by itself or used in the following manner: chop the frozen crunch into 1/2-inch pieces and fold it into a semifrozen dark chocolate ice cream; freeze for several hours before serving. Now you have Double Chocolate Honey Almond Crunch Ice Cream!*

*If the chocolate pieces do not completely melt on top of the honey-almond mixture, pop the baking sheets back into the oven for 10 to 15 seconds.*

*Although we suggest freezing the Chocolate Honey Almond Crunch for 20 minutes before breaking it into irregular pieces, it is also possible to set this candy in the refrigerator for 45 minutes or keep it at room temperature (68 to 72 degrees Fahrenheit) for 2 hours before breaking it into pieces.*

# CHOCOLATE PEANUT BUTTER CHOCOLATE CHIP COOKIES

MAKES 3 DOZEN COOKIES

*This is a cookie lover's cookie. I love to watch the expression elicited by the first bite into this sweet. At the risk of sounding like a politician, I can guarantee smiles whenever you offer these goober- and chocolate-chip-laden morsels.*

*We use the same peanut butter at The Trellis that I have been enjoying for more years than I like to admit— Skippy Creamy Peanut Butter.*

*It is not necessary to use parchment paper, nor is it necessary to butter the baking sheets for these cookies. If you are the proud owner of nonstick baking sheets, you may certainly use them. I suggest using a baking sheet with sides for toasting the peanuts; this will prevent you from scrambling around for itinerant peanuts.*

*You may bake these cookies two baking sheets at a time on the top and middle shelves of your oven. Rotate the baking sheets from top to bottom about halfway through the baking time. Since the recipe makes 3 dozen cookies, you will have one more baking sheet of cookies to bake. Be certain the baking sheet is at room temperature before using it to bake the final dozen cookies.*

$1/2$ cup unsalted shelled Virginia peanuts
6 ounces semisweet chocolate, broken into $1/2$-ounce pieces
1 cup creamy peanut butter
$3/4$ cup tightly packed light brown sugar
$1/4$ pound unsalted butter
1 egg
1 teaspoon pure vanilla extract
2 cups chocolate chips
$1 1/2$ cups all-purpose flour
$3/4$ teaspoon baking soda

### EQUIPMENT

*Measuring cup, measuring spoons, 2 baking sheets (1 with sides), food processor fitted with a metal blade, double boiler, film wrap, electric mixer with paddle, rubber spatula, 2 tablespoons, dinner fork, cooling rack*

Preheat the oven to 300 degrees Fahrenheit.

Toast the peanuts on a baking sheet with sides in the preheated oven until golden brown, about 8 minutes. Remove from the oven and allow to cool to room temperature.

In the bowl of a food processor fitted with a metal blade, chop the peanuts into pieces $1/8$ inch in size. Set aside until needed.

Heat 1 inch of water in the bottom half of a double boiler over medium heat. Place the semi-sweet chocolate in the top half of the double boiler (see page 151). Tightly cover the top with film wrap and allow to heat for 6 to 7 minutes. Remove from heat and stir until smooth. Keep at room temperature until needed.

Place the peanut butter, brown sugar, and butter in the bowl of an electric mixer fitted with a paddle. Beat on low for 2 minutes, then on high for $2 1/2$ minutes. Scrape down the bowl and beat on high for an additional 2 minutes. Add the egg and beat on high for 1 minute. Scrape down the bowl.

Continuing to beat on high, add the vanilla extract and beat for 30 seconds. Add the melted chocolate and beat for 30 seconds more. Scrape down the bowl and beat for an additional 30 seconds. Add the chocolate chips, flour, baking soda, and chopped peanuts and combine on low for 45 seconds. Remove the bowl from the mixer and mix thoroughly with a rubber spatula.

Portion by rounding 2 tablespoons of dough into 1 dough ball, approximately $1 1/4$ inch in diameter. Place 12 balls on each baking sheet. Using the back of a dinner fork, gently press each ball to slightly flatten the dough. Place the cookies in the preheated oven and bake for 20 to 22 minutes. Allow the cookies to cool for 3 to 4 minutes on the baking sheets. Transfer the cookies to a cooling rack to cool thoroughly.

# CHOCOLATE TRINITY PARFAITS

MAKES 8 PARFAITS

12 ounces semisweet chocolate (8 ounces broken into 1/2-ounce pieces and 4 ounces finely grated)
6 1/2 cups heavy cream

3/4 cup granulated sugar
2 tablespoons unsweetened cocoa
1 teaspoon pure vanilla extract

**EQUIPMENT**

*Measuring cup, measuring spoons, hand grater, double boiler, film wrap, whisk, 3 stainless steel bowls, electric mixer with balloon whip, rubber spatula, film wrap, pastry bag, 8 12-ounce brandy snifters*

To prepare the dark chocolate cream, heat 1 inch of water in the bottom half of a double boiler over medium heat. Place the 8 ounces semisweet chocolate broken into pieces in the top half of the double boiler (see page 151). Tightly cover the top with film wrap and allow to heat for 8 to 10 minutes. Remove from the heat and stir until smooth. Transfer the melted chocolate to a stainless steel bowl and set aside until needed.

Place 2 1/2 cups heavy cream and 2 tablespoons sugar in the well-chilled bowl of an electric mixer fitted with a well-chilled balloon whip (see page 151). Whisk on high until stiff peaks form, about 1 1/2 minutes. Remove the bowl from the mixer. Use a hand whisk to combine 1/4 of the whipped cream into the melted chocolate until smooth and completely incorporated. Add the combined whipped cream and chocolate to the remaining whipped cream and use a rubber spatula to fold together. Transfer the dark chocolate cream to a stainless steel bowl. Tightly cover the top with film wrap and refrigerate until needed.

To prepare the cocoa cream, place 2 cups heavy cream, 1/2 cup sugar, the cocoa, and 1/2 teaspoon vanilla extract in the well-chilled bowl of an electric mixer fitted with a well-chilled balloon whip. Mix on medium until stiff peaks form, about 4 to 5 minutes. Transfer the cocoa cream to a stainless steel bowl. Tightly cover the top with film wrap and refrigerate until needed.

To prepare the speckled chocolate cream, place the remaining 2 cups heavy cream, 2 tablespoons sugar, and 1/2 teaspoon vanilla extract in the well-chilled bowl of an electric mixer fitted with a well-chilled balloon whip. Mix on high until stiff peaks form, about 1 1/4 minutes. Remove the bowl from the mixer and use a rubber spatula to fold in the 4 ounces grated chocolate. Transfer the cream to a stainless steel bowl. Tightly cover the top with film wrap, and refrigerate for at least 30 minutes before assembling the parfaits.

To assemble the parfaits, fill a pastry bag (without a tip) with the dark chocolate cream. Pipe an even layer of about 1/2 cup of the cream into each of the brandy snifters. Then fill a clean pastry bag with the cocoa cream and pipe an even layer of it onto the layer of dark chocolate cream. For the final layer of cream, fill a clean pastry bag with the speckled chocolate cream and pipe an even layer of the cream onto the cocoa cream. Refrigerate the parfaits until just a few minutes before serving.

**THE CHEF'S TOUCH**

*Most Americans think of a tall, slender glass filled with ice cream when a parfait is mentioned. Actually, a classic parfait is prepared with whipped cream.*

*On July 4, 1985, at the idiosyncratic Paris restaurant Le Vivarois, I had a delightfully light-tasting, parfait-like dessert made with whipped cream that had been combined with fresh red raspberries and raspberry puree. The top of the confection had been sprinkled with broken pieces of puff pastry. The concept of this dessert was pure simplicity, yet the appearance and eating experience suggested a much more complex preparation. Since that time, we have done many variations on this theme at The Trellis. As you might guess, my favorite is prepared with chocolate.*

*The cocoa cream is mixed on medium speed to allow sufficient time to dissolve the larger amount of sugar. This recipe may also be prepared using a hand-held mixer (mixing time may increase slightly), or by hand using a wire whisk (mixing time may double).*

*If using one pastry bag to pipe the 3 layers, the bag must be thoroughly cleaned and wiped dry before being filled with the different creams. If available, it would be more convenient to use 3 pastry bags.*

*Although we use large brandy snifters as parfait glasses at The Trellis, you may use any type and size glass you wish. Keep in mind that using a smaller glass will increase the number of portions in the recipe.*

*The snifters may be filled with the layers of cream 2 to 3 hours before serving. Cover the top of each with film wrap and keep in the refrigerator until a few minutes before serving. To serve, garnish as desired and present with a long-handled dessert spoon.*

*For a knockout dessert, top the parfaits with fresh berries and white- and dark-chocolate curls.*

# DEEP DARK CHOCOLATE FUDGE COOKIES

## (INCLUDING THE RECIPE FOR ABSOLUTELY DEEP DARK)

MAKES 3 TO 3 1/2 DOZEN COOKIES

*If a nocturnal lust for chocolate has you making furtive movements towards the kitchen, I suggest a few Absolutely Deep Dark Chocolate Fudge Cookies, each one dipped into your favorite chocolate ganache (there are several to choose from in this book). It is a fact that this confection will assuage even the most passionate chocophile, regardless of the hour.*

*I have specified Nestlé cocoa for this recipe because it delivers the deep dark chocolate flavor implied by the name of the cookie.*

*One and a half cups of tightly packed light brown sugar will weigh 12 ounces.*

*If you are making Absolutely Deep Dark Chocolate Cookies (and I highly recommend that you do so), the yield will remain the same—about 3 to 3 1/2 dozen cookies.*

*The cookies will be crisp around the edges following baking and cooling. Storing in an airtight plastic container after cooling will reduce the crispness of the cookies. Decide which texture you prefer and store accordingly (in or out of a sealed container).*

*This cookie was made for traveling: do not hesitate to send them to chocophiles everywhere.*

1 1/2 cups all-purpose flour
1/2 cup Nestlé unsweetened cocoa
1 teaspoon baking soda
1 teaspoon salt
8 ounces semisweet chocolate, broken into 1/2-ounce pieces
4 ounces unsweetened chocolate, broken into 1/2-ounce pieces

1 1/2 cups tightly packed light brown sugar
12 tablespoons unsalted butter
3 eggs
1 teaspoon pure vanilla extract

### ABSOLUTELY DEEP DARK

3 cups semisweet chocolate chips

### EQUIPMENT

*Measuring cup, measuring spoons, sifter, waxed paper, double boiler, film wrap, whisk, electric mixer with paddle, rubber spatula, 2 nonstick baking sheets, flexible pancake turner, cooling rack, plastic container with lid*

Preheat the oven to 325 degrees Fahrenheit.

Sift together the flour, cocoa, baking soda, and salt onto the waxed paper. Set aside.

Heat 1 inch of water in the bottom half of a double boiler over medium heat. Place the semisweet and the unsweetened chocolates in the top half of the double boiler (see page 151). Tightly cover the top with film wrap and allow to heat for 12 to 15 minutes. Remove from the heat and stir until smooth. Keep at room temperature until needed.

Place the light brown sugar and butter in the bowl of an electric mixer fitted with a paddle. Beat on medium for 1 minute. Scrape down the bowl and beat on high for an additional 30 seconds. Scrape down the bowl. Add the eggs, one at a time, while beating on medium, and stopping to scrape down the bowl after incorporating each addition. Add the vanilla extract and beat on medium for 30 seconds. Add the melted chocolate and beat on low for 10 seconds more. Scrape down the bowl and beat for an additional 30 seconds. Add the sifted flour, cocoa, and baking soda (also add the chocolate chips if making the Absolutely Deep Dark Chocolate Fudge Cookies), and beat on low until thoroughly combined, about 20 to 30 seconds. Remove the bowl from the mixer and mix thoroughly with a rubber spatula.

Portion 6 to 8 cookies per baking sheet by dropping 2 level tablespoons of batter per cookie onto each of the 2 baking sheets. Place the cookies on the top and middle shelves of the preheated oven and bake for 18 to 22 minutes, rotating the sheets from top to bottom about halfway through the baking time. Allow the cookies to cool for 5 to 6 minutes on the baking sheets. Transfer the cookies to a cooling rack to thoroughly cool before storing in a sealed plastic container. Repeat this procedure until all the cookies have been baked.

# "HOT" CHOCOLATE CAKE

SERVES 12 to 18

| | |
|---|---|
| 2 | cups plus 1 tablespoon all-purpose flour |
| 1¹/₂ | teaspoons baking powder |
| 1 | teaspoon baking soda |
| 1 | teaspoon salt |
| 3¹/₂ | ounces semisweet chocolate, broken into ¹/₂-ounce pieces |
| 1¹/₂ | ounces unsweetened chocolate, broken into ¹/₂-ounce pieces |
| ¹/₄ | cup brewed coffee, full-strength |
| 2 | tablespoons orange juice |
| 1 | teaspoon orange zest |
| 1 | teaspoon instant espresso powder |
| 1 | teaspoon cinnamon |
| ¹/₂ | teaspoon cayenne pepper |
| ¹/₄ | teaspoon cracked black pepper |
| 13 | tablespoons unsalted butter |
| 1 | cup very tightly packed light brown sugar |
| 4 | eggs |
| ¹/₂ | cup sour cream |
| 1 | cup pecan pieces, chopped into ¹/₈-inch pieces |

### EQUIPMENT

*Zester or vegetable peeler, cook's knife, cutting board, measuring cup, measuring spoons, stainless steel bowl, double boiler, film wrap, whisk, 9- by 13- by 2-inch rectangular cake pan, electric mixer with paddle, rubber spatula, cutting board, serrated slicer*

Preheat the oven to 350 degrees Fahrenheit.

Combine 2 cups flour, baking powder, baking soda, and salt in a stainless steel bowl. Set aside.

Heat 1 inch of water in the bottom half of a double boiler over medium heat. Place semisweet chocolate, unsweetened chocolate, coffee, orange juice, orange zest, espresso powder, cinnamon, cayenne pepper, and cracked black pepper in the top half of the double boiler (see page 151). Tightly cover the top with film wrap and heat for 6 to 8 minutes. Remove from heat and stir until smooth.

Coat a 9- by 13- by 2-inch rectangular cake pan with 1 tablespoon butter. Flour the pan with 1 tablespoon flour, shaking out the excess.

Place the brown sugar and remaining butter in the bowl of an electric mixer fitted with a paddle. Beat the sugar and butter on low for 3 minutes, then on high for 2 minutes. Scrape down the sides of the bowl. Beat on high until light and fluffy, about 3 to 4 minutes.

Add the eggs, one at a time, while beating on high for 1 minute after adding each egg. Scrape down the bowl before adding each egg. Add the melted chocolate and beat on high until thoroughly combined, about 30 seconds. Scrape down the bowl. Add the flour mixture and beat on low for 30 seconds. In the stainless steel bowl, vigorously whisk the sour cream. Add the sour cream to the cake mixture and combine on high for 10 seconds. Remove the mixing bowl from the mixer and use a rubber spatula to thoroughly combine.

Pour the batter into the prepared pan, spreading it evenly, including the corners. Sprinkle the chopped pecans evenly over the top of the batter. Bake in the preheated oven, until a toothpick inserted in the center of the cake comes out clean, about 35 to 40 minutes. Remove the cake from the oven and cool in the pan at room temperature for 15 minutes.

Remove the cake from the pan and place upright on a cutting board. Use a serrated slicer to cut the cake lengthwise across the center. To yield 12 portions, make 5 cuts across the width of the cake at 2¹/₄-inch intervals. For 18 servings, cut the cake lengthwise into thirds, then make 5 cuts across the width of the cake at 2¹/₄-inch intervals.

# EBONY AND IVORY CHOCOLATE TRUFFLES

MAKES ABOUT 3 DOZEN

7¹/₂ ounces white chocolate, chopped into
¹/₄-inch pieces
8 ounces semisweet chocolate, chopped into
¹/₄-inch pieces

³/₄ cup heavy cream
5 tablespoons unsweetened cocoa

### EQUIPMENT
*Cutting board, cook's knife, measuring cup, measuring spoons, 2 stainless steel bowls, 1¹/₂-quart saucepan, 2 whisks, baking sheet, parchment paper*

Place the white and dark chocolates into separate stainless steel bowls. Heat the cream in a 1¹/₂-quart saucepan over medium heat. Bring to a boil. Pour ¹/₄ cup of boiling cream over the white chocolate and the remaining ¹/₂ cup over the dark chocolate and allow to stand for 4 to 5 minutes. Stir each with a separate whisk until smooth, and allow to cool for 1 hour at room temperature. Refrigerate the two ganaches for 15 minutes, stirring every 5 minutes.

Line a baking sheet with parchment paper. Portion 36 heaping teaspoons of dark chocolate into separate mounds onto the parchment paper. Top each teaspoon of dark chocolate with a level teaspoon of white chocolate.

To fashion the truffles, roll each portion of chocolate in your palms in a gentle circular motion, using just enough pressure to form smooth rounds.

Roll the rounds of chocolate in cocoa until completely covered.

### THE CHEF'S TOUCH

*M*y first introduction to what many consider to be the quintessential chocolate confection—truffles—came at the women's club on Park Avenue, The Colony Club, where I worked for several months shortly after graduating from The Culinary Institute of America. The Italian-born pastry chef at The Colony was an extraordinary candy maker, and it was not long before I was able to sample many of his creations, including the mysterious dark, plump orbs that so quickly dissolved on the tongue surrendering an exquisite explosion of flavor.

If the heat of the cream is not sufficient to thoroughly melt the chocolate, or if the chocolate does not completely dissolve while you are stirring, then place the bowl of chocolate over very hot water (not simmering or boiling) and continue to stir to a smooth texture.

Frequently wipe your hands clean during the process of rolling the truffles. Some candy makers suggest dusting the palms of your hands with cocoa powder.

It is easier to completely cover the truffles with cocoa if they are rolled around in a substantial amount. The remaining 4 to 4¹/₂ tablespoons of cocoa may be sifted and saved for other uses.

In place of cocoa, you may enrobe the truffles with several other coatings: Deep Dark Chocolate Fudge Cookie Crumbs (see page 28), finely chopped nuts (macadamia nuts are terrific), shredded coconut, or the Ultimate Chocolate Ganache (see page 19). Another ploy for the candy maker is to place a pistachio or hazelnut in the center of the chocolate-truffle mixture and roll the chocolate around the nut.

The truffles may be refrigerated for several days before serving. Do, however, bring the truffles to room temperature before offering them to your guests (this will take 15 to 20 minutes).

If the truffles absorb the cocoa during refrigeration, simply roll them in more cocoa before serving.

# THE ESSENTIAL CHOCOLATE MOUSSES

Y I E L D S   1   Q U A R T   O F   E A C H   M O U S S E

*I*magine the soft, rounded peaks of a balloon glass filled with chocolate mousse. It's an elementary creation, you say. True, but in the hands of a careful and loving cook, it offers a sublime enjoyment for the palate.

For the Dark Chocolate Mousse, it is necessary to whip the cream and sugar on medium, rather than high, in order to provide the time to dissolve the sugar thoroughly.

In addition to the aforementioned balloon glass of mousse, many other presentations are appealing: alternate rings of White and Dark Chocolate Mousse sandwiched between two disks of baked meringue (a quickie dacquoise!); place egg-shaped scoops of both mousses in a pool of red raspberry purée; or fill a chocolate cup with mousse and decorate with chocolate curls.

If a table-model electric mixer is not available, this recipe may also be prepared using a hand-held mixer (mixing time may increase slightly), or by hand, using a wire whisk (mixing time may double).

## DARK CHOCOLATE MOUSSE

3   ounces unsweetened chocolate, broken into ¹/₂-ounce pieces
2   cups heavy cream
³/₄   cup granulated sugar

## WHITE CHOCOLATE MOUSSE

10   ounces white chocolate, broken into ¹/₂-ounce pieces
4   tablespoons water
2   cups heavy cream

## EQUIPMENT

*Measuring cup, measuring spoons, double boiler, film wrap, whisk, 2 stainless steel bowls, rubber spatula, electric mixer with balloon whip, 2 2-quart plastic containers with lids*

To make the Dark Chocolate Mousse, heat 1 inch of water in the bottom half of a double boiler over medium heat. Place the unsweetened chocolate in the top half of the double boiler (see page 151). Tightly cover the top with film wrap and allow to heat for 4 to 5 minutes. Remove from the heat and stir until smooth. Transfer the melted chocolate to a stainless steel bowl, using a rubber spatula to remove all the chocolate from the double boiler.

Place the heavy cream and the sugar in the well-chilled bowl of an electric mixer fitted with a well-chilled balloon whip. Mix on medium until soft peaks form, about 4 to 5 minutes.

Using a hand-held whisk, vigorously whisk 1¹/₂ cups of the whipped cream into the melted chocolate, scrape down the bowl with a rubber spatula, and continue to whisk until the cream and the chocolate are smooth and completely incorporated. Add the combined whipped cream and chocolate to the remaining whipped cream and use the rubber spatula to fold together until smooth.

Transfer the Dark Chocolate Mousse to a plastic container and refrigerate for 2 to 3 hours before serving.

For the White Chocolate Mousse, heat 1 inch of water in the bottom half of a double boiler over low heat. When the water is hot (do not allow to simmer), place white chocolate and 4 tablespoons of water in the top half of the double boiler. Using a rubber spatula, constantly stir the white chocolate and water until melted, about 4 to 5 minutes. Remove from the heat and keep at room temperature until needed.

Place the heavy cream in the well-chilled bowl of an electric mixer fitted with a well-chilled balloon whip. Mix on high until stiff, about 1 minute. Remove the bowl from the mixer. Using a hand-held whisk, vigorously whisk ¹/₃ of the whipped cream into the melted white chocolate. Scrape down the bowl with a rubber spatula, and continue to whisk until smooth and thoroughly combined. Add the combined whipped cream and white chocolate to the remaining whipped cream and use a rubber spatula to fold together until smooth.

Transfer the White Chocolate Mousse to a plastic container and refrigerate for 2 to 3 hours before serving.

# MRS. D'S CHOCOLATE PEANUT FUDGE

### MAKES ABOUT 1 1/2 POUNDS

When I called my mother to ask her if she had any idea when I had my first taste of chocolate, she answered without hesitation that I was about 2 years old when my dad offered me a taste of her chocolate fudge. She was a bit chagrined at my initial reaction, which was less than enthusiastic. Evidently it didn't take long for me to develop an affinity for her fudge, for just moments later she caught me trying to smear a piece into a crack in a wall.

Temperature to time ratio is very important in this recipe. If the fudge mixture takes too long to reach the desired temperature, the liquid in the milk will evaporate, resulting in a grainy-textured fudge. If the cooking temperature is too high, evaporation will take place, and once again you get grainy-textured fudge. With this in mind, it is important to note that the differences in range-top temperature calibration will vary significantly from one range to another, depending on the source of energy as well as the size of the cooking element. The key factor is the time (22 to 25 minutes) it takes to reach the desired temperature (245 degrees Fahrenheit). It may take a batch or two for you to master this, but the results are worthwhile.

You may notice that I did not specify Virginia peanuts in this recipe. You can use any unsalted peanut, or, for that matter, use walnuts, hazelnuts, cashews, or pecans. You can even go crazy and make a mixed-nut chocolate fudge.

The fudge may be stored in a sealed container at room temperature for several days. It will actually keep substantially longer; however, the fudge will get quite hard after a couple of weeks.

1 1/2  cups unsalted shelled peanuts
3  tablespoons plus 1/2 teaspoon unsalted butter
2  cups granulated sugar
1  cup whole milk
1/2  cup Hershey's unsweetened cocoa
Pinch of salt
1  teaspoon pure vanilla extract

### EQUIPMENT
Measuring cup, measuring spoons, baking sheet with sides, 9- by 9- by 2-inch square cake pan, 2 1/2-quart saucepan, whisk, candy/deep frying thermometer, rubber spatula

Preheat the oven to 325 degrees Fahrenheit.

Toast the peanuts on a baking sheet in the preheated oven until golden brown, about 6 to 7 minutes. Remove the peanuts from the oven and set aside until needed.

Lightly coat the insides of a 9- by 9- by 2-inch square cake pan with 1/2 teaspoon butter.

Heat the sugar, milk, cocoa, and salt in a 2 1/2-quart saucepan over medium heat. Stir until the mixture is smooth and the sugar is dissolved. Bring to a boil, then adjust heat to medium-low and allow the mixture to cook until it reaches a temperature of 245 degrees Fahrenheit, about 22 to 25 minutes. Use a rubber spatula to scrape down the sides of the saucepan every 5 to 6 minutes. Remove the pan from the heat. Vigorously stir in the remaining butter and the vanilla. Fold in the peanuts and pour into the prepared cake pan. Allow to cool to room temperature, about 45 minutes. Cut into the desired size and serve.

# White Chocolate "Ice Cream"

YIELDS 1 1/2 QUARTS

12 ounces white chocolate, broken into
    1/2-ounce pieces
3 1/4 cups whole milk
1 cup granulated sugar
3 eggs

### EQUIPMENT

*Measuring cup, double boiler, film wrap, 2 1/2-quart saucepan, whisk, electric mixer with paddle, rubber spatula, instant-read test thermometer, 2 stainless steel bowls (1 large), ice-cream freezer, 2-quart plastic container with lid*

Heat 1 inch of water in the bottom half of a double boiler over medium-high heat. Place the white chocolate and 1/4 cup of milk in the top half of the double boiler (see page 151). Tightly cover the top with film wrap. Heat for 10 to 12 minutes, then remove from the heat and stir until smooth. Set aside until needed.

Heat the remaining 3 cups of milk and 1/2 cup granulated sugar in a 2 1/2-quart saucepan over medium-high heat. Stir to dissolve the sugar. Bring milk to a boil.

While the milk is heating, place the eggs and the remaining 1/2 cup sugar in the bowl of an electric mixer fitted with a paddle. Beat the eggs on high for 2 to 3 minutes. Scrape down the sides of the bowl. Then beat on high until slightly thickened and lemon-colored, 2 1/2 to 3 minutes. (At this point, the milk should be boiling. If not, adjust the mixer speed to low and continue to mix until the milk boils. If this is not done, the eggs will develop undesirable lumps.)

Pour the boiling milk into the beaten eggs and whisk to combine. Return to the saucepan and heat over medium-high heat, stirring constantly. Bring to a temperature of 185 degrees Fahrenheit, 2 to 4 minutes. Remove from the heat and transfer to a stainless steel bowl. Add the melted white chocolate, and whisk to combine. Cool in an ice-water bath (see page 150) to a temperature of 40 to 45 degrees Fahrenheit, about 15 minutes.

When the mixture is cold, freeze in an ice-cream freezer, following the manufacturer's instructions. Transfer the semifrozen "ice cream" to a plastic container. Securely cover the container, then place in the freezer for several hours before serving. Serve within 5 days.

# GRANNY TWICHELL'S
## SECRET CHOCOLATE CUPCAKE RECIPE

MAKES 18 CUPCAKES

### CHOCOLATE CUPCAKE

- 10 ounces semisweet chocolate, broken into $^1/_2$-ounce pieces
- 1 cup heavy cream
- 2 ounces unsweetened chocolate, broken into $^1/_2$-ounce pieces
- 5 eggs
- $^1/_2$ cup granulated sugar
- 1 teaspoon pure vanilla extract
- $^3/_4$ cup cake flour
- $^1/_2$ teaspoon baking soda
- 2 cups semisweet chocolate chips

### CHOCOLATE ICING

- $^1/_2$ cup heavy cream
- 6 ounces semisweet chocolate, broken into $^1/_2$-ounce pieces

### DECORATION

- 1 ounce white chocolate, finely grated

### EQUIPMENT

*Measuring cup, measuring spoons, hand grater, double boiler, film wrap, whisk, electric mixer with paddle, muffin tins, 18 foil-laminated bake cups, 1$^1/_2$-quart saucepan, stainless steel bowl*

Preheat the oven to 325 degrees Fahrenheit.

Heat 1 inch of water in the bottom half of a double boiler over medium heat. Place 10 ounces semisweet chocolate, 1 cup heavy cream, and 2 ounces unsweetened chocolate in the top half of the double boiler (see page 151). Tightly cover the top with film wrap. Allow to heat for 8 minutes. Remove from heat and stir until smooth. Set aside until needed.

Place eggs, sugar, and vanilla extract in the bowl of an electric mixer fitted with a paddle. Beat on medium until lemon-colored and slightly thickened, about 4 minutes. Add the melted chocolate mixture and beat on medium for 15 to 20 seconds more. Add the cake flour, baking soda, and chocolate chips, and beat on low for 10 seconds. Increase to medium and beat for an additional 10 seconds. Remove the bowl from the mixer. Use a rubber spatula and thoroughly combine the batter.

Evenly divide the mixture into 18 bake cups that have already been positioned into muffin tins, filling the cups to $^1/_4$ inch below the rim. Bake in the preheated oven until a toothpick inserted in the center comes out clean, about 25 to 30 minutes. Remove from the oven and allow to cool to room temperature.

To prepare the icing, heat $^1/_2$ cup heavy cream in a 1$^1/_2$-quart saucepan over medium-high heat. Bring to a boil. Place 6 ounces semisweet chocolate in a stainless steel bowl. Pour the boiling cream over the chocolate and allow to stand for 5 minutes. Stir with a whisk until smooth.

One at a time, dip the top of each of Granny's cupcakes into the chocolate icing. Sprinkle the grated white chocolate over the icing on each cupcake, and refrigerate for 30 minutes to set the icing.

Allow the cupcakes to come to room temperature for 15 to 20 minutes before serving.

# Mom's Chocolate Chip Date Cake

SERVES 12 to 18

**THE CHEF'S TOUCH**

*I wish this was my mom's recipe, but it actually belongs to Trellis assistant chef Jon Pierre Peavey's mom. When Mrs. Peavey learned from Jon that we were working on a chocolate cookbook, she sent me one of her extraordinary cakes from the Peavey home in Eau Claire, Wisconsin. The cake was so outstanding that, with Mrs. Peavey's permission, we are including it in our book.*

*This is a wonderful dessert for children. All those chocolate chips perched atop a dark and moist cake immediately grab their attention. But, as far as I am concerned, why let the kids have all the fun? I usually have a couple of scoops of Double Mocha Madness (see page 131) with my cake.*

*If you cannot find dates that have already been chopped, purchase whole dates and chop them into 1/4-inch pieces. Raisins may be substituted for the dates.*

*You may keep this cake in the refrigerator for 3 to 4 days before serving. It can be served cold or at room temperature.*

- 1 1/2 *cups water*
- 2 *cups chopped dates (1 8-ounce package)*
- 1 3/4 *teaspoons baking soda*
- 1/4 *pound plus 1 tablespoon unsalted butter*
- 1 3/4 *cups plus 1 tablespoon all-purpose flour*
- 4 *tablespoons unsweetened cocoa*
- 1/2 *teaspoon salt*
- 1 1/2 *cups granulated sugar*
- 2 *eggs*
- 1 *teaspoon pure vanilla extract*
- 3 *cups semisweet chocolate chips*
- 1 *cup walnut pieces*

**EQUIPMENT**

*Measuring cup, measuring spoons, 2 1/2-quart saucepan, stainless steel bowl, 9- by 13- by 2-inch cake pan, sifter, waxed paper, electric mixer with paddle, rubber spatula, cutting board, serrated slicer*

Preheat the oven to 325 degrees Fahrenheit.

Heat the water in a 2 1/2-quart saucepan over medium-high heat. Bring to a boil. Place the chopped dates and 1 teaspoon of baking soda in a stainless steel bowl. Pour the boiling water over the dates, and allow to stand until needed.

Coat a 9- by 13- by 2-inch cake pan with 1 tablespoon of butter. Flour the pan with 1 tablespoon of flour and shake out the excess. Set aside until needed.

Combine 1 3/4 cups flour, cocoa, remaining baking soda, and salt in a sifter. Sift onto waxed paper and set aside.

Combine 1 cup sugar and the remaining butter in the bowl of an electric mixer fitted with a paddle. Beat on medium for 2 minutes, then scrape down the sides of the bowl. Beat on high for 1 minute, then add the eggs, one at a time, beating on high for 15 seconds after the addition of each egg, and scraping down the bowl after each addition. After the eggs have been incorporated, beat on high for 2 minutes. Scrape down the bowl.

Add the vanilla extract and beat on medium for 15 seconds. Scrape down the bowl. Add the sifted flour mixture and beat on low for 20 seconds. Add the cooled date mixture and continue to beat on low for 20 seconds, then on medium for 10 seconds. Remove the bowl from the mixer and use a rubber spatula to thoroughly combine. Pour into the prepared pan and spread evenly, including the corners. Sprinkle the remaining 1/2 cup sugar over the top of the batter. Bake in the center of the preheated oven for 20 minutes. Remove the cake from the oven and sprinkle the chocolate chips, then the walnut pieces, over the top of the batter. Return the cake to the oven and bake for an additional 20 to 25 minutes, until a toothpick inserted in the center of the cake comes out clean.

Remove the cake from the oven and allow to cool to room temperature, about 30 to 40 minutes. Refrigerate the cake for at least 15 to 20 minutes. Leaving the cake in the pan, use a serrated slicer to cut the cake lengthwise across the center. To yield 12 portions, make 5 cuts across the width of the cake at 2 1/4-inch intervals. For 18 servings, cut the cake lengthwise into equal thirds, then make 5 cuts across the width of the cake at 2 1/4-inch intervals.

# PENNY SOUS

·····················

MAKES ABOUT 24 CHOCOLATE PENNIES

24  whole, unsalted, shelled Virginia peanuts
$^1/_2$  cup heavy cream
6  tablespoons creamy peanut butter
14  ounces semisweet chocolate, broken into
      $^1/_2$-ounce pieces

### EQUIPMENT

*Measuring cup, measuring spoons, 3 baking sheets with sides, 1$^1/_2$-quart saucepan, whisk, 2 stainless steel bowls, film wrap, double boiler, rubber spatula, instant-read test thermometer, cake spatula, 1$^1/_2$-inch round cookie cutter, parchment paper, pastry bag, medium straight tip*

Preheat the oven to 325 degrees Fahrenheit.

Toast the peanuts on a baking sheet in the preheated oven until golden brown, about 6 to 7 minutes. Remove the peanuts from the oven and set aside until needed.

Heat the heavy cream and the peanut butter in a 1$^1/_2$-quart saucepan over medium-high heat. Stir with a whisk to combine thoroughly. Bring the mixture to a boil. Place 6 ounces of semisweet chocolate in a stainless steel bowl. Pour the boiling cream and peanut butter mixture over the chocolate, and allow to stand at room temperature for 5 minutes. Stir until smooth. Refrigerate the peanut butter ganache for 30 minutes.

Cover the bottom of a baking sheet with film wrap.

Heat 1 inch of water in the bottom half of a double boiler over medium heat. Place the remaining 8 ounces of semisweet chocolate in the top half. Heat the chocolate uncovered, while stirring constantly, until it has melted, about 4 to 5 minutes. Transfer the melted chocolate to a stainless steel bowl, and continue to stir until the temperature of the chocolate is reduced to 90 degrees Fahrenheit, about 5 minutes.

Pour the chocolate onto the film-wrapped bottom of the baking sheet. Use a cake spatula to spread the chocolate evenly over the entire surface of the sheet (the chocolate should be about $^1/_8$ inch in depth). Place the baking sheet in the refrigerator until the chocolate has hardened, about 10 minutes. Remove the chocolate sheet from the refrigerator and use a 1$^1/_2$-inch round cookie cutter to cut 48 circles. Remove the circles by placing your hand underneath the film wrap and pushing the circles out, one at a time. Place the cut circles onto 2 baking sheets covered with parchment paper (24 circles per baking sheet), and then put them in the freezer for 20 minutes.

Remove the circles from the freezer. Fill a pastry bag, fitted with a medium-sized straight tip, with the peanut butter ganache. Pipe the equivalent of 2 teaspoons of ganache onto each of 24 chocolate circles. Form the Penny Sous by placing another chocolate circle on top of each portion of peanut butter ganache, using your index finger to gently press the center of the top circle into place. Pipe the equivalent of $^1/_4$ teaspoon of peanut butter ganache onto the finger imprint on the top chocolate circle. Set a single, whole roasted peanut into the ganache. Keep the Penny Sous refrigerated until needed.

## THE CHEF'S TOUCH

*These delicious, coin-shaped candies ("sou" is the French word for "penny") are actually a tribute to my friend Penny Seu, a token of appreciation for her friendship and guidance.*

*Virginia peanuts are not essential, but they certainly are delicious. We use Skippy brand peanut butter at The Trellis—it is my favorite, and has been for more than 4 decades.*

*Because the chocolate circles are fashioned from hardened melted chocolate rather than tempered chocolate, they do not lend themselves to a lot of handling. If the chocolate becomes difficult to work with during the process of cutting the circles, return the sheet to the refrigerator or place it in the freezer for a short time.*

*If the chocolate peanut butter ganache sets up too hard after being refrigerated for 30 minutes, allow it to sit at room temperature for 10 to 15 minutes before piping it onto the chocolate circles.*

*The Penny Sous may be kept refrigerated for several days before using. To serve, place each candy on an individual paper doily. The candies will keep their shape for several hours in an air-conditioned room.*

# SIMPLY THE BEST CHOCOLATE BROWNIE
### SERVES 12

*I was only 19 years old in June of 1965 when I graduated from The Culinary Institute of America. As kids are prone to do (even those with a culinary arts degree), I did not give much thought to my eating habits. By day, I cooked in a fine club on Wall Street, and 5 nights a week I sweated it out in the minuscule kitchen of a small French restaurant on the Upper East Side. When it came time to relax away from work, my favorite snack consisted of chocolate nut brownies from a favorite pastry shop and a couple of cold beers. Now that I am a grown up I am more likely to sip a glass of vintage port with my brownie indulgence.*

*Because of the chocolate chunks, a toothpick inserted in the center of the Simply The Best Macadamia Nut Chocolate Chunk Brownies will probably not come out clean no matter how long you bake the brownies. I suggest pulling them from the oven after 50 minutes baking time.*

*The brownies are wonderful when they are still warm, but they can be served at room temperature. Once cooled to room temperature, the brownies may be refrigerated for several days before serving. Allow the brownies to come to room temperature for 15 to 20 minutes before serving.*

*The fudgelike texture of these brownies makes them a perfect confection to ship to faraway places; that is, if you have the willpower to part with them.*

4 tablespoons plus 1 teaspoon unsalted butter
$^{1}/_{4}$ cup plus 1 teaspoon all-purpose flour
2 tablespoons unsweetened cocoa
1 teaspoon baking powder
$^{1}/_{2}$ teaspoon salt
3 ounces unsweetened chocolate, broken into $^{1}/_{2}$-ounce pieces
2 ounces semisweet chocolate, broken into $^{1}/_{2}$-ounce pieces
3 eggs
1 cup granulated sugar
1 teaspoon pure vanilla extract
$^{1}/_{4}$ cup sour cream

## SIMPLY THE BEST MACADAMIA NUT CHOCOLATE CHUNK BROWNIE

8 ounces semisweet chocolate, chopped into $^{1}/_{4}$-inch chunks
$1^{1}/_{2}$ cups raw, unsalted macadamia nuts

## SIMPLY THE BEST PEANUT RAISIN CHOCOLATE BROWNIE

$1^{1}/_{2}$ cups raisins
$1^{1}/_{2}$ cups unsalted, shelled, toasted Virginia peanuts

### EQUIPMENT
*Measuring spoons, measuring cup, 9- by 9- by 2-inch square cake pan, sifter, waxed paper, double boiler, film wrap, whisk, electric mixer with balloon whip, rubber spatula, serrated slicer*

Preheat the oven to 325 degrees Fahrenheit.

Lightly coat a 9- by 9- by 2-inch square cake pan with 1 teaspoon of butter, then flour the pan with 1 teaspoon flour, shaking out the excess.

Sift together the remaining $^{1}/_{4}$ cup flour, cocoa, baking powder, and salt onto the waxed paper. Set aside.

Heat 1 inch of water in the bottom half of a double boiler over medium-high heat. Place the 3 ounces unsweetened chocolate, remaining 4 tablespoons of butter, and 2 ounces semisweet chocolate in the top half of the double boiler (see page 151). Tightly cover the top with film wrap. Heat for $4^{1}/_{2}$ to 5 minutes, remove from the heat, and stir until smooth.

Place the eggs, sugar, and vanilla in the bowl of an electric mixer fitted with a balloon whip. Mix on high until slightly thickened, about $1^{1}/_{2}$ minutes. Add the melted chocolate mixture to the egg mixture and mix on medium for 30 seconds. Add the sifted ingredients, mix on low for 10 seconds, then on medium for 10 seconds. Add the sour cream and mix on medium for 5 seconds.

Remove the bowl from the mixer and use a rubber spatula to combine thoroughly (also add and combine 4 ounces of chocolate chunks if making the **Macadamia Nut Chocolate Chunk Brownie**, or the raisins if making the **Peanut Raisin Chocolate Brownie**).

Pour the batter into the prepared cake pan, spreading evenly, including the corners. (If making the **Macadamia Nut Chocolate Chunk Brownie**, sprinkle the macadamia nuts and the remaining chocolate chunks evenly over the batter, or if making the **Peanut Raisin Chocolate Brownie**, sprinkle the peanuts evenly over the batter.) Bake in the preheated oven until a toothpick inserted in the center comes out clean, about 40 minutes (bake for 10 to 15 minutes longer if making either one of the brownie varieties).

Remove the brownies from the oven and allow to cool in the pan at room temperature for 10 to 15 minutes. Use a serrated slicer to cut into 12 portions.

# Rose's Chocolate Pots de Crème

1 cup heavy cream
³/₄ cup whole milk
12 ounces semisweet chocolate, finely
   chopped
6 egg yolks
1 tablespoon Kahlúa

## THE CHEF'S TOUCH

*Rose Levy Beranbaum's reputation as America's leading confectioner had not been established when I first met her several years ago. Rose was researching an article on "wild food" foraging for The New York Times, and a colleague in New York had given her my name. That phone call established a friendship based in part on a kindred passion for chocolate. I am very pleased that Rose would reveal her never-before-published recipe for pots de crème here.*

*Rose writes about her pots de crème: "This classic recipe is one of the most satisfying and glorious ways in the world to enjoy chocolate, while being one of the simplest recipes to prepare. Despite its charms, it is not nearly as well known as its fluffier cousin, the chocolate mousse. So my offering to my friend Marcel's delightful collection of chocolate recipes is this perfectly bittersweet, dense, silken chocolate bliss."*

*Rose suggests using her favorite chocolate—Lindt bittersweet—for her pots de crème.*

*To prevent the pots de crème from absorbing refrigerator odors, be certain to cover them tightly with film wrap.*

*If pot de crème forms or custard cups are not available, use espresso cups.*

## EQUIPMENT
*Measuring cup, cook's knife, cutting board, measuring spoons, 2¹/₂-quart saucepan, double boiler, rubber spatula, whisk, instant-read test thermometer, 2 stainless steel bowls (1 large), 8 small* pot de crème *forms or custard cups, film wrap*

Heat the heavy cream and milk in a 2¹/₂-quart saucepan over medium heat. Bring to a boil. While the cream is heating, heat 1 inch of water in the bottom half of a double boiler over medium-high heat. Place the chocolate in the top half and stir with a rubber spatula until melted. Whisk the egg yolks into the melted chocolate. Slowly pour the boiling cream and milk into the chocolate, whisking constantly. Bring to a temperature of 160 degrees Fahrenheit, about 3¹/₂ to 4 minutes. Remove the mixture from the heat and transfer to a stainless steel bowl. Add the Kahlúa. Cool in an ice-water bath (see page 150), stirring constantly with a whisk to a temperature of 90 degrees Fahrenheit, about 4 to 5 minutes.

Evenly divide the mixture into 8 small *pot de crème* forms or custard cups. Cover each with film wrap and refrigerate for 2 to 3 hours to set before serving. Serve within 2 days.

# CHOCOLATE RASPBERRY TOASTED HAZELNUT ICE CREAM

YIELDS 1¹/₂ QUARTS

1 cup hazelnuts
4 ounces semisweet chocolate, broken into
    ¹/₂-ounce pieces
2 ounces unsweetened chocolate, broken
    into ¹/₂-ounce pieces
¹/₂ cup whole milk

¹/₂ pint red raspberries
1¹/₂ cups heavy cream
1 cup half-and-half
³/₄ cup granulated sugar
4 egg yolks

### EQUIPMENT

*Measuring cup, 2 baking sheets with sides, 100-percent-cotton kitchen towel, sauté pan, double boiler, film wrap, 2 stainless steel bowls (1 large), rubber spatula, whisk, ladle or metal spoon, 2¹/₂-quart saucepan, electric mixer with paddle, instant-read test thermometer, ice-cream freezer, 2-quart plastic container with lid*

Preheat the oven to 325 degrees Fahrenheit.

Toast and skin the hazelnuts (see page 151). Lightly crush the nuts with the bottom of a sauté pan.

Heat 1 inch of water in the bottom half of a double boiler over medium-high heat. Place the semisweet and unsweetened chocolates and milk in the top half of the double boiler (see page 151). Tightly cover the top with film wrap. Allow to heat for 8 to 10 minutes, then transfer to a stainless steel bowl and stir until smooth.

Crush the raspberries in a stainless steel bowl using a ladle or metal spoon (be sure to crush, not purée, the berries). Stir crushed berries into chocolate mixture and hold at room temperature.

Heat the heavy cream and half-and-half in a 2¹/₂-quart saucepan over medium-high heat. When hot, add ¹/₄ cup of sugar and stir to dissolve. Bring cream to a boil.

While the cream is heating, place egg yolks and the remaining sugar in the bowl of an electric mixer fitted with a paddle. Beat the eggs on high for 2 to 2¹/₂ minutes. Scrape down the sides of the bowl, then beat on high until slightly thickened and lemon-colored, 2¹/₂ to 3 minutes. (At this point, the cream should be boiling. If not, adjust the mixer speed to low and continue to mix until the cream boils. If this is not done, the egg yolks will develop undesirable lumps.)

Pour the boiling cream into the beaten egg yolks and whisk to combine. Return to the saucepan and heat over medium-high heat, stirring constantly. Bring to a temperature of 185 degrees Fahrenheit, 2 to 4 minutes, then pour over the chocolate mixture, add crushed hazelnuts, and stir to combine. Cool in an ice-water bath (see page 150) to a temperature of 40 to 45 degrees Fahrenheit, about 15 minutes.

When the custard is cold, freeze in an ice-cream freezer following the manufacturer's instructions. Transfer the semifrozen ice cream to a plastic container. Securely cover the container, then place in the freezer for several hours before serving. Serve within 5 days.

# CHAPTER THREE

# A TOUCH OF CHOCOLATE

## *RECIPES UTILIZING CHOCOLATE SPARINGLY, BUT WITH DAZZLING RESULTS*

# Banana, Walnut, and Chocolate Chip Fritters

MAKES 24 FRITTERS

- $1\frac{1}{2}$ *cups all-purpose flour*
- 6 *tablespoons light brown sugar*
- 2 *tablespoons baking powder*
- 2 *tablespoons cornstarch*
- $\frac{1}{2}$ *teaspoon salt*
- $\frac{1}{2}$ *teaspoon cinnamon*
- 1 *pound medium-size bananas, unpeeled*
- $\frac{3}{4}$ *cup Budweiser beer*
- 1 *egg*
- 2 *teaspoons lemon juice*
- $\frac{3}{4}$ *cup walnuts, chopped into $\frac{1}{4}$-inch pieces*
- $\frac{3}{4}$ *cup semisweet chocolate chips*
- 6 *cups vegetable oil*
- 2 *tablespoons confectioners' sugar*

**Equipment**

*Measuring cup, measuring spoons, cook's knife, cutting board, 3 stainless steel bowls (1 large), slotted spoon, whisk, rubber spatula, deep fryer or heavy-gauge 4-quart saucepan, candy/deep frying thermometer, #50 ($1\frac{1}{2}$ tablespoons) ice-cream scoop, tongs, baking sheet, paper towels*

In a large stainless steel bowl, combine the flour, light brown sugar, baking powder, cornstarch, salt, and cinnamon. Set aside.

Peel the bananas. Smash them to a rough-textured consistency in a stainless steel bowl using a slotted spoon (they should yield about 1 cup). In another stainless steel bowl whisk together the beer, egg, and lemon juice. Pour this mixture over the bananas and use the slotted spoon to combine thoroughly.

Add the banana and beer mixture to the dry ingredients and use a rubber spatula to combine thoroughly all the ingredients. Add the chopped walnut pieces and chocolate chips. Thoroughly combine with a rubber spatula and set aside.

Preheat the oven to 325 degrees Fahrenheit.

Heat the vegetable oil in a deep fryer (or high-sided, heavy-duty pot) to a temperature of 350 degrees Fahrenheit. Use a #50 ice cream scoop (or long-handled tablespoon) to portion the batter. Drop 6 scoops of batter into the hot oil and fry until golden brown, about 2 to 3 minutes. Use tongs (or a slotted spoon) to remove the fritters from the hot oil and transfer to a baking sheet lined with paper towels. Repeat this process until all the fritters are fried, then place them in the preheated oven for 10 to 12 minutes, until a toothpick inserted in the center of a fritter comes out clean.

Dust the fritters with confectioners' sugar. Serve hot.

### THE CHEF'S TOUCH

*Much of the pleasure in developing the recipes for this book came from testing the seemingly endless ideas for chocolate concoctions that I received from my staff. Assistant chef Charles "Chet" Flanagan came up with this fritter recipe. Chet is in charge of our lunch production, so he gets to experiment with the different savory fritters that we serve as a garnish to our sandwiches at lunch. Not to be bypassed by the fun involved with the chocolate recipes, Chet surprised us with this incredibly delicious dessert fritter.*

*Be certain to stir the batter in between frying each batch of fritters to prevent the chocolate chips from settling to the bottom of the batter.*

*In between frying each batch of fritters, skim the frying oil with a slotted spoon to remove fried residue.*

*Measure the temperature of the frying oil between batches and adjust the heat as needed to maintain a frying temperature of 350 degrees Fahrenheit.*

*For an elegant dessert, I suggest serving 2 or 3 hot fritters in a pool of White Chocolate Sauce (see page 18), sprinkled with a generous portion of fresh red raspberries.*

# CHILLED ORANGE CAPPUCCINO CREAM WITH GRATED CHOCOLATE

SERVES 8

4 cups heavy cream
1¹/₂ cups half-and-half
6 egg yolks
2 eggs
¹/₂ cup granulated sugar

4 tablespoons cornstarch
4 tablespoons instant espresso powder
2 tablespoons Grand Marnier
¹/₂ ounce chunk semisweet chocolate, finely grated

## EQUIPMENT

Measuring cup, measuring spoons, hand grater, 2¹/₂-quart saucepan, electric mixer with paddle and balloon whip, rubber spatula, whisk, instant-read test thermometer, 2 stainless steel bowls (1 large), pastry bag, 8 8-ounce coffee cups

Heat 1¹/₂ cups of heavy cream and the half-and-half in a 2¹/₂-quart saucepan over medium-high heat. Bring to a boil.

While the cream is heating, combine the egg yolks, eggs, sugar, cornstarch, and instant espresso powder in the bowl of an electric mixer fitted with a paddle. Beat the mixture on high for 2 minutes, scrape down the sides of the bowl, and continue mixing on high until the mixture is slightly thickened, about 1¹/₂ to 2 minutes. (At this point the cream should be boiling. If not, adjust the mixer speed to low and continue to mix until the cream boils. If this is not done, the eggs will develop undesirable lumps.)

Pour the boiling cream into the beaten egg mixture and whisk to combine. Return to the saucepan and heat over medium-high heat, whisking constantly, until the cream reaches a temperature of 180 degrees Fahrenheit, about 5 to 6 minutes. Remove from the heat and transfer to a stainless steel bowl. Cool the espresso-custard mixture in an ice-water bath (see page 150) to a temperature of 40 to 45 degrees Fahrenheit, about 20 to 25 minutes.

While the espresso-custard mixture is cooling, place 1¹/₂ cups of heavy cream in the well-chilled bowl of an electric mixer fitted with a well-chilled balloon whip (see page 151). Whisk the cream on high until stiff peaks form, about 1¹/₂ minutes. Fold the whipped cream into the chilled espresso cream and combine gently but thoroughly.

Transfer the espresso-cream mixture to a pastry bag. Evenly divide the mixture into the 8 coffee cups, filling the cups to ¹/₂ inch below the rim. Refrigerate the cups until ready to top with the whipped cream.

A few minutes before serving, place the remaining 1 cup heavy cream and the Grand Marnier in the well-chilled bowl of an electric mixer fitted with a well-chilled balloon whip. Whisk on high until soft peaks form, about 45 to 50 seconds. Evenly divide the Grand Marnier-flavored cream over the espresso mixture in each cup. Use a teaspoon to spread the cream to the inside edges of each cup, leaving the surface a bit uneven. Sprinkle grated chocolate over each and serve immediately.

# TIPSY CHOCOLATE PECAN CRUNCH ICE CREAM

YIELDS 2 QUARTS

1 cup pecan halves
2 cups granulated sugar
¼ teaspoon lemon juice
1 ounce unsweetened chocolate, broken into
 ½-ounce pieces

2 cups heavy cream
2 cups half-and-half
8 egg yolks
¼ cup Myers's Dark Rum

### EQUIPMENT
*Measuring cup, measuring spoons, baking sheet with sides, 2 2½-quart saucepans, whisk, metal spoon, cook's knife, cutting board, 2-quart plastic container with lid, electric mixer with paddle, rubber spatula, instant-read test thermometer, 2 stainless steel bowls (1 large), ice-cream freezer*

Preheat the oven to 325 degrees Fahrenheit.

Toast the pecan halves on a baking sheet in the preheated oven for 10 to 12 minutes. Cool to room temperature.

Combine 1¼ cups of sugar and the lemon juice in a 2½-quart saucepan. Stir with a whisk to combine (the sugar will resemble moist sand). Caramelize the sugar for 8 to 10 minutes over medium-high heat, stirring constantly with a whisk to break up any lumps (the sugar will first turn clear as it liquefies, then light brown as it caramelizes). Remove the saucepan from the heat. Add the unsweetened chocolate and stir gently to blend. Pour the chocolate-caramel mixture over the pecans and stir with a spoon to completely coat the pecans with the chocolate caramel; spread the mixture evenly over the bottom of the baking sheet. Freeze the chocolate pecan crunch for 20 minutes. Remove from the freezer. Chop the chocolate pecan crunch into ¼-inch pieces. Store in a sealed plastic container in the freezer until needed.

Heat the heavy cream and half-and-half in a 2½-quart saucepan over medium-high heat. When hot, add ½ cup sugar. Stir to dissolve and bring the mixture to a boil, about 10 to 12 minutes.

While the cream is heating, place the egg yolks and the remaining ¼ cup sugar in the bowl of an electric mixer fitted with a paddle. Beat the yolks on high for 2 to 2½ minutes, then scrape down the sides of the bowl. Beat on high, until slightly thickened and lemon-colored, an additional 2½ to 3 minutes. (At this point, the cream should be boiling. If not, adjust mixer speed to low and continue to mix until the cream boils. If this is not done, the egg yolks will develop undesirable lumps.)

Pour the boiling cream into the beaten egg yolks and whisk to combine. Return to the saucepan and heat over medium-high heat, stirring constantly, until the cream reaches a temperature of 185 degrees Fahrenheit, 2 to 4 minutes. Add the rum and combine thoroughly. Remove from the heat and transfer to a stainless steel bowl. Cool the mixture in an ice-water bath (see page 150), to a temperature of 40 to 45 degrees Fahrenheit, about 20 minutes.

When the mixture is cold, freeze in an ice-cream freezer following the manufacturer's instructions. Transfer the semifrozen ice cream to the plastic container that is holding the chocolate pecan crunch. Stir with a rubber spatula to thoroughly combine the crunch with the semifrozen ice cream. Securely cover the container, then place in the freezer for several hours before serving. Serve within 3 days.

see page 150

## THE CHEF'S TOUCH

*I*f more than a small bowl of this ice cream is to be consumed at one seating, I would suggest caution if driving or operating machinery.

In order to deter crystallization, fresh lemon juice is added to the sugar before caramelization.

Sticky business this chocolate pecan crunch. For that reason it is important to keep it in the freezer. Securely covered, the crunch will keep for several days.

Bacardi dark rum may be used as a substitute for the suggested Myers's Rum. Remember that the quality of this ice cream depends on a high-quality rum: use the best.

The egg yolks and sugar may also be prepared using a hand-held mixer (mixing time may increase slightly) or by hand, using a wire whisk (mixing time may double).

# CHOCOLATE ALMOND CRISPS

MAKES 30 CRISPS

## ALMOND MERINGUE CRISPS

3/4 cup sliced almonds
1/2 cup plus 2 tablespoons granulated sugar
2 egg whites
1/8 teaspoon cream of tartar
1/8 teaspoon salt
1/2 teaspoon almond extract
1 teaspoon cornstarch
1 tablespoon confectioners' sugar

## CHOCOLATE GANACHE

6 ounces semisweet chocolate, broken into
    1/2-ounce pieces
7 tablespoons heavy cream
1 teaspoon granulated sugar
1 teaspoon unsalted butter

### THE CHEF'S TOUCH

We first served this cookie at a book-signing for The Trellis Cookbook in September 1988. The celebration was held at the Rizzoli Bookstore with some 600 Trellis fans in attendance. The champagne flowed, lots of cookbooks were signed and sold, and the food (prepared by The Trellis, of course) was quickly consumed, especially these ethereal little meringue crisps.

The meringue crisps can be made 2 days in advance and stored in an airtight container. If the meringues lose their crispness, recrisp in a 200-degree-Fahrenheit oven for 20 to 30 minutes.

The assembled crisps must be served within 3 to 4 hours; otherwise, the meringues will absorb moisture from the ganache and lose their crispness.

### EQUIPMENT

*Measuring cup, measuring spoons, 2 baking sheets, food processor with metal blade, electric mixer with balloon whip, rubber spatula, parchment paper, pastry bag, double boiler, film wrap, whisk, 1 1/2-quart saucepan, small stainless steel bowl, medium star tip*

Preheat the oven to 325 degrees Fahrenheit.

Lightly toast the almonds on a baking sheet in the preheated oven for 5 minutes. Remove from the oven and cool to room temperature. Reduce the oven temperature to 225 degrees Fahrenheit.

In the bowl of a food processor fitted with a metal blade, coarsely process the toasted almonds with 2 tablespoons of sugar into pieces 1/8 inch in size. Set aside until needed.

Line two baking sheets with parchment paper.

Create a meringue by whisking the egg whites on medium speed in the bowl of an electric mixer fitted with a balloon whip. Whisk until frothy, about 1 minute. Add the cream of tartar and salt, increase speed to high, and whisk until the egg whites begin to stiffen, 1 to 1 1/2 minutes. While continuing to whisk on high speed, gradually add 1/2 cup granulated sugar. The egg whites should form peaks that are stiff, but not dry, about 2 to 3 minutes. Add almond extract and whisk on high for an additional 30 seconds. Remove the bowl from the mixer and use a rubber spatula to fold in the chopped almonds and cornstarch.

Fill a pastry bag (with no tip) with the meringue. Pipe 30 1 1/2-inch-high mounds of meringue onto the parchment-covered baking sheets (15 mounds per sheet, evenly spaced). Make an indentation in the center of each meringue by dipping your thumb in 1 tablespoon confectioners' sugar and then into the center of each meringue. Place the meringues in the preheated oven and bake for 30 minutes. Reduce the oven temperature to 200 degrees Fahrenheit and bake for an additional 2 hours. Remove from the oven and allow to cool for 20 minutes before handling.

While the crisps are cooling, prepare the ganache. Heat 1 inch of water in the bottom half of a double boiler over medium-high heat. Place the semisweet chocolate in the top half of the double boiler (see page 151). Tightly cover the top with film wrap and allow to heat for 5 to 6 minutes. Remove from heat and stir until smooth.

Heat the heavy cream, 1 teaspoon sugar, and the butter in a 1 1/2-quart saucepan over medium-high heat. Bring to a boil. Pour the boiling cream over the melted chocolate and stir until smooth. Transfer the ganache from the double boiler to a small stainless steel bowl. Cover with film wrap and refrigerate until the ganache is firm, about 20 minutes.

Transfer the ganache to a pastry bag fitted with a medium-sized star tip. Pipe approximately 1 1/2 teaspoons of ganache in the center of each almond meringue crisp.

# Fresh Berry Tulip with White Chocolate "Ice Cream"

### SERVES 8

**EQUIPMENT**

*Measuring cup, measuring spoons, paring knife, 9-inch cake circle, parchment paper, electric mixer with paddle and balloon whip, rubber spatula, double boiler, whisk, 2 baking sheets, cake spatula, 46-ounce juice can, 100-percent-cotton kitchen towel, food processor with metal blade, ice-cream scoop*

12  tablespoons unsalted butter
2  cups granulated sugar
6  egg whites
1/4  teaspoon pure vanilla extract
2  cups all-purpose flour
1 1/2  pints red raspberries
3  cups heavy cream
  White Chocolate "Ice Cream" (see page 35)
2  pints strawberries, stemmed and quartered
1  pint blueberries, stemmed and washed
1/2  pint blackberries

With a pencil, trace a 9-inch circle on each of 8 sheets of parchment paper (each one cut to fit a baking sheet).

Preheat oven to 350 degrees Fahrenheit.

Combine butter and 1 1/2 cups of sugar in the bowl of an electric mixer fitted with a paddle. Beat the butter on low for 1 minute, on medium for 1 minute, and on high for 1 minute. Scrape down the sides of the bowl and beat on high for 1 additional minute. Once again, scrape down the bowl.

Heat 1 inch of water in the bottom half of a double boiler (see page 151) over high heat. Place the egg whites in the top half of the double boiler and continuously whisk the whites while heating to a temperature of 110 degrees Fahrenheit, about 1 minute. Slowly pour 1/2 of the beaten whites into the butter mixture while mixing on high, about 1 minute. Scrape down the bowl. Slowly add the remaining whites while mixing on high. Scrape down the bowl. Mix on high for 15 more seconds. Add the vanilla extract and beat on high for 5 seconds. Add the flour, mixing on low for 10 to 15 seconds, until the batter pulls away from the sides of the bowl. Remove the bowl from the mixer. Use a rubber spatula to finish mixing the batter, until it is smooth and thoroughly combined.

Place a sheet of parchment paper with the trace mark down on each of 2 baking sheets. Place 4 tablespoons of batter in the center of each circle. Use a cake spatula to smear a uniformly thin coating of batter to completely cover the inside of each circle. Bake both sheets in the preheated oven for 10 to 15 minutes, until most of the surface of each battered circle is golden brown (normally the circle on the bottom shelf will turn golden brown first). Remove from the oven and immediately remove the parchment paper from the baking sheet. Carefully invert the parchment paper over the top (or bottom) of a large (46-ounce) juice can. Remove the parchment from the baked batter, place a 100-percent-cotton towel over the baked batter, then gently pull down the edges of the towel to form the tulip (this must be done while tulips are hot). Remove the tulip and repeat with the second sheet of baked batter. While the finished tulips are cooling, repeat the baking-and-forming procedure until 8 tulip shells have been produced.

To prepare the raspberry sauce, puree 1 pint of red raspberries and the remaining 1/2 cup sugar in a food processor fitted with a metal blade. Refrigerate until ready to use.

Whip the heavy cream in the well-chilled bowl of an electric mixer fitted with a well-chilled balloon whip (see page 151). Whip until firm peaks form, about 1 to 1 1/2 minutes. Refrigerate until needed.

Portion 4 tablespoons of raspberry sauce onto 8 10-inch plates and place a tulip in the center of each plate. Place 2 small scoops of White Chocolate "Ice Cream" in the center of each tulip, cover with whipped cream, and then sprinkle an assortment of berries over the whipped cream in each tulip. Serve immediately.

*I*f you are looking for a summertime dessert that is fairly simple to prepare and is sure to please, then these elegant berry-laden tulips are an excellent choice. Preparation of the baked biscuit tulip does take some skill, acquired after a few attempts at shaping the tulip. Humidity, which can be the bane of a pastry chef's existence, can certainly cause problems with this type of pastry. However, most nonprofessionals will probably have an easier time of it than the professionals who all too often work in an adverse environment.

We use the bottom from a 9-inch springform tin to trace the circles on the greaseproof paper. Any approximately 9-inch diameter form, such as a small dinner plate, may be used instead.

There is enough batter to produce 12 tulips. I recommend baking all 12, since the baked tulips are delicate and it is a good idea to have a few extra in case of breakage.

Be careful not to overbake the tulips, as they will become brittle and possibly break when being formed over the juice can. They are especially fragile when they are being removed from the baking sheet and placed onto the juice can.

Baked tulips will stay crisp for several hours and even overnight depending upon the relative humidity. The drier the air, the longer they will stay at their best. If the baked tulips become soft, crisp them one at a time in a 225-degree-Fahrenheit (110 degrees C/Gas ¼) oven for 5 minutes (the tulips will completely lose their shape and flatten out when reheated). Reshape each tulip over the juice can and allow to cool thoroughly before filling with whipped cream.

The tulip batter may be prepared using a hand-held electric mixer; the preparation time may increase slightly.

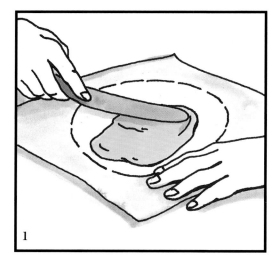

1. Use a cake spatula to apply batter to circle of parchment paper. Smear a thin coating of batter over circle.

2. Carefully invert parchment paper and cooked batter over juice can.

3. Remove paper. Place clean towel over baked batter and pull down edges to form tulip.

4. The formed tulip.

# CARAMEL BANANA CHOCOLATE CHIP ICE CREAM

YIELDS 2 QUARTS

1¼ pounds medium-size bananas, unpeeled
1½ cups granulated sugar
⅛ teaspoon lemon juice
2 cups heavy cream

2 cups half-and-half
6 egg yolks
1 cup semisweet chocolate chips

### EQUIPMENT

*Measuring cup, measuring spoons, 2 stainless steel bowls (1 large), slotted spoon, film wrap, 2½-quart saucepan, whisk, electric mixer with paddle, rubber spatula, instant-read test thermometer, ice-cream freezer, 2-quart plastic container with lid.*

Peel the bananas. Using a slotted spoon, smash them to a rough-textured consistency in a stainless steel bowl. Cover with film wrap and set aside.

Place ½ cup of sugar and the lemon juice in a 2½-quart saucepan. Stir with a whisk to combine (the sugar will resemble moist sand). Caramelize the sugar for 5 to 6 minutes over medium-high heat, stirring constantly with a whisk to break up any lumps (the sugar will first turn clear as it liquefies, then light brown as it caramelizes). Reduce the heat to medium.

Carefully and slowly pour the heavy cream, then the half-and-half into the caramelized sugar (the mixture will steam and boil rapidly as the cream is added). Add ½ cup of sugar and whisk to dissolve. Bring to a boil, about 5 minutes.

While the caramel cream is heating, place the egg yolks and remaining ½ cup of sugar in the bowl of an electric mixer fitted with a paddle. Beat the eggs on high for 2 to 2½ minutes. Scrape down the sides of the bowl then beat on high again until slightly thickened and lemon-colored, 2½ to 3 minutes. (At this point, the caramel cream should be boiling. If not, adjust the mixer speed to low and continue to mix until the cream boils. If this is not done, the eggs will develop undesirable lumps.)

Pour the boiling caramel cream into the beaten egg yolks and whisk to combine. Return to the saucepan and heat over medium-high heat, stirring constantly. Bring to a temperature of 185 degrees Fahrenheit, 2 to 4 minutes. Remove from heat and pour over the smashed bananas; cool in an ice-water bath (see page 150) to a temperature of 40 to 45 degrees Fahrenheit, about 15 to 20 minutes.

When the mixture is cold, fold in the chocolate chips (the mixture *must* be cold; otherwise, the chips will melt) and freeze in an ice-cream freezer following the manufacturer's instructions. Transfer the semifrozen ice cream to a plastic container. Securely cover the container, then place in the freezer for several hours before serving. Serve within 5 days.

## THE CHEF'S TOUCH

*I*n The Very Best Ice Cream and Where to Find It *(The Very Best Publishers, Inc., Boston), ice-cream lovers were directed to The Trellis for this particular treat. Now, for the first time, here is the recipe.*

*To deter crystallization, fresh lemon juice is added to the sugar before caramelization.*

*The egg yolks and sugar may also be prepared using a hand-held mixer (mixing time may increase slightly) or by hand, using a wire whisk (mixing time may double).*

# Red Pear Sorbet and White Chocolate "Ice Cream" with Pralines and Caramel Sabayon

SERVES 4

## Red Pear Sorbet

- 3 ripe red pears (preferably Bartlett)
- 1 tablespoon fresh lemon juice
- 1 cup water
- 6 tablespoons granulated sugar
- 1/4 teaspoon finely chopped lemon zest

## Pralines and Caramel Sabayon

- 1/2 cup plus 2 tablespoons granulated sugar
- 1/8 teaspoon fresh lemon juice
- 16 large pecan halves
- 4 tablespoons heavy cream
- 1 egg
- 2 egg yolks

White Chocolate "Ice Cream"
(see page 35)

### EQUIPMENT

*Measuring spoons, measuring cup, zester or vegetable peeler, paring knife, cutting board, cook's knife, hand grater, 2 stainless steel bowls (1 large), 2 1/2-quart saucepan, whisk, instant-read test thermometer, ice-cream freezer, dinner fork, nonstick baking sheet, 2 2-quart plastic containers, double boiler*

Core and quarter the pears (do not peel). Grate the pear quarters, then place the grated pear in a stainless steel bowl and toss with 1 tablespoon lemon juice. Refrigerate until needed.

Heat the water, sugar, and lemon zest in a 2 1/2-quart saucepan over medium-high heat. Whisk to dissolve sugar. Bring to a boil and boil for about 5 minutes until slightly thickened.

Pour the hot sugar mixture over the grated pear and stir. Cool in an ice-water bath (see page 150) to a temperature of 40 to 45 degrees Fahrenheit, about 15 minutes.

When cold, freeze in an ice-cream freezer following the manufacturer's instructions. Transfer the semifrozen sorbet to a plastic container then freeze for several hours. Serve within 2 days.

To prepare the pralines, combine 1/2 cup of sugar and 1/8 teaspoon of lemon juice in a 2 1/2-quart saucepan. Stir with a whisk. (The sugar will resemble moist sand.) Caramelize the sugar for 2 to 2 1/2 minutes over medium-high heat, constantly stirring to break up any lumps (the sugar will first turn clear as it liquefies, then brown as it caramelizes). Remove the saucepan from the heat. Using a dinner fork, dip the pecans one at a time into the caramelized sugar. Place pecans on a nonstick baking sheet, spaced so they are not touching. Allow the caramelized sugar to harden around the pecans, about 1 minute. Transfer the pralines to a sealed plastic container and store in the freezer until needed. Add the heavy cream to the remaining caramelized sugar and stir to combine. Transfer the caramel to a stainless steel bowl and keep at room temperature until needed.

Make the sabayon just before serving. Heat 1 inch of water in the bottom half of a double boiler over medium heat. Place the egg, egg yolks, and 2 tablespoons of sugar in the top half of the double boiler. Vigorously whisk until soft peaks form and the mixture is light and airy, about 6 to 8 minutes. Remove from the heat and continue to whisk the sabayon while gradually adding the caramel.

Portion 4 tablespoons of sabayon onto 4 plates. Place 2 scoops of White Chocolate "Ice Cream" and 2 scoops of sorbet onto the sauce on each plate. Decorate with 4 pralines. Serve immediately.

*If red Bartlett pears are not available, you may use any other good-to-eat pear that is ripe (pears are usually sold a bit underripe; to ripen, store in a room with a temperature of 70 to 80 degrees Fahrenheit for 2 to 5 days).*

*Use a zester or a vegetable peeler to zest the lemon. Be careful to remove only the colored skin and not the bitter white pith which lies beneath the skin. If using a vegetable peeler, cut the peeled rind with a sharp cook's knife.*

*In order to prevent crystallization, a little fresh lemon juice is added to the sugar before caramelization.*

*By organizing the production of this dessert, it can be easily prepared for your next dinner party. The "ice cream" may be produced several days in advance. Prepare the sorbet a day or two before serving (it is at its best when served within 48 hours of preparation). Caramelize the pecans days or even 2 to 3 weeks before serving. Simply store the pralines in a sealed container in the freezer. The caramel should be prepared just prior to whisking the eggs for the sabayon. And the sabayon should be prepared moments before serving. The sabayon may be prepared using a hand-held electric mixer; the preparation time will be 3 to 4 minutes, rather than 6 to 8 minutes.*

# PORT WINE ICE CREAM WITH HOT "LIQUOR" SAUCE

YIELDS 1¹/₂ QUARTS

1   cup heavy cream
1   cup half-and-half
³/₄   cup granulated sugar
6   eggs
1¹/₂   cups port
3   tablespoons grenadine
Hot "Liquor" Sauce (see page 16)

## THE CHEF'S TOUCH

*T*he task of suggesting a wine to accompany dessert is,
if not formidable, then certainly challenging. My
personal taste is for fruity wines with obvious sugar, be they
sparkling or still. The balance of flavor created by joining a
ruby port with a chocolate dessert is perfect to my palate.

Pastry chef John Twichell's nonplussed expression
when I suggested developing a Port Wine Ice Cream soon
changed to comprehension when I proposed serving it with
a warm dark chocolate sauce.

This is a satisfying and relatively light dessert. It can
be served year-round and is particularly fitting after a
multicourse dinner.

At The Trellis, we produce the Port Wine Ice Cream
using Gallo California port and Wupperman grenadine.

### EQUIPMENT

*Measuring cup, measuring spoons, 2¹/₂-quart saucepan, whisk, electric mixer with paddle,
rubber spatula, instant-read test thermometer, 2 stainless steel bowls (1 large), ice-cream freezer,
2-quart plastic container with lid, ice-cream scoop or paddle*

Heat the heavy cream and half-and-half in a 2¹/₂-quart saucepan over medium-high heat. When hot, add ¹/₄ cup sugar and stir to dissolve. Bring to a boil.

While the cream is heating, place the eggs and the remaining ¹/₂ cup sugar in the bowl of an electric mixer fitted with a paddle. Beat the eggs on medium for 2 to 2¹/₂ minutes. Scrape down the bowl, then beat on medium until slightly thickened and lemon-colored, 2¹/₂ to 3 minutes. (At this point, the cream should be boiling. If not, adjust mixer speed to low and continue to mix until the cream boils. If this is not done, the eggs will develop undesirable lumps.)

Pour the boiling cream into the beaten eggs and whisk to combine. Return this mixture to the saucepan and heat over medium-high heat, stirring constantly, until the cream reaches a temperature of 185 degrees Fahrenheit, 2 to 4 minutes. Remove from the heat and transfer to a stainless steel bowl. Add the port and grenadine and whisk to combine thoroughly. Cool the mixture in an ice-water bath (see page 150) to a temperature of 40 to 45 degrees Fahrenheit, about 10 to 15 minutes.

Freeze in an ice-cream freezer following the manufacturer's instructions. Transfer the semi-frozen ice cream to a plastic container, securely cover the container, then place in the freezer for several hours before serving. Serve within 2 days.

To serve, use an ice-cream scoop or paddle to portion the ice cream into the serving dish. Top the Port Wine Ice Cream with a generous amount of warm Hot "Liquor" Sauce and serve immediately.

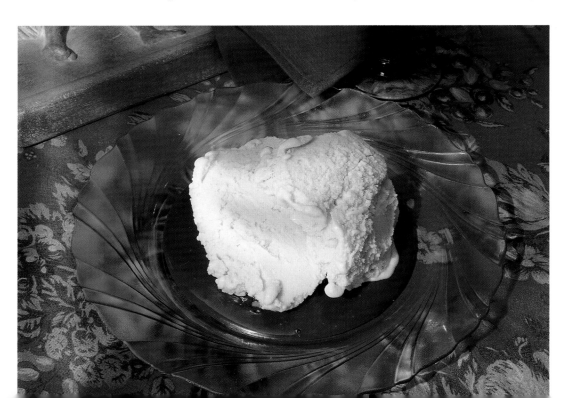

# CHOCOLATE DIPPED HOKEY POKEY COOKIES

MAKES 8 COOKIES

$^1/_2$  cup sliced almonds
$^1/_4$  cup granulated sugar
 2  tablespoons all-purpose flour
 1  egg white
 1  teaspoon unsalted butter, melted

$^1/_4$  teaspoon salt
$^1/_4$  teaspoon pure almond extract
 3  ounces semisweet chocolate, chopped into
    $^1/_4$-inch pieces

### EQUIPMENT

*Measuring cup, measuring spoons, small nonstick sauté pan, baking sheet, stainless steel bowl, rubber spatula, parchment paper, cake spatula, pizza cutter, double boiler, instant-read test thermometer*

Preheat the oven to 325 degrees Fahrenheit.

Toast the almonds on a baking sheet in a preheated oven until golden brown, about 8 minutes, then remove from the oven and cool. Do not turn off the oven.

Combine the sugar, flour, egg white, butter, salt, and almond extract in a stainless steel bowl. Stir the mixture until smooth. Gently fold in the almonds until coated with the batter. Hold the batter at room temperature for 20 minutes before using, stirring occasionally. This is done in order to dissolve the sugar. If this step is bypassed, the cookies will not have the desired taste and texture.

Trace 2 6-inch circles onto a piece of parchment paper (cut to fit a baking sheet). Place the parchment paper, trace marks down, on a baking sheet. Evenly divide the batter between the circles. Use a cake spatula to evenly spread the batter to entirely cover each circle. Bake in the preheated oven for 20 to 24 minutes, until uniformly golden brown. Turn the baking sheet 180 degrees about halfway through the baking time. Remove the pan from the oven and allow to cool for 3 to 4 minutes. Use a pizza cutter to cut each baked circle into 4 wedge-shaped cookies. Cool for 30 minutes before removing the cookies from the parchment paper.

Heat 1 inch of water in the bottom half of a double boiler over medium heat. Place the semisweet chocolate in the top half of the double boiler (see page 151). Heat the chocolate uncovered, constantly stirring with a rubber spatula until the chocolate is melted and smooth, about 2 minutes. Remove the chocolate from the heat and continue to stir until the temperature of the chocolate is reduced to 90 degrees Fahrenheit.

Dip $^1/_2$ inch of the rounded edge of each cookie into the melted chocolate. Place the cookies onto parchment paper and allow the chocolate to set at room temperature (74 to 78 degrees Fahrenheit) for 20 to 25 minutes. (The cookies may be placed in the refrigerator for 5 minutes to quickly set the chocolate.)

# Zio Ciccio's Cassata

SERVES 8

### Marsala Cake

- 2 *teaspoons unsalted butter, melted*
- 1/2 *cup cake flour*
- 2 *tablespoons cornstarch*
- 3 *eggs*
- 1/2 *cup granulated sugar*
- 3 *egg yolks*
- 1 *teaspoon pure vanilla extract*
- 2 *egg whites*
- 1 *cup Marsala wine (set aside until the assembly of the cake)*

### Chocolate Chunk Custard

- 1 *cup whole milk*
- 1 *cup heavy cream*
- 1/2 *cup granulated sugar*
- 2 *eggs*
- 4 *egg yolks*
- 4 *tablespoons cornstarch*
- 2 *teaspoons pure vanilla extract*
- 2 *ounces semisweet chocolate, chopped into 1/4-inch pieces*

### Decoration

- 2 *tablespoons unsweetened cocoa*

**Equipment**

*Measuring spoons, small nonstick frying pan, measuring cup, cutting board, cook's knife, 9- by 1 1/2-inch cake pan, parchment paper, sifter, wax paper, electric mixer with balloon whip, 2 stainless steel bowls (1 large), whisk, rubber spatula, 2 cardboard cake circles, 2 1/2-quart saucepan, instant-read test thermometer, serrated slicer, cake spatula*

Lightly coat the insides of a 9- by 1 1/2-inch cake pan with melted butter. Line the pan with parchment paper, then lightly coat the parchment with more melted butter.

Preheat the oven to 325 degrees Fahrenheit.

Sift together the cake flour and 2 tablespoons cornstarch onto the wax paper. Set aside.

Place 3 eggs, 1/2 cup sugar, 3 egg yolks, and 1 teaspoon vanilla extract in the bowl of an electric mixer fitted with a balloon whip. Whisk on high until slightly thickened and lemon-colored, about 3 to 4 minutes. Adjust mixer speed to low and continue to mix while whisking the egg whites.

Whisk 2 egg whites in a stainless steel bowl until stiff but not dry, about 2 to 3 minutes.

Add the sifted dry ingredients to the egg mixture in the mixing bowl. Mix on medium for 10 seconds. Increase the speed to high and whisk for an additional 5 seconds. Remove the bowl from the mixer and use a rubber spatula to vigorously fold in the beaten egg whites.

Pour the batter into the prepared cake pan, spreading evenly. Bake in the preheated oven until a toothpick inserted in the center comes out clean, about 25 to 30 minutes. Remove the cake from the oven, and allow to cool in the pan for 20 minutes. Invert onto a cake circle, then immediately reinvert onto another cake circle (the cake is now right side up).

To prepare the custard, heat the milk and cream in a 2 1/2-quart saucepan over medium heat. Bring to a boil. While the cream is heating, place 1/2 cup sugar, 2 eggs, 4 egg yolks, and 4 tablespoons of cornstarch in the bowl of an electric mixer fitted with a balloon whip. Whisk on high until slightly thickened and lemon-colored, about 3 1/2 to 4 minutes. (At this point the cream should be boiling. If not, adjust the mixer speed to low and continue to mix until the cream boils. If this is not done, the egg yolks will develop undesirable lumps.)

**THE CHEF'S TOUCH**

*Ristorante Zio (uncle) Ciccio in Marsala, Sicily, faces the glimmering late-afternoon sunshine. We arrived here on our second day of a two-week gastronomic tour of Sicily with Giuliano Bugialli. Those of us seated facing the sea had to wear sunglasses to shield our eyes from the bright rays. Given the agreeableness of the situation, we could have settled for a tin of sardines and a bit of bread; however, as the remainder of the afternoon unfolded we took great delight in the cooking and hospitality of Zio Ciccio. Wonderful antipasti were followed by fragrant shellfish* cucucs *(couscous), then grilled* ariciola *(a meaty fish) liberally doused with olive oil and sprinkled with rough-cut herbs. A simple salad preceded an extravagant slice of Zio Ciccio's Cassata. This interpretation of a classic dish played flavors and textures against each other in a fashion that accentuated the whole.*

*I was driven to create my own rendition in Williamsburg. This version is most definitely an idiosyncratic interpretation, as it contains no ricotta cheese in the filling.*

*A sweet Pellegrino Marsala Dolce Superiore was sipped as the accompaniment to Zio Ciccio's Cassata. I leave the choice of Marsala for soaking the cake up to you. We use a dry Marsala on our cake at The Trellis.*

*The cake will shrink from the sides of the pan after removal from the oven. Not to worry, it just does!*

*The assembled cassata is best eaten within 24 hours. If you care to spread out the preparation of this dessert, I suggest that the cake and the custard be prepared on day 1, followed by the assembly of the cake 2 to 3 hours before serving it on day 2 or even day 3.*

*Use a sifter, dredger, or strainer to uniformly dust the cocoa onto the top of the cake.*

*For a more attractive slice of cassata, lift the sliced portion up and away from the cake rather than backing it out.*

Remove the bowl from the mixer, then pour the boiling cream into the beaten egg mixture, and whisk to combine. Return this mixture to the saucepan and heat over medium heat, stirring constantly, until the mixture reaches a temperature of 185 degrees Fahrenheit, about 3 minutes. Remove from the heat, add 2 teaspoons vanilla extract, and whisk to combine. Transfer the custard to a stainless steel bowl. Cool the custard in an ice-water bath (see page 150) to a temperature of 40 to 45 degrees Fahrenheit, about 25 minutes. When the custard is cold, use a rubber spatula to fold in the chopped semisweet chocolate and combine thoroughly. Refrigerate until needed.

To assemble the cake, first slice it horizontally into 2 equal layers. Place the top layer onto a separate cake circle. Sprinkle each layer with ¹/₂ cup of the reserved Marsala (it will take a little longer for the top cake layer to absorb the Marsala). Evenly spread the chilled chocolate chunk custard over the top cake layer. Invert the bottom layer onto the custard (the top of the cake should be the smooth bottom of the original baked cake), and gently press the layer into place. Use a cake spatula to smooth the custard around the sides of the cake. Refrigerate for 2 hours before slicing and serving.

To serve, dust the top of the cake with the cocoa. Cut the cake with a serrated slicer, wiping the blade clean before cutting each slice. Serve immediately.

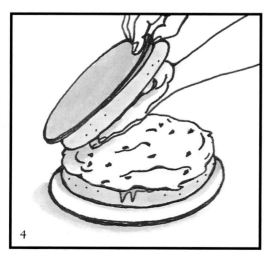

1. Slice cake into two equal layers.

2. Place layers on separate plates and sprinkle each with Marsala.

3. Evenly spread chilled custard over top layer.

4. Invert bottom layer onto custard.

5. Smooth custard evenly around sides of cake.

# SLICED BLOOD ORANGES WITH WHITE CHOCOLATE SAUCE

### SERVES 8

**EQUIPMENT**

*Zester or vegetable peeler, cutting board, cook's knife, serrated slicer*

Zest 2 of the oranges to yield 3 tablespoons of zest. Peel, then slice (about ¼ inch thick) all the oranges. Refrigerate until needed.

To serve, portion 5 to 6 tablespoons of White Chocolate Sauce onto each of 8 chilled 10-inch plates. Arrange 7 to 8 blood orange slices (one slice slightly overlapping the one before it) in a semicircle along a border of each of the plates. Sprinkle about 1 teaspoon of zest over the sauced area not covered by the orange slices. Serve immediately.

12  (3 pounds) blood oranges
 3  tablespoons blood orange zest
White Chocolate Sauce
    (see page 18)

### THE CHEF'S TOUCH

*T*he contrast of the strikingly vivid color of the blood oranges against the rich White Chocolate Sauce makes this dessert a visually impressive and delicious finale to an evening of fine dining. This dessert may be prepared with other sweet oranges, although the drama of the presentation will be diminished.

The intensity of both the flavor and color of blood oranges varies tremendously from one variety of this sweet orange to another. Unfortunately, it is not possible to gauge the color of the flesh based on the pigmentation of the skin. However, with a little luck and by asking the produce dealer about the quality of the product on hand, it is possible to purchase extremely juicy and intensely flavored fruit of a dazzling scarlet color.

If possible, purchase blood oranges that weigh about 4 ounces (¼ pound) each. This size should yield 5 to 6 ¼-inch-thick slices.

Use a zester or a vegetable peeler to zest the oranges. Be careful to remove only the colored skin and not the bitter white pith that lies beneath the skin. If using a vegetable peeler, cut the peeled rind with a sharp cook's knife.

# CHAPTER FOUR

# OBVIOUSLY CHOCOLATE

*RECIPES THAT DEFEAT THE CONSCIENCE*
*AND SEDUCE THE SENSES*

# "BITTERSWEET" CHOCOLATE CUSTARD TART
# WITH ZINFANDEL SOAKED PEARS

SERVES 12

## CHOCOLATE TART SHELL DOUGH

1½ cups all-purpose flour
½ cup granulated sugar
6 tablespoons unsalted butter, cut into
   1-tablespoon pieces
4 tablespoons unsweetened cocoa
Pinch of salt
3 tablespoons brewed coffee, chilled
1 cup rice

## ZINFANDEL SOAKED PEARS

1½ cups Zinfandel wine
½ cup water
½ cup granulated sugar
1 teaspoon lemon juice
1 teaspoon orange juice
4 ripe Bartlett pears

## "BITTERSWEET" CHOCOLATE
## CUSTARD FILLING

2 Zinfandel Soaked Pear halves
1 cup heavy cream
6 ounces semisweet chocolate, broken into
   ½-inch pieces
2 ounces unsweetened chocolate, broken
   into ½-inch pieces
4 eggs
¼ cup granulated sugar
1 teaspoon pure vanilla extract

## EQUIPMENT

*Measuring cup, measuring spoons, cook's knife, cutting board, electric mixer with paddle, film wrap, parchment paper, rolling pin, 9½- by ¾-inch false-bottom tart pan, aluminum foil, 2½-quart saucepan, vegetable peeler, parisienne scoop (also known as a melon baller), slotted spoon, stainless steel bowl, 2 baking sheets, paper towels, food processor with a metal blade, double boiler, rubber spatula, instant-read test thermometer, serrated slicer*

To prepare the chocolate tart shell, mix 1 cup flour, ½ cup sugar, butter, cocoa, and salt in the bowl of an electric mixer fitted with a paddle. Mix on low for 5 minutes, until the butter is "cut into" the flour and the mixture develops a fine, mealy texture. Add coffee and continue to mix on low until the dough comes together, about 1 minute. Remove the dough from the mixer and form it into a smooth round ball. Wrap in film wrap and refrigerate for at least 3 hours.

After the tart shell dough has relaxed in the refrigerator for 3 hours, transfer it to a clean, dry, lightly floured sheet of parchment paper. Roll the dough (using the extra ½ cup of flour as necessary to prevent the dough from sticking) into a circle about 12 inches in diameter and ⅛ inch to ¼ inch thick. Refrigerate the rolled dough (leave it on the parchment paper) for 10 to 15 minutes. Invert the rolled dough into the tart pan. Carefully remove the parchment paper and gently press the dough around the bottom and sides of the pan. Cut away excess dough, leaving a ¾-inch border that should be crimped around the top edge of the pan. Refrigerate for 30 minutes.

Preheat the oven to 325 degrees Fahrenheit.

Line the dough with an 18- by 18-inch piece of aluminum foil (use 2 pieces of foil if necessary); weigh down the foil with 1 cup of rice (evenly spread the rice over the surface of the foil). Bake the tart shell in the center of the preheated oven for 30 minutes, rotating it 180 degrees after 20 minutes. Remove the baked tart shell from the oven, discard the foil and rice, and allow to cool at room temperature. Lower the oven temperature to 300 degrees Fahrenheit.

To prepare the Zinfandel Soaked Pears, place the Zinfandel, water, ½ cup sugar, lemon juice, and orange juice in a 2½-quart saucepan. Whisk to dissolve the sugar. Set aside.

Peel a pear. Cut the pear in half from stem end to bottom. Use a parisienne scoop to core each half. Place the 2 halves into the Zinfandel mixture. Repeat this procedure with the remaining pears, immediately placing the peeled and cored pear halves into the Zinfandel. Heat the pears over medium-low heat until they are cooked through, about 35 to 40 minutes (turn the pears once or twice while they are cooking).

Use a slotted spoon to transfer the pear halves to a bowl of ice water. When cool, remove the pears from the water and drain them on a baking sheet lined with paper towels. Reserve 2 pear halves for the chocolate custard filling. Cover the remaining pears with film wrap and refrigerate until needed.

To prepare the chocolate custard filling, place 2 pear halves in a food processor fitted with a metal blade. Puree the pears by pulsing for 20 to 30 seconds. Hold at room temperature until needed.

Heat 1 inch of water in the bottom half of a double boiler over medium heat. Place the heavy cream, semisweet chocolate, and unsweetened chocolate in the top half of the double boiler (see page 151). Tightly cover the top with film wrap. Allow to heat for 8 to 9 minutes. Remove from the heat and stir until smooth. Set aside until needed.

Place the eggs, pureed pear, 1/4 cup sugar, and vanilla in the bowl of an electric mixer fitted with a paddle. Beat on high for 1 minute. Add the melted chocolate mixture and beat on medium for 20 seconds. Remove the bowl from the mixer and use a rubber spatula to combine thoroughly. Pour the filling into the prebaked tart shell. Place the tart on a baking sheet and bake on the middle shelf of the preheated oven for 45 minutes, until the internal temperature of the tart filling reaches 170 degrees Fahrenheit. Remove the tart from the oven and cool at room temperature for 1 hour. Refrigerate the tart for 1 hour (do not remove the tart from the pan).

To serve, cut the tart with a serrated slicer. Heat the blade of the slicer under hot running water before making each slice. Remove the pear halves from the refrigerator. Cut each half into a quarter by slicing the half from stem end to bottom. Make a fan out of each quarter by cutting 1/8-inch slices starting 1/4 inch from the stem end. Gently press down on the slices to produce a fan effect. Decorate the top of each tart slice with a pear fan and serve immediately.

### THE CHEF'S TOUCH

*T*he chocolate tart shell dough is very delicate: be gentle in handling. If the dough does become difficult to work with, especially while placing in the tart pan or while crimping the border, return it to the refrigerator for a few minutes.

Use a vegetable peeler to carefully peel the pears so that their natural shape is retained.

Depending on the size of the fruit, it may be necessary to add up to 1 cup of water to poach the pears. In any case, the poaching liquid should almost cover the pears.

Handle the soaked pears gently when cooling in ice water. If the pears are moved too vigorously into the ice water, the surface will become cut and bruised.

If the pears discolor after being removed from the ice water, they probably were not cooked through; otherwise, they should not discolor for at least 24 hours.

The tart may be kept in the refrigerator for 2 to 3 days before serving. The pears should be cooked and used within 24 hours.

# CHOCOLATE CARAMEL SURPRISE
# WITH BOURBON ANGLAISE
................................................
SERVES 8

## MOCHA HAZELNUT MOUSSE

12  ounces semisweet chocolate, broken into
    $^1/_2$-ounce pieces
3   ounces unsweetened chocolate, broken
    into $^1/_2$-ounce pieces
4   tablespoons hazelnut liqueur
2   tablespoons brewed coffee, full strength
5   egg whites
2   tablespoons granulated sugar
$^3/_4$  cup heavy cream

## VANILLA COOKIE

$^1/_4$  pound unsalted butter, softened
$^1/_2$  cup granulated sugar
$^1/_4$  teaspoon salt
3   egg whites
$^1/_4$  teaspoon pure vanilla extract
$^3/_4$  cup all-purpose flour

## GOLDEN SUGAR

$^1/_4$  cup granulated sugar
$^1/_8$  teaspoon lemon juice

## CARAMEL FILLING

1   cup granulated sugar
$^1/_4$  teaspoon lemon juice
$^1/_2$  cup heavy cream

## BOURBON ANGLAISE

$^3/_4$  cup heavy cream
$^3/_4$  cup whole milk
5   egg yolks
$^1/_4$  cup granulated sugar
2   tablespoons bourbon

## DECORATION

2   tablespoons unsweetened cocoa

## EQUIPMENT

*Measuring cup, measuring spoons, double boiler, film wrap, whisk, 4 stainless steel bowls (1 large), electric mixer with balloon whip and paddle, rubber spatula, parchment paper, 3 baking sheets (1 non-stick), cake spatula, 2 plastic containers with lids, cutting board, cook's knife, 2$^1/_2$-quart saucepan, instant-read test thermometer, pastry bag, medium star tip, sifter*

To prepare the Mocha Hazelnut Mousse, heat 1 inch of water in the bottom half of a double boiler over medium-high heat. Place the semisweet chocolate, unsweetened chocolate, hazelnut liqueur, and brewed coffee in the top half of the double boiler (see page 151). Tightly cover the top with film wrap. Heat for 6 to 8 minutes, then remove from the heat. Stir the mixture until smooth. Transfer to a large stainless steel bowl. Keep at room temperature while whisking the 5 egg whites.

In the bowl of an electric mixer fitted with a balloon whip, whisk the egg whites on high until soft peaks form, 1 to 1$^1/_2$ minutes. Continue to whisk while gradually adding 2 tablespoons sugar. Whisk until stiff but not dry, about 30 seconds.

Whip $^3/_4$ cup heavy cream in a well-chilled stainless steel bowl until stiff. Use a rubber spatula to fold a quarter of the egg whites into the melted chocolate mixture, then fold in the whipped cream. When combined, fold in the remaining egg whites. Cover the bowl with film wrap and refrigerate until needed.

Preheat the oven to 325 degrees Fahrenheit.

Trace 6 3$^1/_2$-inch circles with a pencil on each of 4 sheets of parchment paper cut to fit a baking sheet.

To prepare the cookie batter combine the butter, $^1/_2$ cup sugar, and the salt in the bowl of an electric mixer fitted with a paddle. Beat on medium for 1 minute. Scrape down the sides of the bowl and beat on high for 2 minutes. Once again, scrape down the bowl. Add the 3 egg whites, one at a time, while beating on high, stopping to scrape down the bowl after incorporating each egg white. Add the vanilla extract and beat on high for 10 seconds. (Do not be concerned about the appearance of the batter at this juncture; quite frankly, it looks rather unappetizing.) Add flour, mixing on low for 15 to 20 seconds, until the batter pulls away from the sides of the bowl. Remove bowl from mixer. Use a rubber spatula to finish mixing the batter until it is smooth and thoroughly combined.

Place a sheet of parchment paper, trace marks down, on a baking sheet. Place 1 tablespoon of batter in the center of each circle. Use a cake spatula to smear a uniformly thin coating of the batter to entirely cover each circle. Repeat this procedure on the second baking sheet. Bake the cookies on the top and middle shelves of the preheated oven until evenly golden brown, about 14 to 16 minutes. Rotate the baking sheets from top to bottom about halfway through the baking time. Remove from the oven and slide the parchment paper with the cookies onto a flat surface, allowing the cookies to cool to room temperature before handling. Store the cookies in an airtight plastic container. Prepare the remaining cookies by repeating the above procedure. If the baking sheets are still warm, it will take 2 to 3 minutes less baking time to bake the cookies until golden. Store all the cookies in a plastic container at room temperature until needed. (They will keep several days if the container is tightly sealed.)

*In December of 1981, The Trellis inaugurated its concept for a seasonal preview dinner. Held the night before the change in the seasonal menu, these preview dinners showcase new menu items for all but the summer season. At the preview dinner we try to outdo ourselves with wickedly delicious chocolate creations. On the occasion of the twenty-fifth seasonal preview dinner, December 19, 1989, pastry chef John Twichell astounded our guests with what appeared to be a subtle stack of cookies. Upon tasting the first morsel, they came to realize what we have known for some time—this young man is a cunning confectioner.*

*As with several other recipes offered in this book, I recommend that you stagger the production of this dessert over 2 days. DAY 1: Prepare the vanilla cookies and store in an airtight plastic container at room temperature until the dessert is assembled. Also, make the golden sugar and store it in an airtight plastic container in your freezer until assembly of the dessert. The Bourbon Anglaise may also be prepared on day 1 and stored, covered with film wrap, in the refrigerator until assembly.*

*DAY 2: Prepare the mousse early in the day and keep refrigerated until 30 to 45 minutes before assembly. Prepare the caramel filling last and hold at room temperature (70 to 75 degrees Fahrenheit) until assembly. If your room temperature is running on the cool side and the caramel gets too thick, place the bowl containing the caramel in a pan with hot water and gently stir until the caramel liquefies enough to spoon into the mousse circles. Be certain that the caramel is not too warm or it will melt the mousse.*

*In order to deter crystallization, fresh lemon juice is added to the sugar before caramelization.*

*The golden sugar quickly becomes tacky at room temperature. If this happens and it becomes difficult to handle, return it to the freezer for a few minutes.*

*For a final sublime touch, place 1 or 2 fresh red raspberries in each layer of caramel filling as you are assembling the cookie stack.*

To prepare the golden sugar, place $1/4$ cup sugar and $1/8$ teaspoon of lemon juice in a $2^1/2$-quart saucepan. Stir with a whisk to combine (the sugar will resemble moist sand). Caramelize the sugar for 3 to 4 minutes over medium-high heat, stirring constantly with a whisk to break up any lumps (the sugar will first turn clear as it liquefies, then brown as it caramelizes). Pour the caramelized sugar onto a nonstick baking sheet, then harden in the freezer, about 4 minutes. Turn the hardened sugar out onto a cutting board, then finely chop by hand with a cook's knife. Store the golden sugar in an airtight container in the freezer until ready to use. (The sugar will keep several weeks if the container is tightly sealed.)

For the caramel filling, combine 1 cup sugar and $1/4$ teaspoon lemon juice in a $2^1/2$-quart saucepan and stir to combine. Heat over medium-high heat. Caramelize the sugar for 4 to 6 minutes, constantly stirring with a whisk to break up any lumps. Remove the saucepan from the heat and slowly add $1/2$ cup heavy cream, stirring to combine. Transfer the caramel filling to a stainless steel bowl and allow to cool to room temperature.

To prepare the Bourbon Anglaise, heat $3/4$ cup heavy cream and the milk in a $2^1/2$-quart saucepan over medium heat. Bring to a boil. While the cream is heating, place the egg yolks and $1/4$ cup sugar in the bowl of an electric mixer fitted with a paddle. Beat on high for 2 to $2^1/2$ minutes. Scrape down the sides of the bowl, then beat on high until slightly thickened and lemon-colored, an additional 2 to $2^1/2$ minutes. (At this point, the cream should be boiling. If not, adjust the mixer speed to low and continue to mix until the cream boils. Otherwise, the egg yolks will develop undesirable lumps.)

Pour the boiling cream into the beaten egg yolks and whisk to combine. Return to the saucepan and heat over medium-high heat, stirring constantly, until the cream reaches a temperature of 185 degrees Fahrenheit, $1^1/2$ to 2 minutes. Remove from the heat and transfer to a stainless steel bowl. Add bourbon and stir to combine. Cool the anglaise in an ice-water bath (see page 150) for about 15 minutes.

To assemble, fill a pastry bag fitted with a medium-sized tip with the Mocha Hazelnut Mousse. Pipe a $3/4$-inch-wide ring of mousse along the outside edge of 16 of the cookies. Portion 1 tablespoon of the caramel filling into the center of each mousse ring. Stack 2 of the caramel-filled cookies (mousse side up) on top of each other, then cover with a plain cookie. Repeat until all the cookies are stacked. Lightly sift 2 tablespoons of cocoa over all the cookie stacks.

Portion 4 tablespoons of Bourbon Anglaise onto each of 8 10-inch plates. Place a cookie stack in the center of each plate and finish by sprinkling golden sugar onto the Anglaise.

# MOCHA JAVA SORBET

YIELDS 2 QUARTS

2 cups water
2 cups granulated sugar
1½ cups brewed coffee, full strength
6 ounces unsweetened chocolate, broken into ½-ounce pieces

2 ounces semisweet chocolate, broken into ½-ounce pieces
1 teaspoon pure vanilla extract

## EQUIPMENT
*Measuring cup, measuring spoons, 2½-quart saucepan, 2 stainless steel bowls (1 large), whisk, spoon, instant-read test thermometer, ice-cream freezer, rubber spatula, 2-quart plastic container with lid*

Heat the water, sugar, and coffee in a 2½-quart saucepan over medium-high heat. Whisk to dissolve the sugar. Bring the mixture to a boil. Place the unsweetened and semisweet chocolates in a stainless steel bowl. Remove the boiling liquid from the heat and pour 1 cup over the chocolate. Allow to stand for 5 minutes. Vigorously whisk until completely smooth, about 3 minutes. Add the remaining hot liquid and whisk until smooth. Cool in an ice-water bath (see page 150) to a temperature of 40 to 45 degrees Fahrenheit, about 18 to 20 minutes. When cold, add the vanilla and stir to incorporate.

Freeze in an ice-cream freezer following the manufacturer's instructions. Transfer semifrozen sorbet to a plastic container, securely cover the container, then place in freezer for several hours before serving. Serve within 2 days.

### THE CHEF'S TOUCH

*The simplicity of this recipe belies the years of trial and error spent by pastry chef John Twichell, to achieve the texture and flavor balance, which is the secret to the "eating quality" of this sorbet. The concept of a chocolate sorbet was conceived from the idea of offering a dairy-free product. I felt that many of our guests who eschewed ice cream would enthusiastically order and enjoy a chocolate sorbet. Of course, our Mocha Java Sorbet is not fat-free (due to the cocoa butter in the chocolate), nor is it low in calories (due to the substantial amount of sugar). What this sorbet has going for it is the fact that it is deliciously refreshing and overwhelmingly chocolate, and yes, I will mention once again, no dairy products—ergo that frequently heard cry, "no cholesterol."*

*The importance of the stated amount of sugar in this recipe cannot be overemphasized. It is essential for the smooth texture of the frozen sorbet.*

*The coffee we brew at The Trellis is a blend called mocha java, purchased from the First Colony Coffee & Tea Company of Norfolk, Virginia (see page 153). The flavor and aroma of this coffee, and its use in this recipe, inspired me to rename what we had called Dark Chocolate Sorbet for years, to its now-popular moniker: Mocha Java Sorbet.*

*It is very important to vigorously whisk the mixture when incorporating the cup of boiling liquid into the chocolate. If the mixture is not smooth, the sorbet will be grainy.*

*I would suggest that the mixture be constantly stirred while cooling in the ice bath. This will speed up the time necessary to chill the mixture and seems to have an effect on the eventual texture of the frozen sorbet.*

# CHOCOLATE CASHEW BROWNIE CAKE

SERVES 12

## CHOCOLATE BROWNIE CAKE

4$^1/_2$  ounces semisweet chocolate, broken into $^1/_2$-ounce pieces

6  tablespoons plus 1 teaspoon unsalted butter

2$^1/_2$  ounces unsweetened chocolate, broken into $^1/_2$-ounce pieces

$^3/_4$  cup plus 1 teaspoon all-purpose flour

5  eggs

1  cup granulated sugar

1  teaspoon pure vanilla extract

$^3/_4$  teaspoon salt

$^3/_4$  teaspoon baking powder

3  tablespoons sour cream

## CHOCOLATE GANACHE

3  cups cashews

1$^1/_2$  cups heavy cream

3  tablespoons unsalted butter

3  tablespoons granulated sugar

12  ounces semisweet chocolate, broken into $^1/_2$-ounce pieces

## EQUIPMENT
*Measuring cup, measuring spoons, double boiler, film wrap, whisk, 9- by 1$^1/_2$-inch cake pan, electric mixer with balloon whip, rubber spatula, 2 stainless steel bowls (1 large), cardboard cake circle, baking sheet with sides, food processor with metal blade, 2$^1/_2$-quart saucepan, serrated slicer, 9- by 3-inch springform pan, serrated knife, cake spatula*

Preheat the oven to 325 degrees Fahrenheit.

Heat 1 inch of water in the bottom half of a double boiler over medium heat. Place 4$^1/_2$ ounces semisweet chocolate, 6 tablespoons butter, and the unsweetened chocolate in the top half of the double boiler (see page 151). Tightly cover the top with film wrap and allow to heat for 8 to 9 minutes. Remove from the heat and stir until smooth.

Coat a 9- by 1$^1/_2$-inch cake pan with 1 teaspoon butter. Flour the pan with 1 teaspoon flour, shaking out the excess.

Combine the eggs, 1 cup sugar, and the vanilla extract in the bowl of an electric mixer fitted with a balloon whip. Whip on high until slightly thickened and doubled in volume, about 4 to 5 minutes. Add the melted chocolate and whip on medium for 15 seconds. Remove the bowl from the mixer. Fold in $^3/_4$ cup flour, the salt, and the baking powder, using a rubber spatula to combine thoroughly. In a stainless steel bowl, vigorously whisk the sour cream. Add the sour cream to the brownie cake mixture and thoroughly combine.

Pour the brownie cake batter into the prepared pan, spreading the batter evenly. Bake in the preheated oven until a toothpick inserted in the center of the cake comes out clean, about 1 hour. Remove the cake from the oven and cool in the pan for 20 minutes at room temperature. Turn out onto a cake circle and refrigerate, uncovered, for 1 hour.

Lower the oven temperature to 300 degrees Fahrenheit.

Toast the cashews on a baking sheet in the 300 degree Fahrenheit oven until golden, about 15 to 18 minutes. Remove from the oven and allow to cool to room temperature. Reserve 36 cashews to decorate the cake. Chop $^1/_2$ cup toasted cashews into pieces no larger than $^1/_8$ inch in a food processor fitted with a metal blade (to be used to decorate the sides of the brownie cake). Chop the remaining cashews in the food processor into $^1/_4$-inch pieces (to combine into the ganache).

To prepare the chocolate ganache, heat the heavy cream, 3 tablespoons butter, and 3 tablespoons sugar in a 2$^1/_2$-quart saucepan over medium-high heat, stirring to dissolve the sugar. Bring the mixture to a boil. Place 12 ounces of semisweet chocolate in a stainless steel bowl and pour the boiling cream over the chocolate. Allow to stand for 5 minutes, then stir until smooth.

Remove 1 cup of ganache and keep at room temperature. Combine the remaining ganache and the $^1/_4$-inch pieces of cashews. Keep at room temperature until needed.

Remove the brownie cake from the refrigerator. Turn the cake top side up and place on a clean, dry surface. Slice the brownie cake horizontally into 3 equal layers. Place the top layer of the brownie cake, cut side down, onto the bottom of a closed springform pan. Using a rubber spatula, spread 1$^1/_2$ cups of the ganache and cashew mixture over the brownie cake layer in the springform pan, spreading the ganache evenly to the edges. Place the center layer of the brownie cake on top of the ganache in the springform pan and gently press into place.

Spread the remaining ganache and cashew mixture over the center brownie cake layer, again spreading evenly to the edges. Place the bottom layer of the brownie cake, cut side down, on top of the last ganache layer, pressing gently but firmly into place. Refrigerate the brownie cake for at least 1 hour before final assembly.

To remove the brownie cake from the springform pan, cut around the inside edges of the pan with a serrated knife. Pour the reserved cup of ganache over the top of the brownie cake, spreading the ganache with a cake spatula to create an even coating on both the top and the sides. Press the ⅛-inch chopped cashews into the ganache on the sides of the brownie cake, coating the cake evenly all around.

Evenly space the reserved whole cashews around the top of the brownie cake, ½ inch inside the outer edge of the top. Refrigerate the cake for 1 hour before serving.

To serve, cut the Chocolate Cashew Brownie Cake with a serrated slicer. Heat the blade of the slicer under hot running water before making each slice. Allow the slices to come to room temperature for 15 to 20 minutes before serving.

*A caveat regarding the roasting time of the cashews: the suggested time of 15 to 18 minutes may vary considerably, depending on the coloration of the cashews as purchased. In any case, keep a close eye on the cashews while roasting; they are expensive, and easy to over-roast.*

*Use several toothpicks inserted in the sides of the cake as guides to accurately cut the cake horizontally.*

*If the cup of ganache needed to coat the cake becomes too firm, warm it over a pan of warm water, stirring until smooth.*

*When placing the whole cashews on top of the cake, first set 12 as if they were numbers on a clock. Then place 2 cashews between each of the 12 so that you will have 36 perfectly placed cashews.*

*After assembly, you may keep this cake in the refrigerator for 2 to 3 days before serving. Allow the slices to come to room temperature for 15 to 20 minutes before serving.*

# CHOCOLATE HARLEQUIN BIRTHDAY CAKE

SERVES 8

## EQUIPMENT

*Measuring spoons, measuring cup, 9-inch cardboard cake circle, 2 baking sheets, parchment paper, electric mixer with balloon whip, rubber spatula, pastry bag, large straight tip, double boiler, film wrap, whisk, large stainless steel bowl, large star tip, cardboard diamond template (see page 78), dredger, serrated slicer*

Using a 9-inch cake circle (or cake plate) as a guide, trace a circle on each of 2 sheets of parchment paper (cut to fit the baking sheets) with a pencil. Turn each sheet of parchment paper over and place with the trace mark down on a baking sheet.

Preheat the oven to 225 degrees Fahrenheit.

To prepare the meringues, place 6 egg whites, the cream of tartar, and salt in the bowl of an electric mixer fitted with a balloon whip. Whisk on high until soft peaks form, about 1 minute. Gradually add 6 tablespoons sugar while whisking on high, until stiff but not dry, about $1^1/2$ to 2 minutes. Remove the bowl from the mixer and use a rubber spatula to fold in and thoroughly combine 1 tablespoon cornstarch.

Fill a pastry bag fitted with a large-sized straight tip with about half of the meringue. Fill a traced circle with meringue: start in the center and pipe a $^3/_4$-inch-wide spiral toward the outside of the circle. Repeat this procedure with the remaining circle.

Place the meringues in the preheated oven and bake for 1 hour. Reduce the oven temperature to 200 degrees Fahrenheit and bake for an additional 3 hours. Remove from the oven and allow to cool on the baking sheets for 30 minutes before handling.

While the meringues are cooling, prepare the double chocolate mousse. Heat 1 inch of water in the bottom half of a double boiler over medium heat. Place the semisweet and unsweetened chocolates in the top half of the double boiler (see page 151). Tightly cover the top with film wrap. Allow to heat for 10 to 12 minutes. Remove from the heat and stir until smooth. Keep at room temperature until needed.

Place the heavy cream in the well-chilled bowl of an electric mixer fitted with a well-chilled balloon whip (see page 151). Whisk on high until peaks form, about 1 minute. Set aside until needed.

Whisk 3 egg whites in a large stainless steel bowl, until soft peaks form, about 3 minutes. Add 2 tablespoons sugar and continue to whisk until stiff peaks form, about 2 to $2^1/2$ minutes. Add a quarter of the whipped cream to the chocolate and whisk quickly, vigorously, and thoroughly, then add to the egg whites. Now add the remaining whipped cream. Fold all together, gently but thoroughly. Transfer the mousse to a standard size (3-quart) stainless steel bowl and refrigerate for 15 to 20 minutes.

To assemble the Chocolate Harlequin Birthday Cake, transfer the mousse to a pastry bag fitted with a large-sized star tip. Place a dab of mousse in the center of a cardboard cake circle. Place a meringue, top side up, on the circle. Gently press down on the meringue so that the mousse will hold it in place. Pipe a circle of stars (each touching the other) along the outside edge of the meringue on the cake circle. Continue to pipe out circles of stars until the meringue is covered. Place the remaining meringue, top side up, on top of the mousse stars, gently pressing down on the meringue to set it into place.

## MERINGUE

- 6 egg whites
- $^1/_4$ teaspoon cream of tartar
- $^1/_8$ teaspoon salt
- 6 tablespoons granulated sugar
- 1 tablespoon cornstarch

## DOUBLE CHOCOLATE MOUSSE

- 8 ounces semisweet chocolate, broken into $^1/_2$-ounce pieces
- 4 ounces unsweetened chocolate, broken into $^1/_2$-ounce pieces
- $1^1/_2$ cups heavy cream
- 3 egg whites
- 2 tablespoons granulated sugar

## DECORATIONS

- 3 tablespoons confectioners' sugar
- 1 tablespoon unsweetened cocoa birthday candles

*T*he week I spent at the Lenotre Pastry School in July 1986, was a rewarding professional experience. The instructional kitchen at Lenotre was state of the art and the level of teaching was first-rate. All of the students in my class were food professionals, including the corporate chef from Möet & Chandon, a culinary instructor from Cairo, Egypt, 2 pastry chefs from Montreal, and a Vietnamese woman married to a German who owned and operated a Chinese restaurant in New Orleans. I also had lots of fun and learned a tremendous amount, including these tips.

The meringues should be rotated once every hour during the baking time in order to assure that they are uniformly baked.

Baked meringues may be prepared a day or two in advance of assembly. Store baked meringues in a closed container in a dry place at room temperature.

Baked meringues are brittle: Handle with care. To avoid cracking the top layer of meringue, be very careful to press gently down on it when pressing it into place on the double chocolate mousse stars.

Although the meringues can be baked a day or two in advance, the mousse should be prepared just before the assembly (if refrigerated for more than the suggested 15 to 20 minutes, the mousse sets up quite hard, making it virtually impossible to pipe through the pastry bag). The assembly of the cake is a fairly quick operation, so I suggest that it be done as close to the point of serving as possible. If the cake is assembled too far in advance of serving, the meringues will absorb some of the moisture from the mousse and lose some of their crisp texture.

Use a dredger to dust the sugar and cocoa diamonds onto the top of the cake.

Birthday candles may be pressed into the crisp surface of the meringue. Position several candles near the outside edge of the cake, or perhaps a single candle in the center.

Dust the top of the cake with the confectioners' sugar. Place the diamond template on top of the cake and dust the diamonds with the cocoa. Remove the template, then refrigerate the cake for no less than 1 hour and no more than 12 hours before serving.

To serve, place as few birthday candles on the top of the cake as your conscience will allow. Cut the cake with a serrated slicer. Heat the blade of the slicer under hot running water before making each slice. Allow the slices to come to room temperature for 10 to 15 minutes before serving.

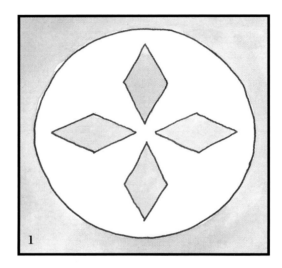

1. The sides of each diamond measure 1³/₄ inches (7 cm).

2. Dust the top of the cake with confectioner's sugar.

3. Place template on top of cake and dust diamonds with cocoa.

4. Remove template.

# CHOCOLATE CHIPPY CRUNCH SOUFFLÉ

MAKES 8 INDIVIDUAL SOUFFLÉS

### EQUIPMENT

*Measuring spoons, measuring cup, 8 8-ounce ovenproof soufflé cups, double boiler, film wrap, large stainless steel bowl, whisk, electric mixer with balloon whip, rubber spatula, long-handled tablespoon*

Preheat the oven to 350 degrees Fahrenheit.

Lightly coat the inside of each soufflé cup with the butter. Sprinkle the inside of each cup with 1 1/2 teaspoons granulated sugar. Set aside until needed.

Heat 1 inch of water in the bottom half of a double boiler over medium heat. Place the semisweet and unsweetened chocolate in the top half of the double boiler (see page 151). Tightly cover the top with film wrap. Heat for 6 to 8 minutes. Remove from the heat and stir until smooth. Transfer the chocolate to a large stainless steel bowl. Use a whisk to stir in the egg yolks and heavy cream until thoroughly combined. Set aside.

Place the egg whites in the bowl of an electric mixer fitted with a balloon whip. Whisk on high until soft peaks form, about 1 minute. Add the remaining sugar and continue to whisk on high until stiff peaks form, about 45 to 50 seconds. Remove the bowl from the mixer. Use a rubber spatula to fold 1/4 of the whipped egg whites into the melted chocolate mixture, then fold in the remaining egg whites.

Evenly divide the soufflé mixture into the prepared soufflé cups (about 4 heaping long-handled tablespoons), filling them to 1/2 inch below the rim of the cup. Evenly divide and sprinkle the cookie pieces and chocolate chips over the tops of the soufflé mixture.

Place the soufflés on the center shelf of the preheated oven. Bake until a toothpick inserted in the center comes out clean, about 22 to 26 minutes.

Remove from the oven and serve immediately.

1 tablespoon unsalted butter
8 tablespoons granulated sugar
6 ounces semisweet chocolate, broken into 1/2-ounce pieces
2 ounces unsweetened chocolate, broken into 1/2-ounce pieces
4 egg yolks
1/4 cup heavy cream
8 egg whites
3 Deep Dark Chocolate Fudge Cookies, chopped into 1/2-inch pieces (see page 28)
1/2 cup semisweet chocolate chips

### THE CHEF'S TOUCH

*My skin gets frissons as I imagine a sterling silver spoon, laden with Mocha Anglaise (see page 17) breaking through the surface of the soufflé to deposit its treasure of pleasure. And for those inclined to more demure infusions, I suggest a similar insertion with White Chocolate "Ice Cream" (see page 35).*

# CHOCOLATE STRAWBERRY MOUSSE CAKE

SERVES 12

## CHOCOLATE CAKE

- 1/2  pound unsalted butter (2 tablespoons melted)
- 8  ounces semisweet chocolate, broken into 1/2-ounce pieces
- 8  egg yolks
- 3/4  cup granulated sugar
- 4  egg whites

## CHOCOLATE STRAWBERRY MOUSSE

- 2  pints strawberries, stems removed
- 16  ounces semisweet chocolate, broken into 1/2-ounce pieces
- 4  ounces white chocolate, broken into 1/2-ounce pieces
- 6  egg whites
- 2  tablespoons granulated sugar
- 1  cup heavy cream

## SEMISWEET CHOCOLATE GANACHE

Semisweet Chocolate Ganache (see page 19)

### EQUIPMENT
*Measuring cup, measuring spoons, 3 9- by 1¹/₂-inch cake pans, parchment paper, double boiler, film wrap, whisk, electric mixer with paddle and balloon whip, rubber spatula, 3 stainless steel bowls (1 large), 9- by 3-inch springform pan, 2 9-inch cake circles, food processor with metal blade, cake spatula, pastry bag, large star tip, serrated slicer*

Lightly coat the insides of 3 9- by 1¹/₂-inch cake pans with melted butter. Line each pan with parchment paper, then lightly coat the parchment with more melted butter. Set aside.

Preheat the oven to 325 degrees Fahrenheit.

Heat 1 inch of water in the bottom half of a double boiler over medium heat. Place remaining butter and 8 ounces semisweet chocolate in the top half of the double boiler (see page 151). Tightly cover the top with film wrap. Allow to heat for 10 to 12 minutes. Remove from heat, stir until smooth, and hold at room temperature.

Place the egg yolks and 3/4 cup sugar in the bowl of an electric mixer fitted with a paddle. Beat on high until slightly thickened and lemon-colored, about 4 minutes. Scrape down the sides of the bowl and beat on high for an additional 2 minutes.

While the egg yolks are beating, whisk 4 egg whites in a large stainless steel bowl until stiff but not dry, about 3 to 4 minutes.

Using a rubber spatula, fold the melted chocolate mixture into the beaten egg yolk mixture. Add a quarter of the beaten egg whites and stir to incorporate, then gently fold in the remaining egg whites.

Divide the batter between the prepared pans, spreading evenly, and bake in the preheated oven until a toothpick inserted in the center comes out clean, about 25 to 30 minutes. Remove the cakes from the oven and allow to cool in the pans for 15 minutes. (During baking, the surface of the cakes will form a crust; this crust will normally collapse when the cakes are removed from the oven.) Invert 1 of the cakes onto the bottom of a springform pan. Invert the other 2 cakes onto cake circles. Remove parchment paper and refrigerate cakes for 30 minutes.

To prepare the chocolate strawberry mousse, reserve the 12 best-looking strawberries to decorate the top of the cake. In a food processor fitted with a metal blade, purée 4 ounces of strawberries (12 medium-sized berries should yield 1/2 cup—4 ounces—of puree). Set aside until needed. Refrigerate the remaining berries until needed (that includes the 12 berries for decoration).

Heat 1 inch of water in the bottom half of a double boiler over medium heat. Place 16 ounces semisweet chocolate, the white chocolate, and the strawberry puree in the top half of the double boiler. Tightly cover the top with film wrap. Allow to heat for 12 to 14 minutes. Remove from the heat and stir until smooth. Transfer to a stainless steel bowl, using a rubber spatula to remove all of the melted chocolate mixture. Keep at room temperature until needed.

In the bowl of an electric mixer fitted with a balloon whip, whisk the 6 egg whites on high until soft peaks form, about 2 minutes. Continue to whisk on high while gradually adding 2 tablespoons sugar. Whisk until stiff but not dry, about 30 seconds. Set aside at room temperature until needed.

Using a hand-held whisk, whip the heavy cream in a well-chilled stainless steel bowl (see page 151) until stiff. Fold a quarter of the egg whites into the melted chocolate mixture, then fold

*Strawberries are normally sold by the pint. Depending on the time of the year and the country of origin, the size may vary substantially. The California berries we prefer at The Trellis are of a fairly uniform size and number about 18 to 20 per pint. Sometimes we receive Mexican berries that have 25 or more berries per pint. For this recipe, I hope that you will be able to pick 12 berries that are about 1 inch wide at the stem end to decorate the top of the cake. Additionally, if you have exceptionally pretty berries with nice green stems, you may want to leave the stems on the 12 that you use for decoration. In this case, place the strawberries stem side up on the top of the cake.*

*Regrettably, the Chocolate Strawberry Mousse Cake has a short shelf life. After assembly, this cake can be kept in the refrigerator for no more than 24 hours before serving. Held longer, the strawberries will leach moisture into the mousse. The cake will taste fine, but the appearance will be disfigured.*

*Always allow the slices to come to room temperature for 20 to 30 minutes before serving.*

*For a final touch, serve each slice on top of 2 to 3 tablespoons of fresh strawberry purée.*

in the whipped cream. Now fold in the remaining egg whites. Set aside at room temperature until needed.

Assemble the springform pan. Spread ¹/₂ cup of chocolate strawberry mousse onto the cake layer in the assembled springform pan. Arrange ¹/₂ the amount of reserved strawberries (not including the 12 for decoration), stem side down, into the mousse. The berries should be arranged in 2 rings: the first ring being ³/₄ inch from the outside edge of the cake, and the second, inside ring, ³/₄ inch away from the first. Distribute 3 cups of mousse over the berries, being careful to keep the berries in position. Holding the pan by the top rim, gently but firmly tap the bottom of the pan 2 to 3 times on your work surface (this will eliminate air pockets). Position a cake layer on top of the mousse, then repeat the process used on the first cake layer (¹/₂ cup mousse, remaining strawberries, and 3 more cups mousse). Top the mousse with the remaining cake layer and gently press into position. Refrigerate the cake for 2 hours (do not freeze).

Refrigerate 1 cup of Semisweet Chocolate Ganache for at least 1 hour. Keep the remaining ganache at room temperature until needed.

Remove the sides from the springform pan (do not remove the bottom of the pan from the cake; this will make it easier to handle later). Use a cake spatula to smooth and fill in the sides of the cake with 2 to 3 tablespoons of room-temperature ganache. Evenly spread the remaining amount of this ganache over the top and sides of the cake. Refrigerate the cake for 1 hour.

Transfer the chilled cup of ganache to a pastry bag fitted with a large-sized star tip. Remove the cake from the refrigerator. Pipe a circle of 12 evenly spaced stars along the outside edge of the top of the cake. Place a strawberry, stem side down, into each ganache star. Refrigerate the cake for 30 minutes.

Cut the cake with a serrated slicer, heating the blade of the slicer under hot running water before making each slice. Allow the slices to come to room temperature for 20 to 30 minutes before serving.

# WHITE CHOCOLATE "CHOCOLATE JUNK" ICE CREAM

### YIELDS 2 QUARTS

8 ounces white chocolate, broken into
   1/2-ounce pieces
1 cup whole milk
2 cups heavy cream
1/2 cup half-and-half
1/2 cup granulated sugar

4 egg yolks
3/4 cup cashew pieces
6 ounces semisweet chocolate, broken into
   1/2-ounce pieces
3/4 cup raisins

### EQUIPMENT

Measuring cup, double boiler, film wrap, whisk, 2 stainless steel bowls (1 large), 2½-quart saucepan, electric mixer with paddle, rubber spatula, instant-read test thermometer, baking sheet with sides, ice-cream freezer, 9- by 1½-inch cake pan, metal spoon, cook's knife, cutting board, 2-quart plastic container with lid

Heat 1 inch of water in the bottom half of a double boiler over medium-high heat. Place the white chocolate and milk in the top half of the double boiler (see page 151). Tightly cover the top with film wrap. Heat for 6 to 8 minutes, then transfer to a stainless steel bowl and stir until smooth.

Preheat the oven to 300 degrees Fahrenheit.

Heat the heavy cream and half-and-half in a 2½-quart saucepan over medium-high heat. When hot, add ¼ cup of sugar and stir to dissolve. Bring the cream to a boil.

While the cream is heating, place the egg yolks and the remaining ¼ cup of sugar in the bowl of an electric mixer fitted with a paddle. Beat the eggs on high for 2 to 2½ minutes. Scrape down the sides of the bowl, then beat on high until slightly thickened and lemon-colored, 2½ to 3 minutes. (At this point, the cream should be boiling. If not, adjust the mixer speed to low and continue to mix until the cream boils. If this is not done, the egg yolks will develop undesirable lumps.)

Pour the boiling cream into the beaten egg yolks and whisk to combine. Return to the saucepan and heat over medium-high heat, stirring constantly; bring to a temperature of 185 degrees Fahrenheit, 2 to 4 minutes. Remove from the heat, pour into the melted chocolate mixture, and stir to combine. Cool in an ice-water bath (see page 150) to a temperature of 40 to 45 degrees Fahrenheit, about 15 minutes.

While the custard is cooling, toast the cashew pieces on a baking sheet in the preheated oven until golden brown, about 15 to 18 minutes. Remove from oven and hold at room temperature until needed.

When the custard is cold, freeze in an ice-cream freezer following the manufacturer's instructions.

While the ice cream is freezing, heat 1 inch of water in the bottom half of a double boiler over medium-high heat. Place the semisweet chocolate in the top half of the double boiler. Tightly cover the top with film wrap. Heat for 8 to 10 minutes, then transfer to a stainless steel bowl and stir until smooth. Stir in the toasted cashew pieces and the raisins and combine thoroughly.

Pour this "chocolate junk" mixture into a cake pan and refrigerate until cold, about 40 minutes. Remove solidified chocolate from the pan and break (or cut) into ½-inch pieces.

Transfer the semifrozen ice cream to a plastic container. Fold in the "chocolate junk." Securely cover the container, then place in the freezer for several hours before serving. Serve within 5 days.

*The richness of the white chocolate ice cream combined with the crunchiness of the "chocolate junk" is highly seductive. Fortunately, addiction to this ice cream is legal.*

*For a "lesser grade" of "chocolate junk," use peanuts; on the other end of the spectrum, use macadamia nuts.*

*The "chocolate junk" may be made several days in advance and kept in the refrigerator until needed. We have scheduled it for production in this recipe while the ice cream is being made, to fill the time it normally takes to produce ice cream in an electric ice-cream freezer.*

*The egg yolks and sugar may be prepared using a hand-held mixer (mixing time may increase slightly) or by hand, using a wire whisk (mixing time may double).*

# CHOCOLATE PECAN CHOCOLATE CHUNK PIE

SERVES 12

**EQUIPMENT**

*Measuring cup, measuring spoons, cook's knife, cutting board, electric mixer with paddle, film wrap, rolling pin, 9- by 1½-inch false bottom pan, serrated knife, 2½-quart saucepan, metal spoon, rubber spatula, baking sheet, instant-read test thermometer, serrated slicer*

To prepare the tart shell, mix 1¼ cups flour, butter, sugar, and salt in the bowl of an electric mixer fitted with a paddle. Mix on low for 5 minutes, until the butter is "cut into" the flour and the mixture develops a mealy texture. Add ice water and continue to mix on low for 10 to 15 seconds, until the dough comes together. Remove the dough from the mixer and form it into a smooth, round ball. Wrap in film wrap and refrigerate for at least 4 hours.

After 4 hours, transfer it to a clean, dry, lightly floured work surface. Roll the dough (using the extra ½ cup of flour as necessary to prevent the dough from sticking) into a circle about 15 inches in diameter and ⅛ inch thick. Line the 9- by 1½-inch false bottom pan with the dough, gently pressing it around the bottom and sides. Use a serrated knife to trim the excess dough, leaving a ¾-inch border, which should be crimped around the top edge of the pan. Refrigerate the pastry crust for 30 minutes.

Preheat the oven to 325 degrees Fahrenheit.

To prepare the filling, heat the butter and sugar in a 2½-quart saucepan over medium-high heat. Stir constantly while bringing the mixture to a boil. Allow the mixture to boil for 1½ minutes. Remove from heat and transfer to the bowl of an electric mixer. Use a rubber spatula to stir in 6 ounces semisweet chocolate and the unsweetened chocolate. Continue to stir until the chocolate has melted. Add dark corn syrup, vanilla extract, and salt. Now add the eggs and place the mixer bowl onto an electric mixer fitted with a paddle. Combine on medium until the eggs are incorporated and the mixture is smooth. Remove the bowl from the mixer. Use a rubber spatula to finish combining the mixture.

Remove the pie shell from the refrigerator and place it on a baking sheet. Evenly disperse the 3 cups of pecan halves over the bottom of the shell. Spread the remaining 6 ounces semisweet chocolate over the pecan halves. Slowly pour the chocolate batter over the chopped chocolate and pecan halves. Bake the pie (leaving it on the baking sheet) on the middle shelf of the preheated oven for 1 hour. Reduce the temperature to 300 degrees Fahrenheit and bake for an additional 45 to 55 minutes, until the internal temperature of the pie filling reaches 170 degrees Fahrenheit. Remove from the oven and cool at room temperature for 1 hour. Refrigerate the pie for at least 2 hours (do not remove the pie from the pan).

To serve, cut the pie with a serrated slicer. Heat the blade of the slicer under hot running water before making each slice. Serve immediately.

## TART SHELL DOUGH

- 1¾ cups all-purpose flour
- 6 tablespoons unsalted butter, cut into 1-tablespoon pieces
- 1 tablespoon granulated sugar
- Pinch of salt
- ¼ cup ice water

## CHOCOLATE PECAN CHOCOLATE CHUNK FILLING

- ¼ pound unsalted butter
- ½ cup granulated sugar
- 12 ounces semisweet chocolate, chopped into ¼-inch pieces
- 2 ounces unsweetened chocolate, chopped into ¼-inch pieces
- 1½ cups dark corn syrup
- 1 tablespoon pure vanilla extract
- ¼ teaspoon salt
- 8 eggs
- 3 cups pecan halves

### THE CHEF'S TOUCH

*A*s described in the recipe, you may roll the pie dough after it has been refrigerated for 4 hours; however, it will be much easier to work with if it has relaxed overnight.

It is important to pour the chocolate batter slowly over the pecan halves and chocolate chunks.

This dessert can be served chilled, at room temperature, or—for a really exquisite taste and texture —warmed.

I suggest that this pie be prepared the day before it is served. Although it may be served after 2 hours of refrigeration, the texture of the pie is perfect after 24 hours of refrigeration. Once it is assembled it can keep for 2 to 3 days in the refrigerator.

# LUCY'S CHOCOLATE DIAMONDS

MAKES 36 DIAMONDS

## CHOCOLATE CAKE

$^1/_2$ pound unsalted butter (2 tablespoons melted)
6$^1/_2$ ounces semisweet chocolate, broken into $^1/_2$-ounce pieces
9 egg yolks
1 cup granulated sugar
4 egg whites

## CHOCOLATE GANACHE

1 cup hazelnuts
3$^1/_2$ cups heavy cream
4 tablespoons unsalted butter
$^1/_4$ cup granulated sugar
2 pounds semisweet chocolate, broken into $^1/_2$-ounce pieces

## RASPBERRY FILLING

$^1/_2$ pint red raspberries
2 tablespoons granulated sugar

### EQUIPMENT

*Measuring cup, measuring spoon, small nonstick pan, 2 10- by 15-inch baking sheets with sides, parchment paper, double boiler, film wrap, whisk, electric mixer with paddle, 3 stainless steel bowls (1 large), rubber spatula, 2 baking sheets with sides, 2 100-percent-cotton kitchen towels, food processor with metal blade, large cutting board, 2$^1/_2$-quart saucepan, metal spoon, medium-gauge strainer, cake spatula, serrated knife, serrated slicer, yardstick, cooling rack, fork, pastry bag, medium star tip*

Lightly coat the bottom and sides of 2 10- by 15-inch baking sheets with melted butter. Line each sheet with parchment paper, then lightly coat the parchment paper with more melted butter. Set aside.

Preheat the oven to 325 degrees Fahrenheit.

Heat 1 inch of water in the bottom half of a double boiler over medium heat. Place the remainder of the $^1/_2$ pound of butter and 6$^1/_2$-ounces semisweet chocolate in the top half of the double boiler (see page 151). Tightly cover the top with film wrap. Allow to heat for 10 to 12 minutes. Remove from heat, stir until smooth, and hold at room temperature.

Place the egg yolks and 1 cup sugar in the bowl of an electric mixer fitted with a paddle. Beat on high until lemon-colored and slightly thickened, about 4 minutes. Scrape down the sides of the bowl and beat on high for 2 more minutes.

While the egg yolks are beating, whisk the egg whites in a large stainless steel bowl until stiff but not dry, about 3 to 4 minutes.

Using a rubber spatula, fold the melted chocolate mixture into the beaten egg yolk mixture. Add a quarter of the beaten egg whites and stir to incorporate, then gently fold in the remaining egg whites.

Divide between the prepared baking sheets, spreading evenly, and bake on the top and middle shelves in the preheated oven, until a toothpick inserted in the center comes out clean, about 20 to 22 minutes. Rotate the cakes from top to bottom about halfway through the baking time. Remove cakes from the oven and allow to cool in the baking sheets for 30 minutes.

While the cakes are cooling, toast the hazelnuts for the ganache. Skin the toasted hazelnuts (see page 151), and allow the nuts to cool to room temperature. In a food processor fitted with a metal blade, chop the nuts into $^1/_8$-inch pieces.

Invert 1 of the sheet cakes onto a large cutting board (or use corrugated cardboard cut to slightly overlap a 10- by 15-inch baking sheet), and refrigerate for 30 minutes. Hold the remaining sheet cake at room temperature until needed.

To prepare the ganache, heat the heavy cream, 4 tablespoons butter, and $^1/_4$ cup sugar in a 2$^1/_2$-quart saucepan over medium-high heat, stirring to dissolve the sugar. Bring the mixture to a boil. Place 2 pounds of semisweet chocolate in a stainless steel bowl. Pour the boiling cream over the chocolate and allow to stand for 6 to 7 minutes. Stir until smooth.

Combine 3 cups ganache with the chopped hazelnuts. Hold this mixture at room temperature to use for filling. Remove 1 more cup of ganache and refrigerate for 1 hour (this will be used to decorate the diamonds). Keep the remaining ganache at room temperature until needed.

My sister Denise is a child psychologist who is also an accomplished cook and baker. She does quite a bit of entertaining, and never hesitates to call me for advice or suggestions. It was a query from Denise regarding the feasibility of using the recipe for our Chocolate Temptation Cake (which is a circular cake that serves 8) for a large dinner party that led to the development of this recipe.

At The Trellis, we save all the trimmings from this cake and fold them into semifrozen White Chocolate "Ice Cream" and call it White Chocolate Temptation "Ice Cream."

This is a great dessert for a party. Use the diamonds with other items on a dessert buffet, or serve 2 diamonds in a pool of red raspberry puree and garnish with 2 small scoops of White Chocolate "Ice Cream" (see page 35).

After assembly, the diamonds may be kept in the refrigerator for 2 to 3 days before serving. Bring the diamonds to room temperature for 15 to 20 minutes before serving.

Now make the raspberry filling by pureeing the raspberries and 2 tablespoons sugar in a food processor fitted with a metal blade for 12 to 15 seconds. Strain the puree directly into a stainless steel bowl. Cover with film wrap and refrigerate until needed.

To assemble and decorate the diamonds, first remove the cake from the refrigerator. Using a cake spatula, spread the raspberry pureé over the chilled, inverted cake layer. Spread evenly to the edges. Spread the ganache and hazelnut mixture over the raspberry puree, evenly to the edges of the cake. Invert the other cake layer on top of the ganache-covered cake. Remove the parchment paper and gently press the cakes together. Place the entire cake in the freezer for 1 hour.

Remove the cake from the freezer. Using a very sharp serrated knife, cut away the uneven edges of the cake so that it will measure 9 by 13½ inches. Use a serrated slicer to cut the cake widthwise into 9 1½-inch-wide strips. Trim a 1-inch, diagonally cut piece from each end of each strip, then cut the strip diagonally 3 times to form 4 uniformly sized diamonds from each strip.

Place a cooling rack on a baking sheet with sides. Put 9 to 12 diamonds onto the cooling rack. Spoon 2 tablespoons of room-temperature ganache over each diamond, allowing the flowing ganache to coat the top and sides of each diamond. Using a fork, remove the ganache-covered diamonds from the cooling rack and place them on a baking sheet covered with parchment paper and refrigerate. Scrape the ganache from the first baking sheet and return it to the bowl of room-temperature ganache. Warm the ganache to the proper consistency over a pan of hot water. Continue this procedure until all the diamonds are covered with ganache and have been refrigerated for a minimum of 20 minutes.

Transfer the reserved refrigerated ganache to a pastry bag fitted with a medium-sized star tip. Decorate each diamond with a ganache star. Refrigerate the diamonds for at least 1 hour before serving.

Allow the diamonds to come to room temperature for 15 to 20 minutes before serving.

1. Cut the cake widthwise into even strips.

2. Cut each strip diagonally to form diamonds.

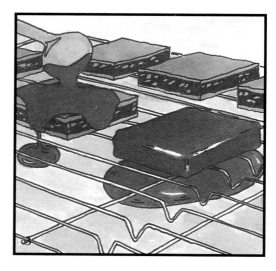

3. Spoon ganache liberally over each diamond.

# CHOCOLATE–WHITE CHOCOLATE CHUNK "ICE CREAM"

### YIELDS 2 QUARTS

6 ounces semisweet chocolate, broken into
  ½-ounce pieces
2 ounces unsweetened chocolate, broken
  into ½-ounce pieces
3½ cups whole milk

1 cup granulated sugar
3 eggs
6 ounces white chocolate, cut into
  ⅜-inch pieces

### EQUIPMENT

*Measuring cup, cook's knife, cutting board, double boiler, film wrap, 2½-quart saucepan, whisk, electric mixer with paddle, rubber spatula, instant-read test thermometer, 2 stainless steel bowls (1 large), ice-cream freezer, 2-quart plastic container with lid*

Heat 1 inch of water in the bottom half of a double boiler over medium-high heat. Place both chocolates and ½ cup milk in the top half of the double boiler (see page 151). Tightly cover the top with film wrap. Heat for 8 to 10 minutes, then remove from heat and stir until smooth. Set aside until needed.

Heat the remaining 3 cups of milk and ½ cup sugar in a 2½-quart saucepan over medium heat. Stir to dissolve the sugar. Bring milk to a boil.

While the milk is heating, place the eggs and the remaining sugar in the bowl of an electric mixer fitted with a paddle. Beat the eggs on high for 2 to 3 minutes. Scrape down the sides of the bowl, then beat on high until slightly thickened and lemon-colored, 2½ to 3 minutes. (At this point, the milk should be boiling. If not, adjust the mixer speed to low and continue to mix until the milk boils. If this is not done, the eggs will develop undesirable lumps.)

Pour the boiling milk into the beaten eggs and whisk to combine. Return to the saucepan and heat over medium-high heat, stirring constantly. Bring to a temperature of 185 degrees Fahrenheit, 2 to 4 minutes. Remove from the heat and transfer to a stainless steel bowl. Add the melted chocolate and whisk to combine. Cool in an ice-water bath (see page 150) to a temperature of 40 to 45 degrees Fahrenheit, about 15 to 20 minutes.

When the mixture is cold, freeze in an ice-cream freezer following the manufacturer's instructions. Transfer the semifrozen "ice cream" to a plastic container and fold in the white chocolate chunks. Securely cover the container, then place in the freezer for several hours before serving. Serve within 5 days.

### THE CHEF'S TOUCH

*At The Trellis, we have a penchant for "high-test" desserts; that is, sweets that usually have lots of butter, sugar, cream, and of course, chocolate. No sense equivocating about it—the bulk of our desserts are outrageously decadent. On the flip side, however, we do have some "low-test" items; these are desserts that are deceptive in appearance: they look and taste like high-test confections, but they deliver intense flavor with a minimum amount of fat. Our Chocolate–White Chocolate Chunk "Ice Cream" fits into the low-test category. Prepared with whole milk, which is only 4 percent fat, this "ice cream" falls substantially below the fat level needed for authentic ice cream, which has a minimum of 10 percent fat.*

*The eggs and sugar may also be prepared using a hand-held mixer (mixing time may increase slightly) or by hand, using a wire whisk (mixing time may double).*

# DARK CHOCOLATE AND PUMPKIN CHEESECAKE

SERVES 12

## CHOCOLATE PECAN COOKIE CRUST

- 1 cup pecan pieces
- 6 Deep Dark Chocolate Fudge Cookies (see page 28)
- 1 teaspoon unsalted butter, melted

## CHOCOLATE CHEESECAKE

- 8 ounces semisweet chocolate, broken into $^1/_2$-ounce pieces
- $^1/_4$ cup brewed coffee, full strength
- $^3/_4$ pound cream cheese, softened
- $^3/_4$ cup granulated sugar
- $^1/_2$ teaspoon salt
- 3 eggs
- 1 teaspoon pure vanilla extract

## PUMPKIN CHEESECAKE

- 2 teaspoons unsalted butter, melted
- 1 pound cream cheese, softened
- $^3/_4$ cup granulated sugar
- 2 tablespoons all-purpose flour
- $^1/_2$ teaspoon salt
- 3 eggs
- 1 teaspoon pure vanilla extract
- 1 cup pumpkin puree
- $^1/_4$ teaspoon ground cinnamon
- $^1/_4$ teaspoon ground allspice
- $^1/_8$ teaspoon ground cloves

## SEMISWEET CHOCOLATE GANACHE

Semisweet Chocolate Ganache (see page 19)

### EQUIPMENT

*Measuring cup, measuring spoons, small nonstick pan, baking sheet, food processor with metal blade, 9- by 3-inch springform pan, double boiler, film wrap, whisk, electric mixer with paddle, rubber spatula, 2 9- by 1$^1/_2$-inch cake pans, parchment paper, instant-read test thermometer, large 100-percent-cotton towel, cake spatula, serrated slicer*

Preheat the oven to 325 degrees Fahrenheit.

Toast the pecan pieces on a baking sheet in the preheated oven for 6 to 8 minutes. Remove from the oven and allow to cool to room temperature. Lower the oven temperature to 300 degrees Fahrenheit. In a food processor fitted with a metal blade, chop the cookies and the pecans until they are in crumbs (to yield 2 cups of crumbs), about 20 to 30 seconds. Set aside until needed.

Coat the bottom of a 9- by 3-inch springform pan with 1 teaspoon melted butter. Use your hands to press 1 cup of crumbs to a uniform and level thickness on the buttered bottom of the pan. Set aside.

To prepare the chocolate cheesecake, heat 1 inch of water in the bottom half of a double boiler over medium-high heat. Place the semisweet chocolate and coffee in the top half of the double boiler (see page 151). Tightly cover the top with film wrap and allow to heat for 6 to 8 minutes. Remove from the heat and stir until smooth.

Place $^3/_4$ pound softened cream cheese, $^3/_4$ cup sugar, and $^1/_2$ teaspoon salt in the bowl of an electric mixer fitted with a paddle. Beat on low for 1 minute and on medium for 2 minutes. Scrape down the sides of the bowl, then beat on medium for 2 more minutes and on high for 2 minutes. Scrape down the bowl. Add 3 eggs, one at a time, beating on high for 20 seconds and scraping down the bowl after each addition. Then beat the mixture for 1 minute more on high. Add 1 teaspoon vanilla extract and beat on medium for 15 seconds. Add the melted chocolate mixture, then beat on medium for 30 seconds. Remove the bowl from the mixer. Use a rubber spatula to finish mixing the batter until it is smooth and thoroughly combined. Pour the cheesecake mixture into the prepared springform pan, spreading evenly. Keep at room temperature while preparing the pumpkin cheesecake batter.

To prepare the pumpkin cheesecake, coat the inside of a 9- by 1$^1/_2$-inch cake pan with 1 teaspoon butter. Line the pan with an 8-inch square of parchment paper. Coat the parchment paper with the remaining teaspoon butter. Set aside until needed.

Place 1 pound softened cream cheese, $^3/_4$ cup sugar, the flour, and $^1/_2$ teaspoon salt in the bowl of an electric mixer fitted with a paddle. Beat on low for 1 minute and on medium for 2 minutes. Scrape down the sides of the bowl, then beat on medium for 2 more minutes and on high for 3 minutes. Scrape down the bowl. Add 3 eggs, one at a time, beating on high for 20 seconds and scraping down the bowl after each addition. Add 1 teaspoon vanilla extract and beat on medium for 15 seconds, then beat for 2 more minutes on high. Add the pumpkin puree, cinnamon, allspice, and cloves, then beat on medium for 30 seconds. Remove the bowl from the mixer. Use a rubber spatula to finish mixing the batter until it is smooth and thoroughly combined. Pour the pumpkin cheesecake mixture into the prepared cake pan, spreading evenly.

Place a 9- by 1$^1/_2$-inch cake pan partially filled with 4 cups of hot water on the bottom rack of the 300 degree Fahrenheit oven (the bottom rack should be at least 3 inches below the center rack).

Place both cheesecakes on the center rack of the oven and bake for 1 hour and 10 minutes, until the internal temperature of the cheesecake fillings reaches 170 degrees Fahrenheit. Turn off the oven and allow the cheesecakes to remain in the oven for an additional 20 minutes. Remove from the oven and cool at room temperature for 20 minutes. Refrigerate the chocolate cheesecake for 1 hour, but keep the pumpkin cheesecake at room temperature (do not remove either cake from the pan).

Pour 1 cup of Semisweet Chocolate Ganache over the top of the chilled chocolate cheesecake. Spread the ganache evenly over the top of the cake. Invert the pumpkin cheesecake onto the layer of ganache. Gently press down on the cake to set in place. Wrap the entire springform pan with film wrap and refrigerate for 3 hours to set.

The cheesecake can now be released from the springform pan. Remove the film wrap and wrap a damp, hot towel around the sides of the pan (the towel should be large enough to completely wrap around and cover the sides of the pan) and hold around the pan for about 1 minute. Carefully release and remove the springform pan. Using a cake spatula, smooth the sides of the cake with 2 to 3 tablespoons ganache. Spread the remaining amount of ganache evenly across the top of the cake. Press the remaining cookie/pecan crumbs into the sides of the cake, coating evenly. Refrigerate for at least 30 minutes before cutting and serving.

Heat the blade of the serrated slicer under hot water before cutting, and run it under hot water after making each slice. Place a piece of cheesecake in the center of each plate and serve.

## THE CHEF'S TOUCH

*Rather than conjuring up images of goblins and dark nights, a field of colorful pumpkins never fails to make me smile. Each bright orange globe seems to have its own personality.*

*This combination of chocolate and pumpkin works, and it is certain to elicit delighted expressions when tasted.*

*If fresh pumpkin is available, use 1 pound of peeled pumpkin meat cut into 1/2-inch pieces. Heat 1/2 cup water and 2 tablespoons tightly packed light brown sugar in a 2 1/2-quart saucepan over medium-high heat. When hot, add the pumpkin pieces and 1 teaspoon salt. Heat for 5 minutes, then reduce heat to medium and allow to cook for 25 minutes, stirring occasionally. Transfer the pumpkin mixture to a stainless steel bowl and cool in an ice-water bath (see page 150) for about 15 minutes. Puree the cooled pumpkin mixture in a food processor fitted with a metal blade until smooth, about 1 minute, to yield about 1 to 1 1/4 cups purée.*

*When fresh pumpkin is not available, be certain to purchase solid pack pumpkin, rather than "pumpkin pie filling." The spices in the latter would overwhelm the flavor balance in this recipe.*

*The production of this cheesecake can be spread out over a 2-day time period. DAY 1. Assuming that you keep a stash of Deep Dark Chocolate Fudge Cookies in the freezer, move on to baking the cheesecakes. If not, bake the cookies before baking the cheesecakes. Allow cheesecakes to cool and refrigerate until assembly. DAY 2. Prepare the ganache and assemble the cake.*

*After assembly, this may be kept in the refrigerator for 2 to 3 days before serving.*

*For an extra-special touch, decorate the top of the uncut cake with sour cream and brown sugar; whisk together in a stainless steel bowl 3/4 cup sour cream and 2 tablespoons light brown sugar. Pour the mixture onto the center area of the cake. Using a spatula, spread the sour cream to within 2 inches of the outside edge of the top of the cake. Now for the final touch: evenly space 12 pecan halves 1/2-inch from the outer edge of the top. Refrigerate for an hour before cutting and serving.*

# DANIELLE'S TEMPTATION

SERVES 10 TO 12

## CHOCOLATE CAKE

chocolate cake from Lucy's
Chocolate Diamonds (see page 86)

## CHOCOLATE GANACHE

3/4 cup heavy cream
2 tablespoons unsalted butter
2 tablespoons granulated sugar
8 ounces semisweet chocolate, broken into
1/2-ounce pieces

## DECORATIONS

3/4 cup sliced toasted almonds
1 ounce white chocolate curls
(see page 150)
1 ounce semisweet chocolate curls
(see page 150)

## EQUIPMENT

*Measuring cup, measuring spoons, small nonstick pan, vegetable peeler, 9- by 3-inch springform pan, parchment paper, double boiler, film wrap, whisk, electric mixer with paddle, 2 stainless steel bowls (1 large), rubber spatula, 9-inch cardboard cake circle, baking sheet, 1 1/2-quart saucepan, cake spatula, serrated slicer*

Preheat the oven to 325 degrees Fahrenheit.

Prepare the chocolate cake recipe from Lucy's Chocolate Diamonds, but use only 1 tablespoon of melted butter to prepare the springform pan, rather than the 2 tablespoons specified in that recipe. Lightly coat a 9- by 3-inch springform pan with some of the melted butter. Line the pan with parchment paper, then lightly coat the paper with more melted butter.

Pour the chocolate cake batter into the prepared pan, spreading evenly. Bake the cake in the preheated oven until a toothpick inserted in the center comes out clean, about 1 hour and 15 minutes. (During baking, the surface of the cake will form a crust; this crust will normally collapse when the cake is removed from the oven.) Invert the cake onto a cardboard cake circle and refrigerate for 1 hour.

To prepare the ganache, heat the heavy cream, butter, and sugar in a 1 1/2-quart saucepan over medium-high heat. Bring to a boil. Place 8 ounces semisweet chocolate in a stainless steel bowl. Pour the boiling cream over the chocolate and allow to stand for 5 minutes. Stir with a whisk until smooth.

Use a cake spatula to smooth the sides of the cake with 2 tablespoons ganache. Pour the remaining ganache over the cake, spreading with a spatula to create an even coating of ganache on both the top and sides of the cake. Refrigerate the cake for 30 minutes. Press the toasted almonds into the ganache on the sides of the cake, coating evenly. Decorate the top of the cake with white and dark chocolate curls. Serve the cake immediately or refrigerate until 20 minutes before serving.

To serve, cut the cake with a serrated slicer. Heat the blade of the slicer under hot running water before cutting each slice. If the cake has been refrigerated, allow the slices to come to room temperature for 15 minutes before serving.

*In July 1986, I spent a wonderful week as the chef on a barge cruising the Yonne River in the Burgundy area of France, an experience enhanced by having my daughter Danielle, who was then only 16 years old, as my assistant. Every day for a week, we prepared lunch and dinner for the eight guests and the crew of six. Danielle had spent the 2 previous summers working in The Trellis kitchen and, prior to the trip to France, had worked for a few weeks assisting Trellis pastry chef Andrew O'Connell. So, she was responsible for preparing desserts for the trip, the most popular being her adaptation of a signature Trellis dessert—Chocolate Temptation. We served it on the second evening of the cruise and as a command performance on the last evening, when the French were celebrating Bastille Day.*

*On the barge, I pureed fresh fraises des bois (wild strawberries) to use as a sauce with Danielle's Temptation. I would also suggest serving the Temptation with a purée of fresh red raspberries or perhaps in a pool of Bittersweet Chocolate Sauce (see page 16) with a cloud or two of unsweetened whipped cream.*

*Danielle's Temptation may be kept in the refrigerator for 2 to 3 days before serving. Bring the cake slices to room temperature for 15 minutes before serving.*

# FROSTY CARAMEL "TIN ROOF" ICE CREAM SANDWICHES

MAKES 12 SANDWICHES

## CHOCOLATE COOKIE

4 tablespoons unsalted butter
2 1/2 ounces unsweetened chocolate, broken
    into 1/2-ounce pieces
2 ounces semisweet chocolate, broken into
    1/2-ounce pieces
1 cup granulated sugar
3 eggs
1/2 cup all-purpose flour
3/4 teaspoon baking powder
1/2 teaspoon salt
1/4 cup sour cream

## CARAMEL PEANUT ICE CREAM

1 cup unsalted shelled Virginia peanuts
3/4 cup granulated sugar
1/4 teaspoon lemon juice
2 cups heavy cream
1 cup whole milk
3 egg yolks

## FUDGE FILLING

1/2 cup heavy cream
3 tablespoons unsalted butter
1/3 cup granulated sugar
5 tablespoons dark brown sugar
1/2 cup unsweetened cocoa, sifted
1/8 teaspoon salt

## EQUIPMENT

*Measuring cup, measuring spoons, sifter, double boiler, film wrap, whisk, electric mixer with paddle, rubber spatula, 2 stainless steel bowls (1 large), 2 baking sheets with sides, airtight plastic container, 2 1/2-quart saucepan, instant-read test thermometer, ice-cream freezer, 2-quart plastic container with lid, parchment paper*

Preheat the oven to 325 degrees Fahrenheit.

Heat 1 inch of water in the bottom half of a double boiler over medium-high heat. Place 4 tablespoons butter and the unsweetened and semisweet chocolates in the top half of the double boiler (see page 151). Tightly cover the top with film wrap and allow to heat for 3 to 4 minutes. Remove from the heat and stir until smooth.

Combine 1 cup sugar and 3 eggs in the bowl of an electric mixer fitted with a paddle. Beat on medium until slightly thickened and doubled in volume, about 4 minutes. Add the melted chocolate and beat on medium for 20 seconds. Scrape down the bowl. Add the flour, baking powder, and 1/2 teaspoon salt and beat on medium until incorporated, about 15 seconds. In a stainless steel bowl, vigorously whisk the sour cream. Remove the bowl from the mixer and fold in the sour cream.

Portion the cookies by dropping 2 tablespoons of batter into 6 mounds on each of the 2 baking sheets. Place the sheets on the top and middle shelves of the preheated oven and bake for 20 to 22 minutes, rotating from top to bottom about halfway through the baking time. Allow the cookies to cool for 10 minutes on the baking sheets. Portion the remaining batter for 12 more cookies and repeat the baking procedure used for the first batch. Store the cookies in an airtight plastic container until needed.

To prepare the ice cream, first toast the peanuts on a baking sheet in the preheated oven for 10 to 12 minutes. Remove from the oven and set aside until needed.

Combine 1/2 cup sugar and the lemon juice in a 2 1/2-quart saucepan. Stir with a whisk to combine (the sugar will resemble moist sand). Caramelize the sugar for 3 to 5 minutes over medium-high heat, stirring constantly with a whisk to break up any lumps (the sugar will first turn clear as it liquefies, then brown as it caramelizes).

Remove the saucepan from the heat, carefully add 1/2 cup heavy cream, and stir to combine (the mixture will steam and boil rapidly as the cream is being added). Transfer the caramel to a stainless steel bowl and allow to cool to room temperature.

Heat the remaining 1 1/2 cups cream and the milk in a 2 1/2-quart saucepan over medium heat. Bring to a boil.

While the cream is heating, place 3 egg yolks and remaining 1/4 cup sugar in the bowl of an electric mixer fitted with a paddle. Beat the eggs on high for 2 to 3 minutes. Scrape down the sides of the bowl. Beat on high for an additional 2 to 3 minutes until slightly thickened and lemon-colored. (At this point, the cream should be boiling. If not, adjust mixer speed to low and continue to mix until cream boils. If this is not done, the egg yolks will develop undesirable lumps.)

Pour the boiling cream into the beaten egg yolks and whisk to combine. Return to the saucepan and heat over medium-high heat, stirring constantly. Bring to a temperature of 185 degrees Fahrenheit, about 2 to 4 minutes. Remove from heat and transfer to a stainless steel bowl. Add the caramel and whisk to combine. Cool in an ice-water bath (see page 150) to a temperature of 40 to 45 degrees Fahrenheit, about 15 minutes.

When the mixture is cold, freeze in an ice-cream freezer following the manufacturer's instructions. Transfer the semifrozen ice cream to a 2-quart plastic container, and fold in the peanuts. Securely cover the container, then place in the freezer for 1 hour.

To prepare the fudge filling, heat $^1/_2$ cup heavy cream and 3 tablespoons butter in a $2^1/_2$-quart saucepan over medium heat. Bring to a simmer. Add $^1/_3$ cup granulated sugar and the dark brown sugar; stir to dissolve. Remove from the heat and add the sifted cocoa and salt. Whisk until smooth. Transfer the fudge filling to a stainless steel bowl and allow to cool to room temperature.

To assemble the Frosty Caramel "Tin Roof" Ice Cream Sandwiches, place 12 cookies upside down on a baking sheet lined with parchment paper. Portion 3 to 4 heaping tablespoons of caramel peanut ice cream in a mound onto each of the cookies. Make an indentation in the ice cream using the back of the tablespoon. Portion a heaping tablespoon of fudge filling into the indentation. Immediately place the tray of cookies in the freezer, and freeze for 30 minutes. Remove from freezer and form the sandwich by placing another cookie, top side up, on each portion. Very gently press the cookie into place. Freeze the sandwiches for 1 hour, then individually film-wrap each sandwich and keep frozen for up to 6 days before serving.

*Our pastry chef John Twichell created this ice cream sandwich. John, who hails from Elkhart, Indiana, tells me that a tin roof sundae is the ice cream concoction of choice when you visit the soda fountain at Judd's Drugstore there. The "Classic" tin roof sundae at Judd's has vanilla ice cream and hot fudge topped off by Spanish red peanuts.*

*To deter crystallization, fresh lemon juice is added to the sugar before caramelization.*

*The ice cream must be frozen to the point that it does not immediately melt and run off the cookie. If it is too soft, return it to the freezer. Conversely, if the ice cream is too hard, it will be difficult to handle. In this instance, place the container of ice cream in the refrigerator until it is manageable.*

*Be certain that the fudge filling is not so warm that it will melt the ice cream on contact.*

*These sandwiches may be prepared over a period of 2 to 3 days. The ice cream can be prepared 2 to 3 days before assembly, then stored in the refrigerator for 30 to 45 minutes before assembling the cookies. The cookies can be baked a day or two before assembly and the fudge filling can be made several days in advance. (Store fudge filling in the refrigerator, but bring it to room temperature before using.)*

*The egg yolks and sugar for the ice cream may also be prepared using a hand-held mixer (mixing time may increase slightly) or by hand, using a wire whisk (mixing time may double).*

# "OLD-FASHIONED" CHOCOLATE LAYER CAKE

SERVES 12

## EQUIPMENT

*Measuring spoons, small nonstick pan, measuring cup, sifter, wax paper, food processor with grating blade (or hand grater), 2 9- by 1¹/₂-inch cake pans, parchment paper, double boiler, whisk, electric mixer with balloon whip and paddle, large stainless steel bowl, rubber spatula, 2 cardboard cake circles, serrated slicer, cake spatula*

Lightly coat the insides of 2 9- by 1¹/₂-inch cake pans with melted butter. Line each pan with parchment paper, then lightly coat the parchment with more melted butter. Set aside.

Preheat the oven to 325 degrees Fahrenheit.

Heat 1 inch of water in the bottom half of a double boiler over medium heat. Place ¹/₂ pound butter in the top half of the double boiler (see page 151). Heat the butter slowly, stirring continuously until the butter is melted but not separated. Remove the butter from the heat.

Place the egg yolks and ³/₄ cup granulated sugar in the bowl of an electric mixer fitted with a balloon whip. Whisk on high until slightly thickened and lemon-colored, about 1 minute. Adjust the mixer speed to low and continue to mix while whisking egg whites.

Whisk the egg whites in a large stainless steel bowl until soft peaks form, about 3 minutes. Add the remaining ¹/₂ cup sugar and continue to whisk until stiff but not dry, about 2 to 3 minutes.

Gradually add the flour to the egg yolks while mixing on low. Add the melted butter and continue to mix on low for 10 seconds. Increase the speed to medium and mix for 5 seconds. Remove the bowl from the mixer and use a rubber spatula to thoroughly combine the ingredients. Add a third of the beaten egg whites and stir to incorporate, then gently fold in the remaining egg whites. Fold in 8 ounces of the grated chocolate (refrigerate the remaining 2 ounces until needed).

Divide the batter between the prepared pans, spreading evenly, and bake in the preheated oven, until a toothpick inserted in the center comes out clean, about 25 to 30 minutes. Remove cakes from oven and cool in pans for 20 minutes. Invert the cakes onto cake circles; cool to room temperature, about 20 minutes. Remove parchment and refrigerate for 30 minutes.

To prepare the icing, place ¹/₂ pound butter, the cocoa, and salt in the bowl of an electric mixer fitted with a paddle. Cream the mixture on low until thoroughly combined, about 3 minutes. Add the confectioners' sugar, half-and-half, and vanilla. Combine on low for 10 seconds, then increase to medium and beat for 10 seconds. Readjust the speed to high and beat until the icing is light and fluffy, about 3 minutes. Scrape down the sides of the bowl and beat for an additional 1 minute. Remove from mixer and keep at room temperature until needed.

To assemble the cake, remove the chilled cakes from the refrigerator. Slice each cake horizontally into 2 layers of equal size. Place a tablespoon of icing in the center of a cake circle. Place a bottom layer of an inverted cake onto the dab of icing and gently press into place. Evenly spread ³/₄ cup of icing over the cake layer. Place the top layer of the cake onto the icing and gently press into place. Evenly spread ³/₄ cup of icing over the cake layer. Place the bottom layer of the second inverted cake onto the icing, and gently press into place. Evenly spread ³/₄ cup of icing over the cake layer. Place the top layer of the cake on the third layer of icing, gently pressing into place. Evenly spread the remaining icing over the top and sides of the cake. Press the reserved 2 ounces of grated chocolate into the icing on the sides of the cake, coating evenly.

Cut the cake with a serrated slicer. Heat the blade under hot water before each slice.

## SPECKLED CHOCOLATE CAKE

- ¹/₂ pound plus 2 tablespoons unsalted butter (2 tablespoons melted)
- 8 egg yolks
- 1¹/₄ cups granulated sugar
- 6 egg whites
- 1¹/₂ cups cake flour, sifted
- 10 ounces semisweet chocolate, finely grated

## CHOCOLATE ICING

- ¹/₂ pound unsalted butter
- ³/₄ cup unsweetened cocoa
- ¹/₄ teaspoon salt
- 4 cups confectioners' sugar
- ¹/₃ cup half-and-half
- 1 teaspoon pure vanilla extract

*To produce a successful cake, it is critical to melt the butter precisely as directed. If the water in the double boiler is too hot, the butter will separate, and will make the batter greasy.*

*Refrigerate the chocolate for 30 minutes before grating; otherwise, you are going to end up with chocolate fondue.*

*In addition to grating the chocolate in the food processor or by hand, you may also chop the chocolate very finely using a cook's knife.*

*Place a large piece of parchment paper or a baking sheet under the cake while you are applying the chocolate shavings to the sides of the cake. The cake circle holding the cake should be held in the palm of one hand, about 8 to 10 inches above the paper, while a large handful of chocolate shavings is applied with the free hand. Allow the shavings that do not adhere to the cake to fall free, then scoop them up and reapply.*

*After assembly, this cake may be kept in the refrigerator for 2 to 3 days before serving. Bring the slices to room temperature for 15 minutes before serving.*

*For a final touch, pastry chef John Twichell recommends ladling 3 to 4 tablespoons of Bittersweet Chocolate Sauce (see page 16) onto the plate. The glistening sheen of the sauce bathes the cake in a lustrous glow of dark chocolate.*

1. Slice each cake horizontally into equal halves.

2. Evenly spread icing over inverted cake layer.

3. Place top layer of cake onto icing and press into place.

4. Repeat with remaining layers then spread icing over top and sides of cake.

5. Press grated chocolate into icing on sides of cake.

# WHITE AND DARK CHOCOLATE PISTACHIO CAKE

SERVES 12

## EQUIPMENT

*Measuring cup, measuring spoons, cook's knife, cutting board, sifter, wax paper, 9- by 3-inch springform pan, double boiler, film wrap, whisk, electric mixer with paddle and balloon whip, rubber spatula, 1½-quart saucepan, 2½-quart saucepan, colander or medium strainer, 100-percent-cotton kitchen towel, baking sheet with sides, 3 stainless steel bowls (1 large), instant-read test thermometer, serrated slicer, cake spatula, pastry bag, medium star tip*

Preheat the oven to 325 degrees Fahrenheit.

Combine together in a sifter 1½ cups all-purpose flour, the cocoa, baking soda, and salt. Sift onto the wax paper and set aside until needed.

Coat a 9- by 3-inch springform pan with 2 teaspoons butter. Flour the pan with 1 tablespoon all-purpose flour, shaking out the excess. Set aside.

Heat 1 inch of water in the bottom half of a double boiler over medium heat. Place the unsweetened chocolate in the top half (see page 151). Tightly cover the top with film wrap. Allow to heat for 3 to 4 minutes. Remove from the heat and stir until smooth. Set aside until needed.

Place 1 cup sugar and 4 ounces butter in the bowl of an electric mixer fitted with a paddle. Beat on medium for 1 minute, then on high for 1 minute. Scrape down the sides of the bowl, then beat on high for 1 additional minute. Scrape down the sides of the bowl. Add the eggs, one at a time, beating on high for 15 seconds after adding each egg and scraping down the bowl after each addition.

Add the vanilla extract and the red raspberry vinegar and beat on high for 20 seconds. Add the melted chocolate and mix on low for 10 seconds. Scrape down the sides of the bowl.

Heat 1 cup water to a boil in a 1½-quart saucepan. Operate the mixer on low while adding the sifted dry ingredients, then mix for 10 seconds. Add the boiling water and continue to mix on low for 10 seconds. Increase the speed to medium and beat for 5 seconds. Remove the bowl from the mixer. Use a rubber spatula to mix the batter until it is smooth and thoroughly combined.

Pour the cake batter into the prepared springform pan. Bake in the center of the preheated oven until a toothpick inserted in the center comes out clean, about 45 to 50 minutes. Remove the cake from the oven and allow to cool in the pan for 20 minutes. Remove the sides of the springform pan and refrigerate the cake for at least 1 hour.

To prepare the white chocolate buttercream and the pistachio buttercream, shell the pistachios (this should yield 1½ cups shelled nuts). Bring 6 cups of water to a boil in a 2½-quart saucepan. Blanch the nuts in the boiling water for 3 minutes, then drain in a colander. Place the drained nuts in the center of a cotton towel. Fold the towel over the nuts and rub vigorously to remove the skins. Toast the skinned pistachios on a baking sheet with sides in the preheated oven for 15 minutes. Remove the nuts from the oven and allow to cool to room temperature. Reserve 24 whole pistachios to decorate the cake. Finely chop the remaining nuts and set aside until needed.

Heat 1 inch of water in the bottom half of a double boiler over medium heat. Place the white chocolate in the top half of the double boiler. Tightly cover the top with film wrap. Heat for 6 to 8 minutes, then remove from the heat and stir until smooth. Transfer the melted white chocolate to a large stainless steel bowl and set aside.

## JOE'S CHOCOLATE CAKE

- 1½ cups plus 1 tablespoon all-purpose flour
- 6 tablespoons unsweetened cocoa
- 1 teaspoon baking soda
- 1 teaspoon salt
- 4 ounces plus 2 teaspoons unsalted butter
- 2 ounces unsweetened chocolate, broken into ½-ounce pieces
- 1 cup granulated sugar
- 2 eggs
- 1 teaspoon pure vanilla extract
- 1 teaspoon red raspberry vinegar
- 1 cup water

## WHITE CHOCOLATE BUTTERCREAM AND PISTACHIO BUTTERCREAM

- 3 cups unshelled pistachios
- 8 ounces white chocolate, broken into ½-ounce pieces
- 12 ounces unsalted butter, cut into 6 pieces
- 3 egg whites
- ½ cup granulated sugar

## GANACHE

- 6 tablespoons heavy cream
- 1 teaspoon granulated sugar
- 4 ounces semisweet chocolate, broken into ½-ounce pieces

Place the 12 ounces of butter pieces in the bowl of an electric mixer fitted with a paddle. Beat the butter on low for 1 minute. Scrape down the paddle and the sides of the bowl. Beat on medium for 2 minutes, then scrape down the sides of the bowl and beat on high for an additional 5 minutes, until light and fluffy. Use a rubber spatula to thoroughly fold the butter into the melted white chocolate. Set aside until needed.

Heat 1 inch of water in the bottom half of a double boiler over medium heat. Place 3 egg whites and $^1/_2$ cup sugar in the top half of the double boiler. Gently whisk the egg whites until they reach a temperature of 120 degrees Fahrenheit, about 1 to 1$^1/_2$ minutes. Transfer the heated egg whites to the bowl of an electric mixer fitted with a balloon whip. Whisk on high until stiff peaks form, about 4 minutes. Remove the bowl from the mixer.

Use a rubber spatula to fold the egg whites into the white chocolate and butter mixture, and combine thoroughly. Transfer 2 cups white chocolate buttercream to a separate stainless steel bowl. Reserve $^1/_2$ cup finely chopped pistachios to be used to decorate the sides of the cake. Combine the remaining chopped pistachios with the 2 cups of buttercream. Keep both bowls of buttercream at room temperature until needed.

To prepare the ganache, heat the heavy cream and 1 teaspoon sugar in a 1$^1/_2$-quart saucepan over medium-high heat, stirring to dissolve the sugar. Bring the mixture to a boil. Place the semi-sweet chocolate in a stainless steel bowl and pour the boiling cream over the chocolate. Allow to stand for 3 to 4 minutes then stir until smooth. Cover with film wrap and refrigerate the ganache until needed.

To assemble the cake, remove the cake from the refrigerator, and remove the bottom of the springform pan from it. Reassemble the springform pan. Slice the cake horizontally into 3 equal layers.

Place the top layer of the cake, cut side down, onto the bottom of the closed springform pan. Portion half the pistachio buttercream on top of the cake layer and spread it evenly over the cake. Place the center section of the cake on top of the layer of buttercream. Portion the remaining pistachio buttercream over the cake layer and spread evenly. Invert the bottom portion of the cake (smooth side up) on top of the buttercream layer and very gently press down on the cake. Refrigerate the cake for at least 30 minutes before continuing the assembly.

Remove the cake from the refrigerator and remove the sides of the springform pan. (If the cake is difficult to remove from the pan, wrap a damp, hot towel around the pan and hold tightly for about 1 minute; this should free the solidified icing from the insides of the pan.) Using a cake spatula, evenly spread the white chocolate buttercream over the top and sides of the cake. Press the chopped pistachios into the buttercream on the sides of the cake, coating evenly. Return the cake to the refrigerator for 20 minutes.

To complete the assembly of the cake, fill a pastry bag fitted with a medium-sized star tip with the chilled ganache. Pipe a circle of 12 evenly spaced stars $^1/_4$ inch away from the outside edge of the top of the cake. Pipe a circle of 12 more stars inside the first 12. Top each ganache star with a whole pistachio nut. The cake may be served immediately or refrigerated until 25 to 30 minutes before serving.

To serve, cut the cake with a serrated slicer, heating the blade of the slicer under hot running water before making each slice. Bring the slices to room temperature for 15 to 20 minutes before serving.

*T*he American Culinary Federation (ACF) is a national organization open to men and women who choose cooking as their livelihood. As the largest organization of its kind, it has been instrumental in establishing the chef as a professional in the United States.

One of the ACF's most significant developments is the culinary apprenticeship program. At The Trellis, the ACF-certified apprentice training is an integral part of our kitchen organization. Since The Trellis opened in 1980, more than 50 young cooks have successfully completed the 3-year program. A shining example is Joe Wilson, a former engineering student at Virginia Tech, who started as a first-year Trellis apprentice in 1984. Since completing his apprenticeship in 1987, Joe has risen through our kitchen organization to become senior assistant chef.

Joe displayed remarkable talents in baking early in his apprentice training (Joe's Chocolate Cake is a case in point). Although he was only scheduled to spend 6 months developing his baking skills, his talent—and a shortage of bakers—extended his stay at the marble slab to nearly a year.

Although shelled pistachios are available in some retail outlets, I do not recommend using them since we have found that they are not of acceptable quality.

Skinning the pistachios is necessary for this recipe, both for its aesthetic value as well as for the enhancement of the eating experience.

To apply the chopped pistachios to the cake, hold the cake with the plate in the palm of your hand. Scoop up a handful of the chopped nuts with your free hand and gently press the nuts into the side of the cake while rotating the cake until the entire side is covered (this will take several scoops). It is a good idea to do this procedure over a clean baking sheet so that excess chopped nuts may be retrieved and reapplied to the cake.

After assembly, you may keep this cake in the refrigerator for 2 to 3 days before serving. Do not forget to bring the slices to room temperature for 15 to 20 minutes before serving.

# Vanilla Bean-Macadamia Nut Fudge Ice Cream Terrine

SERVES 8

1½  cups raw unsalted macadamia nuts
1  whole vanilla bean
1  cup whole milk
2¼  cups granulated sugar
3½  cups heavy cream
4  tablespoons unsalted butter
1  cup tightly packed dark brown sugar
2  cups unsweetened cocoa, sifted
¼  teaspoon salt
1½  cups half-and-half
10  egg yolks
2  teaspoons pure vanilla extract

## EQUIPMENT
*Measuring cup, measuring spoons, sifter, baking sheet with sides, cutting board, cook's knife, paring knife, 1½-quart saucepan with lid, 2 2½-quart saucepans, whisk, 3 stainless steel bowls, electric mixer with paddle, rubber spatula, ice-cream freezer, 9- by 5- by 3-inch loaf pan, parchment paper, aluminum foil, double boiler, serrated slicer*

Preheat the oven to 325 degrees Fahrenheit.

Toast the macadamia nuts on a baking sheet in the preheated oven until golden brown, about 15 minutes. Remove from the oven and cool to room temperature. Use a cook's knife to chop the nuts into ¼-inch pieces. Set aside until needed.

Use a sharp paring knife to cut the vanilla bean lengthwise. Place the split bean, milk, and ¼ cup of granulated sugar in a 1½-quart saucepan. Cover the pan and heat over low heat for 1 hour. Remove the pan from the heat and set aside, covered, until needed.

To prepare the fudge, heat 2 cups of heavy cream and the butter in a 2½-quart saucepan over medium-high heat. When hot, add the brown sugar and 1 cup granulated sugar. Bring to a boil and boil for 2 to 3 minutes until the sugar has dissolved. Remove from heat and cool at room temperature for 5 minutes.

Whisk the sifted cocoa, ¼ cup at a time, into the cooled cream and sugar mixture. Add the salt and continue to whisk until the fudge is smooth. Refrigerate 2 cups to use as sauce. Keep the remaining fudge at room temperature until needed.

Heat the remaining heavy cream, the half-and-half, and ½ cup granulated sugar in a 2½-quart saucepan over medium-high heat. When hot, stir to dissolve the sugar. Bring to a boil.

While the cream is heating, place the egg yolks and remaining ½ cup granulated sugar in the bowl of an electric mixer fitted with a paddle. Beat the eggs on high for 2 to 2½ minutes. Scrape down the bowl, then beat on high until slightly thickened and lemon-colored, 2½ to 3 minutes. (At this point, the cream should be boiling. If not, adjust mixer speed to low and continue to mix until cream boils. If this is not done, the egg yolks will develop undesirable lumps.)

Pour the boiling cream into the beaten egg yolks and whisk to combine. Return to the saucepan and heat over medium-high heat, stirring constantly. Bring to a temperature of 185 degrees Fahrenheit, about 2 to 4 minutes. Remove from the heat and cool in an ice-water bath (see page 150) to a temperature of 40 to 45 degrees Fahrenheit, about 15 minutes.

Transfer the milk and vanilla mixture to a stainless steel bowl. Remove the vanilla bean. Using the back of a paring knife, scrape the tiny seeds from the 2 bean halves, then discard the scraped halves. Put the seeds into the milk, and whisk vigorously to disperse them. Add 2½ cups of the cooled cream mixture to the milk, then add the pure vanilla extract and stir to combine. Freeze in an ice-cream freezer following the manufacturer's instructions.

Add the chopped macadamia nuts to the remaining cream mixture and refrigerate until needed.

Line the bottom and the 2 narrow sides of a loaf pan with a strip of parchment paper 4 inches wide and 18 inches long. Transfer the semifrozen vanilla bean ice cream into the loaf pan, making an even layer. Evenly spread the fudge over the ice cream layer. Place in the freezer while making the macadamia nut ice cream.

Freeze the macadamia nut and cream mixture in an ice-cream freezer following the manufacturer's instructions. Transfer the semifrozen macadamia nut ice cream to the loaf pan and spread evenly over the fudge. Cover the loaf pan with aluminum foil and freeze the ice cream terrine for 12 hours before serving.

To serve, heat 1 inch of water in the bottom half of a double boiler over medium-high heat. Place the 2 cups of reserved fudge in the top half of the double boiler and heat for 10 minutes (see page 151). Occasionally stir until it has returned to its original consistency. Remove the double boiler from heat and allow to stand while completing the following steps for serving the terrine.

To remove the frozen terrine from the loaf pan, first remove the aluminum foil. Briefly dip (a few seconds) the pan in a sink containing 1 inch of very hot water. Unmold the terrine by inverting it onto a baking sheet lined with parchment paper. Return to the freezer for 5 minutes.

Flood the base of each 10-inch plate with 4 tablespoons of warm fudge sauce. Slice the ends from the terrine (does your kitty have a taste for ice cream?) and cut the terrine into 8 slices about 1 inch thick. Place a slice of terrine in the center of each sauced plate and serve immediately.

*I*f you are unable to purchase raw unsalted macadamia nuts, you may use roasted and salted nuts. They must, however, be dropped in 6 cups of boiling water for 3 to 4 minutes, thoroughly drained, and then toasted for 5 minutes in a 325-degree-Fahrenheit oven. This procedure will result in essentially salt-free nuts, which can be used in any recipe that calls for raw unsalted macadamia nuts.

If the vanilla bean is too brittle to split in half lengthwise, steep and cook it whole.

Vanilla beans may be available in the spice section of your local supermarket. They are generally packaged as a single bean per jar. Bulk vanilla beans (sold by the pound) are sometimes found in the natural food section of some large supermarkets. This is usually a much more economical way to purchase the beans.

After dissolving the sugar in the cream, allow the mixture to cool for 5 minutes before whisking in the sifted cocoa. This prevents the cocoa from scorching, which would occur if it were immediately added to the boiling cream.

Apply the warm fudge sauce to slightly warm plates. The fudge sauce should be warm enough to flow, yet not so warm that it would immediately melt the ice cream.

The egg yolks and sugar may be prepared using a hand-held mixer (mixing time may increase slightly) or by hand, using a wire whisk (mixing time may double).

# WHITE CHOCOLATE CHEESECAKE

SERVES 8 TO 12

## CHOCOLATE COOKIE CRUST

3 tablespoons unsalted butter
(2 tablespoons melted)
10 Deep Dark Chocolate Fudge cookies
(see page 28)

## WHITE CHOCOLATE CHEESECAKE

18 ounces white chocolate, broken into
$^{1}/_{2}$-ounce pieces
$^{1}/_{2}$ cup heavy cream
1$^{3}/_{4}$ pounds cream cheese, softened
1 cup granulated sugar
1 teaspoon salt
6 eggs
1 teaspoon pure vanilla extract

## CHOCOLATE GANACHE

$^{1}/_{3}$ cup heavy cream
1 tablespoon unsalted butter
1 tablespoon granulated sugar
3 ounces semisweet chocolate, broken into
$^{1}/_{2}$-ounce pieces

## WHITE CHOCOLATE CURLS

2 ounces White Chocolate Curls
(see page 150)

### EQUIPMENT

*Measuring cup, measuring spoons, small nonstick sauté pan, 9- by 3-inch springform pan, food processor with metal blade, stainless steel bowl, double boiler, film wrap, whisk, electric mixer with paddle, rubber spatula, baking sheet with sides, instant-read test thermometer, 1$^{1}/_{2}$-quart saucepan, large 100-percent-cotton towel, serrated knife, 12-inch serrated slicer*

Preheat the oven to 325 degrees Fahrenheit.

Coat the inside of a 9- by 3-inch springform pan with 1 tablespoon butter.

In a food processor fitted with a metal blade, chop the cookies in 2 batches. Pulse each batch until all the cookies are in crumbs (this should yield 2$^{1}/_{2}$ cups crumbs), 10 to 15 seconds. Transfer the crumbs to a stainless steel bowl. Combine the cookie crumbs with 2 tablespoons melted butter. Mix by hand until the crumbs bind together. Press the crumbs around the buttered sides of the springform pan, then onto the buttered bottom of the pan. Place the pan in the freezer for 15 minutes.

Heat 1 inch of water in the bottom half of a double boiler over medium-high heat. Place the white chocolate and $^{1}/_{2}$ cup heavy cream in the top half of the double boiler (see page 151). Tightly cover the top with film wrap. Allow to heat for 10 to 12 minutes. Remove from heat and stir until smooth. Set aside until needed.

Place the softened cream cheese, 1 cup sugar, and the salt in the bowl of an electric mixer fitted with a paddle. Beat on low for 1 minute, on medium for 1 minute, and on high for 1 minute. Scrape down the sides of the bowl, then beat on high for 1 more minute. Scrape down the bowl. Add the eggs, 2 at a time, beating on medium for 15 seconds after adding, and scrape down the bowl after each addition. Add the vanilla extract and the melted chocolate mixture, then beat on medium for 15 seconds. Remove the bowl from the mixer. Use a rubber spatula to finish mixing the batter until it is smooth and thoroughly combined. Pour the cheesecake mixture into the prepared springform pan, spreading evenly.

Place a baking sheet with sides partially filled with 4 cups of hot water on the bottom rack of the oven (the bottom rack should be at least 3 inches below the center rack). Place the springform pan on the center rack of the oven and bake for 15 minutes. Lower the temperature to 250 degrees Fahrenheit and bake for 15 minutes. Lower the temperature to 225 degrees Fahrenheit and bake for 15 minutes. Then lower the temperature to 200 degrees Fahrenheit, and bake the cheesecake until the internal temperature of the cheesecake filling reaches 170 degrees Fahrenheit, about 2 hours and 45 minutes. Turn off the oven and allow the cheesecake to remain in the oven undisturbed for an additional 2 hours. Remove from the oven and cool at room temperature for 1 hour. Refrigerate the cheesecake for 12 hours (do not remove the cake from the pan).

After the cheesecake has been refrigerated for 12 hours, prepare the chocolate ganache. Heat $^{1}/_{3}$ cup heavy cream, 1 tablespoon butter, and 1 tablespoon sugar in a 1$^{1}/_{2}$-quart saucepan over medium-high heat. Bring to a boil. Place the semisweet chocolate in a stainless steel bowl. Pour the boiling cream over the chocolate and allow to stand for 3 to 4 minutes. Stir until smooth. Pour over the top of the chilled cheesecake. Use a rubber spatula to spread the ganache evenly over the top of the cake, being careful not to spread it over the edge and down the sides of the cheesecake. Refrigerate for 30 minutes to set.

The cheesecake can now be released from the springform pan. To do this, wrap a damp, hot cotton towel around the sides of the pan (the towel should be large enough to wrap completely around and cover the sides of the pan) and hold it around the pan for about 1 minute. Carefully release and remove the springform pan. Use a serrated knife to trim the crust so that it is level with the ganache (trim the crust away from the cake so that it does not fall into the ganache).

Decorate the top of the cake with white chocolate curls.

Heat the blade of the slicer under hot running water before slicing into the cheesecake. Cut the cheesecake with the serrated slicer, reheating the slicer after each slice. Place a piece of cheesecake in the center of each plate and serve.

*B*ecause of the necessarily long baking time (almost 4 hours), resting time in the oven (2 hours), and cooling time (1 hour at room temperature and 12 hours under refrigeration), it is advisable to organize the production of the White Chocolate Cheesecake over 2 or 3 days. The cookies may be baked several days in advance of making the crust, and stored in a sealed plastic container. The crust may be prepared in the springform pan and kept in the freezer (cover with film wrap) for 1 or 2 days. To apply the crumb crust to the springform pan, first press the crumb mixture onto the buttered sides of the pan. Use your fingers to even the crumbs along the lower edge of the sides, so that the crumb crust is square along the lower edge rather than rounded. Press the remaining crumbs, with your hands, to a uniform and level thickness on the bottom of the pan.

When making the cheesecake, it is important that the mixing bowl is frequently scraped down as directed, and that the mixture is thoroughly combined. Failure to do so will result in a lumpy batter and visible white lumps or streaks of cream cheese in the baked cheesecake.

To accompany this cheesecake, I suggest a fresh berry puree (3 to 4 tablespoons ladled onto each dessert plate) and a glass of Schramsberg, Cuveé de Pinot.

# CHAPTER FIVE

# CHOCOLATE DEMENTIA

*RECIPES THAT WILL CAUSE DELIRIUM TREMENS,*

*EVEN IN THE MOST REFORMED CHOCOHOLICS*

# Caramel Rum Delirium Ice Cream Cake

## Caramel Rum Cake

  1  *cup granulated sugar*
 ¹/₄ *teaspoon lemon juice*
 ¹/₂ *cup heavy cream*
  4  *tablespoons plus 2 teaspoons unsalted*
     *butter*
  2  *cups plus 1 tablespoon all-purpose flour*
  2  *teaspoons baking soda*
 ¹/₂ *teaspoon salt*
  1  *cup very tightly packed light brown*
     *sugar*
 ¹/₂ *pound cream cheese, softened*
  3  *eggs*
  3  *tablespoons Myers's Dark Rum*
  1  *teaspoon pure vanilla extract*

## Double Mocha Madness Ice Cream

 *Double Mocha Ice Cream*
    *(see page 131)*

## Semisweet Chocolate Ganache

 *Semisweet Chocolate Ganache*
    *(see page 19)*

## Equipment

*Measuring cup, measuring spoons, 2¹/₂-quart saucepan, whisk, stainless steel bowl, 9- by 3-inch springform pan, sifter, wax paper, electric mixer with paddle, rubber spatula, red toothpick, 10-inch plate, serrated slicer, metal spoon, film wrap, large 100-percent-cotton kitchen towel, cake spatula*

Preheat the oven to 325 degrees Fahrenheit.

To prepare the caramel flavoring, combine the granulated sugar and lemon juice in a 2¹/₂-quart saucepan and stir with a whisk to combine (the sugar will resemble moist sand). Caramelize the sugar for 5 to 6 minutes over medium-high heat, stirring constantly to break up any lumps (the sugar will first turn clear as it liquefies, then brown as it caramelizes). Remove the saucepan from the heat and carefully add the heavy cream; stir to combine (the mixture will steam and boil rapidly as the cream is added). Transfer the caramel to a stainless steel bowl and allow to cool to room temperature.

Coat a 9- by 3-inch springform pan with 2 teaspoons of butter. Flour the pan with 1 table-spoon of flour, then shake out the excess. Set aside until needed.

Combine together in a sifter 2 cups flour, baking soda, and salt. Sift onto wax paper and set aside.

Combine the brown sugar and 4 tablespoons butter in the bowl of an electric mixer fitted with a paddle. Beat on medium for 2 minutes, then scrape down the sides of the bowl. Add the cream cheese and beat on medium for 1 minute, then scrape down the bowl. Beat on high for 1 minute, then add the eggs, one at a time, beating on high for 15 seconds after adding each egg. Scrape down the bowl after each addition. After the eggs have been incorporated, beat on high for 2 minutes. Now add the caramel, dark rum, and vanilla extract; beat on medium for 15 seconds and scrape down the bowl. Add the sifted flour mixture and beat on low for 20 seconds, then on high for 15 seconds. Remove the bowl from the mixer. Use a rubber spatula and mix until the cake batter is thoroughly combined. Pour into the prepared pan, spreading the batter evenly. Bake in the preheated oven for 60 minutes until a red toothpick inserted in the center of the cake comes out clean. Remove the cake from the oven and allow to cool in the pan for 30 minutes at room temperature. Remove the sides of the springform pan and allow the cake to cool for an additional 60 minutes at room temperature, then refrigerate the cake for 1 hour.

While the cake is cooling, prepare the ice cream. It should be frozen for at least 1 hour before assembling the cake. If the ice cream was prepared the previous day, temper (to soften but not thaw) the ice cream in the refrigerator for 45 to 60 minutes before assembling the cake.

To assemble the cake, remove the bottom of the springform pan from the cake. Keep the cake on a 10-inch plate while thoroughly washing, drying, and reassembling the springform pan. Slice the cake horizontally into 3 equal layers. Place the bottom layer in the springform pan, portion half the ice cream on top of the cake layer, and spread the ice cream evenly over the cake. Place the center section of the cake on top of the layer of ice cream. Portion remaining ice cream over the cake and spread evenly. Place the top portion of the cake on top of the ice cream layer and gently press down on the cake. Cover the springform pan with film wrap and freeze the cake for at least 12 hours.

When the cake has been in the freezer for 12 hours, prepare the ganache.

To remove the cake from the springform pan, first remove the film wrap. Wrap a damp, hot towel around the sides of the pan (the towel should be large enough to completely wrap around and cover the sides of the pan). Hold the towel tightly around the pan for 1 minute, then release the springform and remove the cake. Return the cake to the freezer for 30 minutes.

Remove the cake from the freezer. Pour the ganache over the cake and use a cake spatula to create an even coating of ganache on both the top and sides of the cake. Return the cake to the freezer for at least 15 to 20 minutes.

To serve, cut the cake with a serrated slicer. Heat the blade of the slicer under hot running water before making each slice. Hold the slices at room temperature for 5 to 7 minutes before serving.

*To deter crystallization, a little fresh lemon juice is added to the sugar before caramelization.*

*One cup very tightly packed light brown sugar should weigh ½ pound.*

*Use several toothpicks inserted in the sides of the cake as guides to accurately slice the cake into 3 layers.*

*If the springform pan is not washed and dried as directed in the recipe, the ice cream cake may be difficult to remove from the pan after it is assembled and frozen.*

*To facilitate the spreading of the ice cream layers, heat the back of a large metal spoon under hot running water several times during the ice cream spreading procedure. Shake the excess water off the spoon immediately after heating.*

*The temperature of the components is very important in the assembly of the ice cream cake. The cake must be cool enough not to melt the ice cream. The ice cream needs to be soft enough to spread on the cake, but still frozen. Thawing and refreezing of the ice cream will cause ice crystals to form, and diminish the flavor.*

*To serve as we do at The Trellis, portion 3 to 4 tablespoons of Mocha Rum Sauce (see page 18) on a 10-inch plate, sprinkle 1 tablespoon of golden sugar (see page 70) over the sauce, then place a slice of cake on the sauced plate. A drying out period may be wise after consuming this immoderate dessert.*

# CHOCOLATE DEMISE

SERVES 16

## EQUIPMENT

*Measuring cup, measuring spoons, food processor with metal blade, 2¹/₂-quart saucepan, rubber spatula, 2 nonstick baking sheets, cooling rack, small metal spatula, 8 chopsticks, small nonstick pan, 2 9- by 1¹/₂-inch cake pans, parchment paper, double boiler, film wrap, 2 stainless steel bowls (1 large), instant-read test thermometer, electric mixer with balloon whip, 9-inch cardboard cake circle, 9- by 3-inch springform pan, 2 whisks, 9-inch pie tin, serrated knife, cake spatula, pastry bag, medium star tip, serrated slicer*

Preheat the oven to 325 degrees Fahrenheit.

In the bowl of a food processor fitted with a metal blade, chop 1 cup pecan pieces into pieces ¹/₈ inch in size. Set aside until needed.

Heat the light brown sugar, butter, and light corn syrup in a 2¹/₂-quart saucepan over medium heat. Bring to a boil, then remove from heat. Add the chopped pecans and the cake flour and use a rubber spatula to thoroughly combine.

Portion 4 tablespoons of pecan batter in the center of each of 2 nonstick baking sheets. The batter will spread to 8 inches during baking so it is necessary to portion only 1 large tuile per baking sheet. Place the baking sheets on the top and bottom shelves of your oven and bake for 16 minutes (rotate the baking sheets from top to bottom about halfway through the baking time), until evenly caramel-colored. Allow the baked tuiles to cool on the baking sheet for 7 to 10 minutes before handling, then transfer to a cooling rack to completely cool.

Portion and bake 2 more large tuiles. When all 4 large tuiles have been baked, proceed to baking the smaller tuiles. Portion the batter by the teaspoon (1 teaspoon per small tuile) onto the 2 baking sheets. Portion 8 tuiles per sheet. Bake the tuiles, 1 baking sheet at a time, on the center shelf of the oven. Bake for 6 minutes, until evenly caramel-colored. Remove the tuiles from the oven and allow to cool for 30 seconds before handling. Use a small spatula to lift the tuiles from the baking sheet. Roll each small tuile around a chopstick, and allow to cool for 5 minutes before removing the chopstick. Bake the second sheet of small tuiles and repeat the cooling and rolling procedure. Set the rolled tuiles aside until needed.

Lower the oven temperature to 300 degrees Fahrenheit.

To prepare the truffle cake layers, lightly coat the insides of 2 9- by 1¹/₂-inch cake pans with melted butter. Line each pan with parchment paper, then lightly coat the parchment with more melted butter. Set aside.

Heat 1 inch of water in the bottom half of a double boiler over medium heat. Place the semisweet chocolate and ¹/₂ pound of butter in the top half of the double boiler (see page 151). Tightly cover the top with film wrap. Allow to heat for 15 minutes. Remove from the heat, and stir until smooth. Transfer the chocolate to a stainless steel bowl, using a rubber spatula to remove all the chocolate from the double boiler. Keep at room temperature until needed.

Heat 1 inch of water in the bottom half of a double boiler over medium heat. Place the eggs and egg yolks in the top half of the double boiler. Whisk the eggs until they reach a temperature of 110 degrees Fahrenheit, about 4 to 5 minutes. Transfer the heated eggs to the bowl of an electric mixer fitted with a balloon whip. Whisk on high until the eggs become light and pale in color, about 6 to 7 minutes. Remove the bowl from the mixer. Fold ¹/₃ of the eggs into the melted choco-

## PECAN TUILES (4 large and 16 small)

| | |
|---|---|
| 1 | cup pecan pieces |
| ²/₃ | cup very tightly packed light brown sugar |
| ¹/₄ | pound unsalted butter |
| ¹/₂ | cup light corn syrup |
| ²/₃ | cup cake flour |

## TRUFFLE CAKE

| | |
|---|---|
| ¹/₂ | pound plus 2 tablespoons unsalted butter (2 tablespoons melted) |
| 16 | ounces semisweet chocolate, broken into ¹/₂-ounce pieces |
| 4 | eggs |
| 2 | egg yolks |

## CHOCOLATE GANACHE

| | |
|---|---|
| 3 | cups heavy cream |
| 6 | tablespoons unsalted butter |
| 4 | tablespoons granulated sugar |
| 20 | ounces semisweet chocolate, broken into ¹/₂-ounce pieces |
| 6 | ounces unsweetened chocolate, broken into ¹/₂-ounce pieces |

Pastry chef Don Mack was the first to introduce a Chocolate Demise at The Trellis way back in 1981. Subsequently, both pastry chefs Andrew O'Connell and John Twichell have proffered their own versions. The basic premise behind Chocolate Demise, which actually predated Death By Chocolate in the lexicon of Trellis desserts, was a dessert that would pose the greatest challenge to the maker as well as yield the most intensely chocolate reward to the "end user."

Just a glance at the equipment list necessary for the production of this extravaganza and one can imagine our dessert being the demise of even the most ambitious confectioner. Although some improvisation is possible (see below), I would suggest that you check your equipment cupboard before you get started.

To prevent any distortion in the shape of the large tuiles, use heavy duty nonstick baking sheets.

The tuiles can be prepared the day before the assembly of the Demise. If the tuiles lose their crispness, they may be recrisped in a 300-degree-Fahrenheit oven.

If your chopsticks are out to lunch, roll the small tuiles around pencils.

You must work fast when rolling the small tuiles around the chopsticks, because they lose their pliability as they cool. If you are a bit unsure about this procedure, I would suggest baking only 4 small tuiles at a time rather than the suggested 8 tuiles.

I recommend that you serve this cake on the day it is assembled. Do not forget to allow the slices to come to room temperature for 45 to 60 minutes before serving.

late. Add the remaining eggs and fold together gently but thoroughly. Divide between the prepared pans, spreading evenly, and bake in the preheated oven for 20 to 25 minutes, until the internal temperature of the layers reaches 170 degrees Fahrenheit.

Remove the truffle layers from the oven and allow to cool in the pans for 20 minutes. Invert 1 of the truffle layers onto a cardboard cake circle. Invert the other layer onto the bottom of a closed springform pan. Refrigerate the truffle layers until needed.

To prepare the ganache, heat the heavy cream, 6 tablespoons unsalted butter, and sugar in a 2 1/2-quart saucepan over medium-high heat. When hot, stir to dissolve the sugar. Bring the mixture to a boil. Place 20 ounces semisweet chocolate and the unsweetened chocolate in a large stainless steel bowl. Pour the boiling cream over the chocolate and allow to stand for 5 minutes. Stir until smooth. Reserve and refrigerate 3/4 cup ganache; hold the rest at room temperature.

Begin assembly of the Chocolate Demise. One at a time, dip 1 inch of the tip of each small rolled pecan tuile into the room-temperature ganache; allow the excess ganache to drip from the tuile. Lean each dipped tuile (dry tip up) against the inside edge of the pie tin. Keep the chocolate-dipped tuiles in the pie tin in a cool, dry place until needed.

Remove the truffle layers from the refrigerator. Pour 3/4 cup of ganache over the truffle layer in the springform pan, spreading it evenly to the edges. Place 1 of the large tuiles on top of the ganache, gently pressing it into position. Pour 3/4 cup ganache over the tuile, spreading the ganache evenly to the edges. Top this layer of ganache with another large tuile, gently pressing it into place. Repeat these steps until all 4 large tuiles are used. You should end with a layer of ganache. Slide the remaining truffle layer onto the ganache, gently pressing down on the truffle to set it into position. Cover the springform pan with film wrap and freeze for 1 hour.

Remove the Demise from the freezer. Cut around the inside edges to release the Demise from the springform pan, then use a cake spatula to smooth the sides. Pour the remaining room-temperature ganache over the Demise, spreading with a spatula to create an even coating of ganache on both the top and sides. Refrigerate for 30 minutes.

Transfer the reserved refrigerated ganache to a pastry bag fitted with a medium-sized star tip. Pipe a circle of 16 stars along the outside edge of the top of the Demise. Refrigerate the cake for at least 1 hour before cutting and serving.

Place each of the chocolate-dipped tuiles, with the dipped ends pointing towards the center of the Demise, across each one of the 16 stars (allow the dipped ends to touch the top of the Demise). Cut with a serrated slicer, heating the blade of the slicer under hot running water before making each slice. Allow the slices to come to room temperature for 45 to 60 minutes before serving.

# CHOCOLATE ESPRESSO FUDGE CAKE

SERVES 10 TO 12

**EQUIPMENT**

*Measuring cup, measuring spoons, double boiler, film wrap, whisk, small nonstick pan, 2 9- by 1¹/₂-inch cake pans, sifter, wax paper, electric mixer with paddle and balloon whip, rubber spatula, 1¹/₂-quart saucepan, instant-read test thermometer, 2 cardboard cake circles, 2¹/₂-quart saucepan, 2 stainless steel bowls (1 large), serrated slicer, 9- by 3-inch springform pan, 2 pastry bags, large star tip, serrated knife, cake spatula, medium star tip*

Preheat the oven to 350 degrees Fahrenheit.

Heat 1 inch of water in the bottom half of a double boiler over medium heat. Place 4 ounces unsweetened chocolate in the top half of the double boiler (see page 151). Tightly cover the top with film wrap and allow to heat for 5 to 6 minutes. Remove from the heat and stir until smooth.

Lightly coat the insides of 2 9- by 1¹/₂-inch cake pans with melted butter. Flour each pan with 1 teaspoon cake flour, shaking out the excess. Combine together in a sifter the remaining 2 cups cake flour, the baking soda, and salt. Sift onto wax paper and set aside.

Combine the brown sugar and 8 tablespoons butter in the bowl of an electric mixer fitted with a paddle. Beat on low for 3 minutes. Scrape down the sides of the bowl, then beat on high for 2 minutes. Scrape down the sides of the bowl again and beat on high for an additional 1¹/₂ minutes.

Add 4 eggs, one at a time, beating on high for 30 seconds after adding each egg. Scrape down the bowl after each addition, then beat on high for 2 more minutes. Add the melted chocolate and the vanilla. Beat on low for 30 seconds, then scrape down the bowl.

Heat 1 cup water to a boil in a 1¹/₂-quart saucepan. While the water is heating, operate the mixer on low while adding a third of the sifted flour and ¹/₂ cup sour cream; allow to mix for 30 seconds. Add another third of the flour and the remaining sour cream and mix for another 30 seconds. Add the remaining sifted flour and the boiling water and mix for an additional 30 seconds before removing the bowl from the mixer. Use a rubber spatula to finish mixing the batter, until it is smooth and thoroughly combined.

Pour the cake batter into the prepared pans, spreading it evenly. Bake in the preheated oven until a toothpick inserted in the center comes out clean, 45 to 50 minutes. Remove the cakes from the oven and cool in the pans for 15 minutes at room temperature. Invert onto the cake circles and refrigerate, uncovered, until needed.

To prepare the espresso ganache, heat the heavy cream, 2 tablespoons butter, and 2 tablespoons sugar in a 2¹/₂-quart saucepan over medium-high heat, stirring to dissolve the sugar. Bring the mixture to a boil. Place 8 ounces semisweet chocolate and 1 tablespoon instant espresso powder in a stainless steel bowl. Pour the boiling cream over the chocolate and espresso. Tightly cover the top with film wrap and allow to stand for 10 minutes, then stir until smooth. Keep at room temperature until ready to use.

To prepare the chocolate espresso buttercream, heat 1 inch of water in the bottom half of a double boiler over medium heat. Place 8 ounces semisweet chocolate, 2 ounces unsweetened chocolate, and 2 teaspoons espresso powder in the top half of the double boiler. Tightly cover the top with film wrap. Allow to heat for 8 to 10 minutes, transfer to a stainless steel bowl, and stir until smooth. Set aside until needed.

## CHOCOLATE CAKE

- 4 ounces unsweetened chocolate, broken into ¹/₂-ounce pieces
- 8 tablespoons plus 2 teaspoons unsalted butter (2 teaspoons melted)
- 2 cups plus 2 teaspoons cake flour
- 2 teaspoons baking soda
- ¹/₂ teaspoon salt
- 2 cups very tightly packed light brown sugar
- 4 eggs
- 1 teaspoon pure vanilla extract
- 1 cup water
- 1 cup sour cream

## ESPRESSO GANACHE

- 1 cup heavy cream
- 2 tablespoons unsalted butter
- 2 tablespoons granulated sugar
- 8 ounces semisweet chocolate, broken into ¹/₂-ounce pieces
- 1 tablespoon instant espresso powder

## CHOCOLATE ESPRESSO BUTTERCREAM

- 8 ounces semisweet chocolate, broken into ¹/₂-ounce pieces
- 2 ounces unsweetened chocolate, broken into ¹/₂-ounce pieces
- 2 teaspoons instant espresso powder
- 1 pound unsalted butter, softened
- 5 egg whites
- 1 cup granulated sugar

Place 1 pound of butter in the bowl of an electric mixer fitted with a paddle. Beat the butter on low for 2 minutes, then on medium for 3 minutes. Scrape down the sides of the bowl. Beat on high until light and fluffy, about 4 to 5 minutes. Transfer the butter to a large stainless steel bowl. Set aside until needed.

Heat 1 inch of water in the bottom half of a double boiler over medium heat. Place 5 egg whites and 1 cup sugar in the top half of the double boiler. Gently whisk the egg whites until they reach a temperature of 120 degrees Fahrenheit, about 3 to 5 minutes. Transfer the heated egg whites to the bowl of an electric mixer fitted with a balloon whip. Whisk on high until stiff peaks form, about 4 minutes. Remove the bowl from the mixer.

Fold the melted chocolate into the butter, using a rubber spatula to thoroughly combine. Fold in the whipped egg whites until thoroughly combined. Set aside.

Begin assembly of the cake. Turn the 2 cakes over. Using a slicer, trim off just enough of the top of each cake (snack time!) to make an even surface. Slice each cake horizontally into 2 equal layers. Place the top layer of a cake onto the bottom of a closed springform pan. Evenly spread 1 1/2 cups of the chocolate espresso buttercream over the cake in the springform pan. Place the bottom layer of the first cake onto the buttercream and gently press into place. Pour 1 1/4 cups of ganache over the cake layer, spreading the ganache evenly to the edges. Refrigerate the remaining ganache. Place the top layer of the second cake on top of the ganache and press into place. Spread 1 1/2 cups of the buttercream evenly over this layer. Place the remaining bottom cake layer, cut side down, onto the buttercream and gently press into place. Cover the entire cake and pan with film wrap and freeze for 1 hour.

Fill a pastry bag fitted with a large-sized star tip with 1 1/2 cups of chocolate espresso buttercream.

Remove the cake from the freezer. Cut around the inside edges to release the cake from the springform pan. Using a cake spatula, evenly spread the remaining buttercream over the top and sides of the cake. Refrigerate the cake for 1 hour.

Fill a pastry bag fitted with a medium-sized star tip with the remaining ganache.

To decorate the cake, first pipe a ring of the buttercream stars around the outside edge of the top of the cake. Then pipe a circle of ganache stars (each star touching the other) inside the ring of buttercream. Alternate the rings of buttercream stars and circles of ganache stars, until the entire top of the cake is covered. Refrigerate the cake for at least 1 hour before cutting and serving.

Cut the Chocolate Espresso Fudge Cake with a serrated slicer, heating the blade of the slicer under hot running water before making each slice. Bring the slices to room temperature for 10 to 15 minutes before serving.

*Although it is enjoyed all over the world, espresso is a uniquely Italian beverage. My olfactory senses have been put in high gear walking by espresso bars in Auckland, Berkeley, Paris, and especially in tiny alcoves on crowded streets in Florence and Palermo. It would be over-romanticizing to say the best espresso is made in Italy, but then again the Italians are known for romance. For me, the romance in this confection is the coupling of chocolate and espresso.*

*Two cups of very tightly packed light brown sugar should weigh 1 pound.*

*This is buttercream from hell if you have to prepare it—but buttercream from heaven when you eat it! Although a laborious buttercream icing recipe, the results are sublime.*

*We use Ferrara brand instant espresso powder at The Trellis. It is available in some upscale supermarkets as well as gourmet food stores.*

*Be certain that the melted chocolate to be added to the whipped butter is no more than 80 degrees Fahrenheit; if the chocolate is too warm, it will melt the buttercream.*

*To achieve the volume and texture for this exceptional icing, it is necessary to use an electric mixer with a balloon whip.*

*If properly prepared, the buttercream recipe should yield approximately 6 1/2 cups of icing.*

*To spread the production of this cake over 2 days, I recommend baking the chocolate cake on day 1. After the cakes have cooled to room temperature, cover with film wrap and refrigerate until you have made the ganache and buttercream on day 2.*

*After assembly, you may keep this cake in the refrigerator for 2 to 3 days before serving. Do not forget to allow the slices to come to room temperature for 10 to 15 minutes before serving.*

# CHOCOLATE DEVASTATION

SERVES 12

## CHOCOLATE WHISKEY-SOAKED RAISIN ICE CREAM

- 2 cups raisins
- 1/2 cup Jack Daniel's sour mash whiskey
- 8 ounces semisweet chocolate, broken into 1/2-ounce pieces
- 2 cups heavy cream
- 2 ounces unsweetened chocolate, broken into 1/2-ounce pieces
- 1 cup half-and-half
- 8 egg yolks
- 1/4 cup granulated sugar

## MOCHA MERINGUE

- 1/2 cup confectioners' sugar
- 1 tablespoon cornstarch
- 1 tablespoon unsweetened cocoa
- 8 egg whites
- 3/4 cup granulated sugar
- 2 teaspoons instant espresso powder
- 1/4 teaspoon cream of tartar
- 1/8 teaspoon salt

## BITTERSWEET GANACHE

- 2 cups heavy cream
- 2 tablespoons unsalted butter
- 2 tablespoons granulated sugar
- 8 ounces semisweet chocolate, broken into 1/2-ounce pieces
- 4 ounces unsweetened chocolate, broken into 1/2-ounce pieces

## EQUIPMENT

*Measuring cup, measuring spoons, plastic container with tight-fitting lid, double boiler, film wrap, whisk, 2 stainless steel bowls (1 large), 2 1/2-quart saucepan, electric mixer with paddle and balloon whip, rubber spatula, instant-read test thermometer, 2 8- by 1 1/2-inch cake pans, ice-cream freezer, 2 9-inch cardboard cake circles, 4 baking sheets (1 with sides), parchment paper, sifter, wax paper, pastry bag, medium star tip, serrated slicer*

Combine the raisins and whiskey in a plastic container with a tight-fitting lid. Allow to stand at room temperature for 6 hours or overnight.

Heat 1 inch of water in the bottom half of a double boiler over medium heat. Place 8 ounces semisweet chocolate, 1/2 cup heavy cream, and 2 ounces unsweetened chocolate in the top half of the double boiler (see page 151). Tightly cover the top with film wrap. Heat for 10 minutes, then remove from the heat and stir until smooth. Transfer to a stainless steel bowl and set aside until needed.

Heat the remaining 1 1/2 cups heavy cream and the half-and-half in a 2 1/2-quart saucepan over medium-high heat. Bring the cream to a boil.

While the cream is heating, place 8 egg yolks and 1/4 cup sugar in the bowl of an electric mixer fitted with a paddle. Beat the eggs on high for 2 to 2 1/2 minutes. Scrape down the sides of the bowl. Continue to beat on high until slightly thickened and lemon-colored, about 2 1/2 to 3 minutes. (At this point, the cream should be boiling. If not, adjust the mixer speed to low and continue to mix until the cream boils. If this is not done, the egg yolks will develop undesirable lumps.)

Pour the boiling cream into the beaten egg yolks and whisk to combine. Return to the saucepan and heat over medium-high heat, stirring constantly, until the cream reaches a temperature of 185 degrees Fahrenheit, 2 to 4 minutes. Then pour into the melted chocolate mixture, and stir to combine. Cool the mixture in an ice-water bath (see page 150) to a temperature of 40 to 45 degrees Fahrenheit, about 15 to 20 minutes.

Line 2 8- by 1 1/2-inch cake pans with enough film wrap to cover the insides of the pan. Set aside until needed.

Fold the whiskey-soaked raisins and any residual liquid into the cooled chocolate custard mixture. Freeze in an ice-cream freezer following the manufacturer's instructions.

Transfer the semifrozen ice cream to the 2 cake pans, evenly dividing the ice cream between the 2 pans. Use a rubber spatula to spread the ice cream evenly to the edges of the pans. Tightly cover the tops of the pans with film wrap, then place in the freezer for at least 12 hours before assembling the cake.

Prepare the mocha meringue. Using a 9-inch cake circle (or cake plate) as a guide, trace a circle on each of 3 sheets of parchment paper (cut to fit the baking sheets) with a pencil. Turn each sheet of parchment paper over and place with the trace mark down on a baking sheet.

Preheat the oven to 250 degrees Fahrenheit.

Combine together in a sifter the confectioners' sugar, cornstarch, and cocoa. Sift onto the wax paper and set aside until needed.

Heat 1 inch of water in the bottom half of a double boiler over medium-high heat. Place 8 egg whites, 3/4 cup sugar, the espresso powder, the cream of tartar, and the salt in the top half of the

1. Pour ganache into center of meringue.

2. Press ice-cream disk onto ganache.

3. Pipe chilled ganache from a pastry bag around the sides of the ice-cream disk. Freeze. Repeat procedure with another meringue and ice-cream disk.

4. Remove one section from freezer and pour ganache onto ice-cream disk.

5. Remove second section from freezer and press onto first.

6. Pour remaining ganache onto top ice-cream disk.

7. Press remaining meringue onto ganache.

double boiler. Heat the egg white mixture to a temperature of 120 degrees Fahrenheit while gently and constantly whisking, about 2 to 3 minutes. Transfer the mixture to the bowl of an electric mixer fitted with a balloon whip. Whisk on high until stiff but not dry, about 2 to 2½ minutes. Remove the bowl from the mixer and use a rubber spatula to fold in the sifted dry ingredients.

Fill a pastry bag (with no tip) with about a third of the meringue. Fill a traced circle with meringue: start in the center and pipe a ½-inch-wide spiral toward the outside of the circle. Fill the pastry bag again and repeat this procedure with each of the 2 remaining circles (each circle should be filled with about a third of the original amount of meringue). Place the meringues in the preheated oven and bake for 1 hour. Reduce the oven temperature to 225 degrees Fahrenheit and bake for an additional 2 hours. Remove from the oven and allow to cool on the baking sheets for 30 minutes before handling.

To prepare the ganache, heat 2 cups heavy cream, the butter, and 2 tablespoons sugar in a 2½-quart saucepan over medium-high heat. When hot, stir to dissolve the sugar. Bring the mixture to a boil. Place 8 ounces semisweet chocolate and 4 ounces unsweetened chocolate in a stainless steel bowl. Pour the boiling cream over the chocolate and allow to stand for 5 minutes. Stir until smooth. Reserve 1 cup of ganache and set aside at room temperature. Pour the remaining amount of ganache onto a baking sheet with sides and refrigerate for 35 to 40 minutes.

Pour ¼ cup of the reserved room-temperature ganache onto the center of a baked meringue (supported by a cake circle). Remove an ice-cream disk from the freezer. Unwrap the disk and place it onto the puddle of ganache. Press down on the ice-cream disk gently but firmly (this will spread the ganache). Fill a pastry bag fitted with a medium-sized star tip with one-third of the chilled ganache. Pipe about 28 to 30 individual vertical strips 1½-inches long and ¾-inch wide — all the way around the side of the ice-cream disk (each strip should be touching the other, and each strip should also be wider at the base where it touches the meringue and tapered at the crest where it rises to the top edge of the ice-cream disk). Place this section into the freezer and repeat the preceding procedure with another meringue and ice-cream disk. Place in the freezer after completion for about 10 to 15 minutes.

Remove a meringue and ice-cream section from the freezer. Pour ¼ cup of room-temperature ganache onto the center of the ice cream. Remove the second section from the freezer, and center onto the first. Press down on the ice cream, gently but firmly, to spread the ganache. Pour the remaining ¼ cup of room-temperature ganache onto the top ice-cream disk, and onto this ganache place the remaining baked meringue, once again pressing down gently but firmly to spread the ganache. Place the Devastation in the freezer for about 10 to 15 minutes.

Fill a pastry bag fitted with a medium-sized star tip with the remaining chilled ganache. Remove the Devastation from the freezer. Starting ½ inch inside the edge of the top meringue, pipe a ring of about 28 to 30 individual strips — 1½ inches long and ¾ inch wide — all the way around the top (each strip should be touching the other, and each strip should also be wider at the point closest to the edge and tapered at the point closest to the center).

Return the completed Devastation to the freezer for at least 1 hour before serving.

To serve, cut the Devastation with a serrated slicer. Heat the blade of the slicer under hot running water before making each slice. Allow the slices to come to room temperature and hold for 5 to 7 minutes before serving.

*The first time you place a piece of this confection in your mouth, you will appreciate Chocolate Devastation; the whiskey-laced plump raisins will virtually explode on your palate as the coolness of the ice cream nestled between crisp layers of mocha meringue is eagerly lavished by your tongue—truly devastating!*

*The meringues should be rotated once or twice during the baking time to assure that they are uniformly baked.*

*Baked meringues may be prepared a day or two in advance of assembling the Devastation. Store in a closed container in a dry place at room temperature.*

*Baked meringues are brittle: handle with care. To avoid cracking the top layer of meringue, be very careful to gently press down on the meringue when pressing it into place on the ganache.*

*The ganache for this recipe must be of 2 specific degrees of viscosity. One cup of ganache is reserved and held at room temperature; this ganache must be liquid enough to pour easily. If the ganache is too firm, it will not spread over the different layers as detailed in the recipe. The remaining ganache, which is refrigerated on a baking sheet, must be thick enough so that when piped from a pastry bag, it will maintain its shape.*

*If crowded refrigerator space prohibits chilling the ganache on a baking sheet, then chill the ganache in a stainless steel bowl. This will take substantially more time unless you frequently stir the ganache during the chilling process. Another alternative: Place the ganache in a stainless steel bowl and chill in an ice-water bath (see page 150).*

*After assembly, you may keep this cake in the freezer for up to 24 hours before serving. Hold the slices at room temperature for 5 to 7 minutes before serving.*

# CHOCOLATE WEDLOCK

SERVES 60 TO 120

## THE CAKE

- 12 ounces plus 4 teaspoons unsalted butter
- 5 cups plus 4 teaspoons cake flour
- 1 tablespoon baking powder
- 1 teaspoon salt
- 3 cups granulated sugar
- 8 eggs
- 2 teaspoons pure vanilla extract
- 2 cups whole milk
- 8 ounces semisweet chocolate, finely grated

## CHOCOLATE RASPBERRY MOUSSE

- 2 pints fresh red raspberries
- 1/2 cup granulated sugar
- 32 ounces semisweet chocolate, broken into 1/2-ounce pieces
- 8 ounces unsweetened chocolate, broken into 1/2-ounce pieces
- 12 egg whites
- 3 cups heavy cream

## WHITE CHOCOLATE BUTTERCREAM

- 12 ounces white chocolate, broken into 1/2-ounce pieces
- 12 ounces unsalted butter, cut into 6 2-ounce pieces
- 6 egg whites
- 6 tablespoons granulated sugar

## WHITE CHOCOLATE GANACHE

- 1 1/2 cups heavy cream
- 2 tablespoons unsalted butter
- 24 ounces white chocolate, broken into 1/2-ounce pieces

## DECORATION

- 14 ounces semisweet chocolate
- 1 1/4 cups granulated sugar
- 1/4 teaspoon lemon juice
- 48 lemon leaves, washed and dried (Check with your local florist for these)
- 1/2 pint fresh red raspberries

## EQUIPMENT

*Measuring cup, measuring spoons, hand grater or food processor with fine grating blade, 7- by 1 1/2-inch cake pan, 9- by 1 1/2-inch cake pan, 12- by 1 1/2-inch cake pan, sifter, wax paper, electric mixer with paddle and balloon whip, rubber spatula, 2 7-inch, 2 9-inch, and 2 12-inch cardboard cake circles (each trimmed 1/4 inch less in diameter than the size of each cake), 3 stainless steel bowls (1 large), slotted spoon, double boiler, film wrap, whisk, 12-inch serrated slicer, cake spatula, instant-read test thermometer, 2 1/2-quart saucepan, parchment paper, scissors, nonstick baking sheet, cutting board, cook's knife, storage container with tight-fitting lid, 1-inch pastry brush, 7 5 1/2-inch rigid, clear plastic stir sticks (typically used for mixed drinks), large rigid metal spatula*

Preheat the oven to 325 degrees Fahrenheit.

Lightly coat the insides of the 7-inch cake pan and the 9-inch cake pan with 1 teaspoon each of butter, and the 12-inch pan with 2 teaspoons butter. Flour both the 7-inch and 9-inch pans with 1 teaspoon each cake flour and the 12-inch pan with 2 teaspoons. Shake out the excess.

Combine together in a sifter the remaining 5 cups cake flour with the baking powder and salt. Sift onto wax paper and set aside until needed.

Place 3 cups of sugar and the remaining 12 ounces of butter in the bowl of an electric mixer fitted with a paddle. Beat on low for 1 minute, then beat on high for 2 minutes. Scrape down the sides of the bowl. Add 8 eggs, 2 at a time, beating on high for 30 seconds after adding each 2 eggs. Scrape down the sides of the bowl after each addition. Add the vanilla and beat on high for 30 seconds. Add the sifted dry ingredients and mix on low for 45 to 50 seconds. Add the milk and mix on low for 25 to 30 seconds. Increase the speed to medium and beat until smooth, about 10 to 15 seconds. Remove the bowl from the mixer, add 8 ounces grated semisweet chocolate, and use a rubber spatula to thoroughly combine.

Portion the cake batter into the 3 prepared pans: 2 1/2 cups into the 7- by 1 1/2-inch pan, 4 cups into the 9- by 1 1/2-inch pan, and the remaining amount of batter into the 12- by 1 1/2-inch pan. Place the 12-inch pan on the middle shelf of the preheated oven and the 7-inch and 9-inch pans on the bottom shelf. Bake until a toothpick inserted into the center of the cake comes out clean, about 40 minutes for the 7-inch pan, and 45 to 50 for the 9- and 12-inch pans. Remove the cakes from the oven and allow to cool in the pans for 30 minutes. Invert the cake layers onto the appropriately sized, specially cut, cardboard cake circles. Refrigerate the cake layers for 1 hour before commencing the preparation of the mousse.

To prepare the chocolate raspberry mousse, place the red raspberries and 1/4 cup sugar in a stainless steel bowl. Use a slotted spoon to crush the berries to a rough-textured consistency. Set aside for a few minutes.

Heat 1 inch of water in the bottom half of a double boiler over medium heat. Place 32 ounces semisweet chocolate, 8 ounces unsweetened chocolate, and the crushed raspberries in the top half of the double boiler (see page 151). Tightly cover the top with film wrap. Allow to heat for 22 to 24 minutes. Remove from the heat and stir until smooth. Transfer to a large stainless steel bowl and hold at room temperature until needed.

Place 12 egg whites in the bowl of an electric mixer fitted with a balloon whip. Whisk on high

*Our current pastry chef, John Twichell, holds the record for producing wedding cakes at The Trellis. In fact, John is the only Trellis pastry chef to have produced any wedding cakes over the last 12 years. The reason is that The Trellis is an à la carte restaurant; consequently, we do not normally serve parties larger than 8 to 12 people. Exceptions have been made, however, and John was called upon to prepare his (and The Trellis') first wedding cake a few years ago, for a very small group. The cake, of course, was chocolate. And, although it was only one layer, it was nevertheless quite beautiful. A couple of years later, Laura Seu, the daughter of my good friends Jim and Penny Seu, was married at the Wren Chapel at The College Of William And Mary. A small reception followed at The Trellis and John was able to increase the wedding cake to two layers.*

*Now that John has perfected his wedding cake artistry (several Chocolate Wedlocks were produced for the recipe testing and photography for this book), he has informed me that the next Chocolate Wedlock may be his own!*

*Several methods are utilized to cut wedding cakes, depending on whether the cake is to be used for dessert or for ceremonial purposes only. Additionally, quite often the cake is produced for visual impact, resulting in a cake that is much larger than needed. For dessert, I suggest a 4-ounce slice, resulting in a yield of about 60 servings from the 9-inch and 12-inch tiers. The 7-inch or top layer is quite often retained as a sort of keepsake. If the cake is to be served after a dessert as a ceremonial sweet, then 120 2-ounce servings can be cut from the two tiers.*

until soft peaks form, about 1 minute and 45 seconds. Continue to whisk on high while gradually adding the remaining 1/4 cup sugar. Whisk until stiff but not dry, about 30 seconds. Set aside.

Using a hand-held whisk, whip 3 cups heavy cream in a well-chilled stainless steel bowl (see page 151) until stiff. Use a rubber spatula to fold a quarter of the egg whites into the melted chocolate mixture, then fold in the whipped cream. Now fold in the remaining egg whites. Set aside at room temperature while slicing the cakes into layers.

Slice each cake horizontally into 3 equal layers. Remove and set aside the smooth top layer of each inverted cake (this layer was originally the baked bottom of the cake). Place the center layer of each cake onto the appropriate remaining cake circles.

Portion 3 cups of mousse onto each of 2 12-inch cake layers (the 2 that are on the cake circles) and spread evenly to the edges. Refrigerate the 2 layers for 30 minutes. Remove the 2 layers from the refrigerator. Portion 1 additional cup of mousse onto each layer and spread to the edges. Stack the 2 layers (slide the center layer off the cardboard cake circle onto the bottom layer), then top with the reserved layer, smooth side up. Refrigerate.

Portion 2 cups of mousse onto each of 2 9-inch cake layers (the 2 that are on the cake circles) and spread evenly to the edges. Refrigerate the 2 layers for 20 minutes. Remove the 2 layers from the refrigerator. Portion 1/2 additional cup of mousse onto each layer and spread to the edges. Stack the 2 layers (slide the center layer off the cardboard cake circle onto the bottom layer), then top with the reserved layer, smooth side up. Refrigerate.

Portion 1 cup of mousse onto each of 2 7-inch cake layers (the 2 that are on the cake circles) and spread evenly to the edges. Refrigerate the 2 layers for 10 minutes. Remove the 2 layers from the refrigerator. Portion additional 1/2 cup of mousse onto each layer and spread to the edges. Stack the two layers (slide the center layer off the cardboard cake circle onto the bottom layer), then top with the reserved layer, smooth side up. Refrigerate.

Remove the 12-inch cake from the refrigerator. Use a cake spatula to smooth the mousse around the edges of the cake. Return the cake to the refrigerator and repeat this step with the 9-inch cake, then with the 7-inch cake.

To prepare the white chocolate buttercream, heat 1 inch of water in the bottom half of a double boiler over medium heat. Place 12 ounces white chocolate in the top half of the double boiler. Tightly cover the top with film wrap. Heat for 10 to 12 minutes, then remove from the heat and stir until smooth. Transfer the melted white chocolate to a large stainless steel bowl and set aside.

Place 12 ounces butter pieces in the bowl of an electric mixer fitted with a paddle. Beat on low for 1 minute. Scrape down the paddle and the sides of the bowl. Beat on medium for 2 minutes, scrape down the sides of the bowl, and beat on high for 5 minutes, until light and fluffy. Use a rubber spatula to thoroughly fold the butter into the melted white chocolate. Set aside until needed.

Heat 1 inch of water in the bottom half of a double boiler over medium heat. Place 6 egg whites and 6 tablespoons sugar in the top half of the double boiler. Gently whisk the egg whites in the double boiler until they reach a temperature of 120 degrees Fahrenheit, about 2 1/2 to 3 minutes. Transfer the heated egg whites to the bowl of an electric mixer fitted with a balloon whip. Whisk on high until stiff peaks form, about 4 minutes. Remove the bowl from the mixer.

Use a rubber spatula to fold the egg whites into the combined white chocolate and butter mixture, and combine thoroughly.

Use a cake spatula to evenly spread 1 1/2 cups of white chocolate buttercream over the top and sides of the 7-inch cake. The finished surface should be smooth and free of any specks of dark chocolate (any trace of dark chocolate will show through the final ganache coating). Refrigerate the cake for at least 1 hour. Repeat the preceding procedure with the 2 remaining cakes, spreading

2 cups of buttercream onto the 9-inch cake and 2¹/₂ cups onto the 12 inch cake. Also refrigerate these layers for at least 1 hour.

Prepare the white chocolate ganache. Heat 1¹/₂ cups heavy cream and 2 tablespoons butter in a 2¹/₂-quart saucepan over medium-high heat. Bring to a boil. Place 24 ounces white chocolate in a stainless steel bowl. Pour the boiling cream over the white chocolate and allow to stand for 5 minutes. Stir until smooth. Set aside until needed.

Pour ³/₄ cup White Chocolate Ganache over the 7-inch cake, and use a cake spatula to spread the ganache evenly over the top and sides of the cake. Refrigerate for at least 1 hour. Repeat this procedure with the 2 remaining cakes, pouring 1¹/₄ cups of ganache onto the 9-inch cake and the remaining ganache onto the 12-inch cake. Refrigerate for at least 1 hour before decorating, or apply the decorations several hours later or even the following day.

To decorate, heat 1 inch of water in the bottom half of a double boiler over medium heat. Place 8 ounces semisweet chocolate in the top half of the double boiler. Tightly cover the top with film wrap. Allow to heat for 10 minutes. Remove from the heat and allow to stand for 8 minutes before removing the film wrap. Use a rubber spatula or a whisk to stir the chocolate until smooth, and continue to stir until the temperature of the chocolate is reduced to 90 degrees Fahrenheit.

Form a pastry cone with parchment paper. Transfer the melted chocolate to the pastry cone. Cut off a tip of less than ¹/₈ inch. Decorate 1 cake at a time, keeping the cakes refrigerated when not being decorated. Starting with the 7 inch cake, pipe out a line of chocolate ¹/₄ inch away from the edge of the cake (hold the tip of the cone about ¹/₂ inch away from the surface of the cake and gently squeeze a steady line). Continue to pipe parallel lines of chocolate, each one about ¹/₄ inch away from the other. Repeat until the lines cover the entire surface of the cake to within ¹/₄ inch from the edge opposite the first line. Turn the cake clockwise one-sixth of a turn. Proceed to pipe lines over the first set of lines in the exact manner as the first lines were applied, creating a diamond grid over the surface of the cake. Now "finish" the edge of the cake by piping a border of connecting teardrops around the edge, covering the tips of the chocolate lines. Form these teardrops by squeezing out about ¹/₈ teaspoon of chocolate and then pulling away with the cone to form the tapered tip of the teardrop. Return the decorated cake to the refrigerator and decorate the 9-inch and then the 12-inch cake in the same manner.

Now prepare the caramelized sugar decoration. Place 1¹/₄ cups sugar and ¹/₄ teaspoon lemon juice in a 2¹/₂-quart saucepan. Stir with a whisk to combine (the sugar will resemble moist sand). Caramelize the sugar for 5 to 6 minutes over medium-high heat, stirring constantly with a whisk to break up any lumps (the sugar will first turn clear as it liquefies, then brown as it caramelizes). Pour the caramelized sugar onto a nonstick baking sheet, then harden in the freezer, about 12 to 15 minutes. Turn the hardened sugar out onto a cutting board, then finely chop by hand with a cook's knife. Store the sugar in an airtight container in the freezer until ready to use.

Use scissors to trim the lemon leaves. The leaves should not be any wider than 1 inch at the widest point and no longer than 1³/₄ inches from end to end (not including the stem itself).

Heat 1 inch of water in the bottom half of a double boiler over medium heat. Place the remaining 6 ounces of semisweet chocolate in the top half of the double boiler. Tightly cover the top with film wrap. Allow to heat for 6 minutes.

Remove from the heat and allow to stand for 5 minutes before removing the film wrap. Use a rubber spatula or whisk to stir the chocolate until smooth, and continue to stir until the temperature of the chocolate is reduced to 90 degrees Fahrenheit. Use a pastry brush to coat the underside of each leaf with a smooth ¹/₈-inch-thick coating of chocolate. Place the leaves on a baking sheet and refrigerate for about 15 minutes or freeze for about 5 minutes until the chocolate has hardened. To remove the chocolate leaves from the lemon leaves, carefully peel each lemon leaf away

*Your search for equipment needed to produce a wedding cake of this magnitude should be in the direction of an outlet that retails Wilton performance pans and supplies. It is here that you will be able to find the odd-size pans and cardboard cake circles necessary to produce Chocolate Wedlock.*

*Frankly, this cake should not be made at home unless you have adequate refrigeration and preparation space. Otherwise, your wedlock may turn into gridlock!*

*Create as smooth a surface of buttercream as possible on the cake layers, since peaks or ripples will show through the subsequent coating of ganache. To smooth the surface of your iced cakes, first refrigerate the cakes for 10 minutes. Heat a cake spatula under hot running water, wipe the blade dry, and then run the blade across the surface of the buttercream.*

*Be certain that the White Chocolate Ganache is at room temperature before it is poured on the buttercream. If it is too warm, it will melt the buttercream.*

*You need not be an expert to create the chocolate trellis-like design on the cake layers. It requires concentration more than steady hand or decorating expertise. Confidence is key, so practice with some additional chocolate on a cardboard cake circle.*

*To deter crystallization, fresh lemon juice is added to the sugar before caramelization.*

*When coating the lemon leaves with chocolate, be certain that the more textural stem vein is sufficiently coated, otherwise the chocolate leaf may break in two when separated from the lemon leaf.*

*Additional stir-stick supports may be needed if the cake is to be moved after assembly. The heavy duty stir sticks used for Chocolate Wedlock are the same as used in some of our mixed drinks at The Trellis. They are available from wholesale food and paper distributors. If you are not able to locate this particular stir stick, then consider chopsticks, or locate that Wilton dealer to find a variety of wedding cake supports.*

*One final touch for the pastry chef: please quaff a well-chilled glass of champagne upon completion of the wedlock. You deserve it!*

from the hardened chocolate. Return the chocolate leaves to the refrigerator until needed.

For final assembly, place 3 of the stir sticks 1½ inches away from the edge on the top of the 9-inch cake equidistant from each other forming a triangle. The sticks should be inserted straight up and into the cake to its depth, leaving some 2 inches of stick to elevate the 7-inch cake. Place the remaining 4 stir sticks 2½ inches away from the edge on top of the 12-inch cake, equidistant from each other forming a square. The sticks should be inserted straight up and into the cake to its depth, leaving some 2 inches of stick to elevate the 9-inch cake.

Decorate each support stick by forming clusters of 4 to 5 chocolate leaves and 5 to 6 whole red raspberries around each stick. Form a grouping of leaves and raspberries in the center of the top 7-inch cake.

Apply the chopped caramelized sugar by pressing a ½-inch band of sugar around the bottom edge of each cake.

Use a rigid metal spatula to pick up the 9-inch cake and carefully set it into place on the 4 supports of the 12-inch cake. Repeat this procedure with the 7-inch cake, placing it onto the supports of the 9-inch cake.

After the bride and the groom have enjoyed the first exquisite bite of chocolate wedlock the tiers should be removed and then the cakes may be sliced as desired using a serrated slicer.

# CHOCOLATE TRANSPORTATION

SERVES 12

## EQUIPMENT

*Measuring cup, measuring spoons, small nonstick pan, 6 9- by 1¹/₂-inch cake pans, parchment paper, double boiler, film wrap, whisk, electric mixer with paddle and balloon whip, rubber spatula, 3 stainless steel bowls (1 large), baking sheet with sides, food processor with metal blade, 2¹/₂-quart saucepan, 3 9-inch cake circles, 9- by 3-inch springform pan, cake spatula, serrated slicer*

Lightly coat the insides of 6 9- by 1¹/₂-inch cake pans with melted butter. Line each pan with parchment paper, then lightly coat the parchment with more melted butter. Set aside.

Preheat the oven to 325 degrees Fahrenheit.

Heat 1 inch of water in the bottom half of a double boiler over medium heat. Place ³/₄ pound butter and 10 ounces semisweet chocolate in the top half of the double boiler (see page 151). Tightly cover the top with film wrap. Allow to heat for 10 to 12 minutes. Remove from heat, stir until smooth, and hold at room temperature.

Place 12 egg yolks and 1 cup sugar in the bowl of an electric mixer fitted with a paddle. Beat on high until slightly thickened and lemon-colored, about 4 to 5 minutes. Scrape down the sides of the bowl and beat on high for an additional 2 minutes.

While the egg yolks are beating, whisk 6 egg whites in a large stainless steel bowl until stiff but not dry, about 4 to 5 minutes.

Pour the melted chocolate mixture into the egg yolk mixture. Beat on medium for 30 seconds. Add a quarter of the whipped egg whites and beat on medium for 15 seconds. Remove the bowl from the mixer. Using a rubber spatula, vigorously fold remaining egg whites into batter.

Divide the batter between the prepared pans (about 1 cup of batter per pan), spreading evenly, and bake on the top and middle shelves in the preheated oven, until a toothpick inserted in the center comes out clean, about 20 minutes. Rotate the cakes from top to bottom about halfway through the baking time. Remove the cakes from the oven and allow to cool to room temperature in the pans. (During baking, the surface of the cakes will form a crust; this crust will normally collapse when the cakes are removed from the oven.)

Toast the macadamia nuts on a baking sheet with sides in the preheated 325-degree-Fahrenheit oven until golden brown, about 12 to 14 minutes. Allow the nuts to cool to room temperature. In a food processor fitted with a metal blade, chop the nuts into ¹/₈-inch pieces.

To prepare the ganache, heat 2 cups heavy cream, 4 tablespoons butter, and ¹/₄ cup sugar in a 2¹/₂-quart saucepan over medium-high heat, stirring to dissolve the sugar. Bring the mixture to a boil. Place 16 ounces semisweet chocolate in a stainless steel bowl. Pour the boiling cream over the chocolate and allow to stand for 5 minutes. Stir until smooth.

Remove 2 cups ganache and combine with the chopped macadamia nuts. Turn out 3 of the cake layers onto 3 individual cake circles. Evenly divide the ganache-and-macadamia-nut mixture (about 1 cup per layer) onto the inverted cake layers. Spread the mixture evenly to the edges of each layer and top each with a remaining cake layer. Refrigerate until needed.

To prepare the mocha mousse, heat 1 inch of water in the bottom half of a double boiler over medium heat. Place 10 ounces semisweet chocolate, 2 ounces unsweetened chocolate, and the coffee in the top half of the double boiler. Tightly cover the top with film wrap. Heat for 7 to 10

## CHOCOLATE CAKE

- ³/₄ pound unsalted butter (4 tablespoons melted)
- 10 ounces semisweet chocolate, broken into ¹/₂-ounce pieces
- 12 egg yolks
- 1 cup granulated sugar
- 6 egg whites

## CHOCOLATE GANACHE

- 1¹/₂ cups raw unsalted macadamia nuts
- 2 cups heavy cream
- 4 tablespoons unsalted butter
- ¹/₄ cup granulated sugar
- 16 ounces semisweet chocolate, broken into ¹/₂-ounce pieces

## MOCHA MOUSSE

- 10 ounces semisweet chocolate, broken into ¹/₂-ounce pieces
- 2 ounces unsweetened chocolate, broken into ¹/₂-ounce pieces
- ¹/₄ cup coffee, brewed full strength
- 4 egg whites
- 2 tablespoons granulated sugar
- ³/₄ cup heavy cream

## DEEP DARK CHOCOLATE FUDGE COOKIES

- 4 Deep Dark Chocolate Fudge Cookies (see page 28)

minutes, then remove from the heat. Stir the mixture until smooth. Transfer to a large stainless steel bowl. Keep at room temperature while whisking the egg whites.

In the bowl of an electric mixer fitted with a balloon whip, whisk 4 egg whites on high until soft peaks form, 1 to 1½ minutes. Continue to whisk on high while gradually adding 2 tablespoons sugar. Whisk until stiff but not dry, about 30 seconds.

Whip ¾ cup heavy cream in a well-chilled stainless steel bowl (see page 151) until stiff. Use a rubber spatula to fold a quarter of the egg whites into the melted chocolate mixture, then fold in the whipped cream. Now fold in the remaining egg whites. Cover the bowl with film wrap and set aside for a few minutes until needed.

Remove all cake layers from the refrigerator. Place 1 of the layers onto the bottom of a closed springform pan. Evenly spread half the amount of the mousse over the cake in the springform pan. Place a second cake layer onto the mousse and gently press into position. Evenly spread the remaining amount of mousse on the cake in the pan, then top with the remaining cake layer and press into place. Cover the entire cake and pan with film wrap and refrigerate for 2 hours.

In a food processor fitted with a metal blade, chop the cookies. Pulse until all the cookies are in crumbs (this should yield 1 cup crumbs), 10 to 15 seconds.

For assembly, remove the cake from the springform pan (if necessary, use a serrated knife to cut around the inside edges). Pour the remaining ganache over the cake using a cake spatula to create an even coating of ganache on both the top and sides of the cake. Press the cookie crumbs into the ganache on the sides of the cake, coating evenly. Refrigerate the cake for at least 1 hour before cutting and serving.

To serve, cut the cake with a serrated slicer. Heat the blade of the slicer under hot running water before making each slice. Allow the slices to come to room temperature for 15 to 20 minutes before serving.

# CHOCOLATE PHANTASMAGORIA

SERVES 12

## HAZELNUT BUTTER

1 pound hazelnuts
4 tablespoons unsalted butter

## CHOCOLATE CAKE

2 ounces unsweetened chocolate, broken
   into ½-ounce pieces
4 tablespoons plus 1 teaspoon unsalted
   butter, softened
1 cup plus 1 teaspoon cake flour
¼ cup unsweetened cocoa
1 teaspoon baking soda
½ teaspoon salt
1 cup plus 4 tablespoons very tightly packed
   light brown sugar
2 eggs
½ teaspoon pure vanilla extract
½ cup water
¾ cup sour cream

## CHOCOLATE GANACHE

1¾ cups heavy cream
2 tablespoons granulated sugar
2 tablespoons unsalted butter
14 ounces semisweet chocolate, broken into
   ½-ounce pieces

### EQUIPMENT

*Measuring cup, measuring spoons, 2 baking sheets with sides, food processor with metal blade, rubber spatula, double boiler, film wrap, 9- by 1½-inch cake pan, sifter, wax paper, electric mixer with paddle, small saucepan, cooling rack, 2 large 100-percent-cotton towels, 2½-quart saucepan, whisk, stainless steel bowl, 3 cardboard cake circles, cake spatula, 12-inch serrated slicer*

Preheat the oven to 325 degrees Fahrenheit.

Toast and skin the hazelnuts (see page 151), then finely chop them in a food processor fitted with a metal blade, until the consistency resembles that of coarse peanut butter (scrape down the bowl as necessary). Add 4 tablespoons butter and process until thoroughly combined. Set aside until needed.

Raise the oven temperature to 350 degrees Fahrenheit.

Heat 1 inch of water in the bottom half of a double boiler over medium heat. Place the unsweetened chocolate in the top half of the double boiler (see page 151). Tightly cover the top with film wrap and allow to heat for 4 to 5 minutes. Remove from the heat and stir until smooth.

Coat a 9- by 1½-inch cake pan with 1 teaspoon butter. Flour the pan with 1 teaspoon flour, shaking out the excess. Combine together in a sifter 1 cup flour, the cocoa, baking soda, and salt. Sift onto wax paper and set aside.

Combine the brown sugar and 4 tablespoons butter in the bowl of an electric mixer fitted with a paddle. Beat on low for 2 minutes. Scrape down the sides of the bowl, then beat on high for 1½ minutes. Scrape down the sides of the bowl. Add 1 egg and beat on high for 15 seconds, then scrape down the bowl. Add the remaining egg, beat on high for 15 seconds, then scrape down the bowl. Beat on high for 2 minutes. Add the melted chocolate and the vanilla. Beat on low for 30 seconds, then scrape down the bowl.

Heat ½ cup water to a boil in a small saucepan. While the water is heating, operate the mixer on low while adding a third of the sifted flour and half the sour cream; allow to mix for 30 seconds. Add another third of the flour and the remaining sour cream and mix for another 30 seconds. Add the remaining sifted flour and the boiling water and mix for an additional 30 seconds before removing the bowl from the mixer. Use a rubber spatula to finish mixing the batter, until it is smooth and thoroughly combined.

Pour the cake batter into the prepared pan, spreading it evenly. Bake in the preheated oven until a toothpick inserted in the center of the cake comes out clean, 45 to 50 minutes. Remove the cake from the oven and cool in the pan for 15 minutes at room temperature. Turn out onto a cooling rack and keep at room temperature until needed.

To prepare the chocolate ganache, heat the heavy cream, 2 tablespoons sugar, and 2 tablespoons butter in a 2½-quart saucepan over medium-high heat, stirring to dissolve the sugar. Bring the mixture to a boil. Place the semisweet chocolate in a stainless steel bowl. Pour the boiling cream over the chocolate and allow to stand for 5 minutes. Stir until smooth. Keep at room temperature until ready to use.

Turn the cake over onto a clean dry surface and slice it horizontally into 3 equal layers. Place a dab of ganache in the center of a cake circle. Place the *top* layer of the cake, cut side down, onto the circle, gently pressing down on the cake so that the ganache will hold it in place. Place the *center* layer of the cake on a separate cake circle. Also place the *bottom* layer of the cake, cut side down, on a third cake circle. Evenly spread ³/₄ cup of ganache over the *top* and *center* layers of the cake. Refrigerate these 2 layers for 20 minutes. Remove the 2 layers from the refrigerator and divide and spread the hazelnut butter over the ganache on both cake layers, spreading evenly to the edges. Refrigerate for 20 minutes. Slide the ganached *center* layer onto the ganached *top* layer. Slide the *bottom* layer onto the ganached *center* layer. Pour the remaining ganache over the cake, spreading with a spatula to create an even coating of ganache on both the top and sides of the cake. Refrigerate the cake for at least 2 hours before cutting and serving.

Cut the cake with a serrated slicer, heating the blade of the slicer under hot running water before making each slice. Allow the slices to come to room temperature for 30 to 40 minutes before serving.

*O*ne cup very tightly packed light brown sugar should weigh ¹/₂ pound.

When boiling the cream for the ganache, be certain to watch for the precise moment that the cream begins to boil so that you can remove it at that exact point. Otherwise, in a matter of seconds, the cream may boil out of the pan, creating a major mess.

If cardboard cake circles are not available, use any 9- to 10-inch dinner plates.

If room temperature in your kitchen is too cool, the ganache may set up to the point that you can not pour it onto the assembled cake layers. If this occurs, place the ganache over a pan of very hot water and stir it until it attains the desired viscosity.

Preparation of the cake may be spread out over 2 days. DAY 1: Prepare the hazelnut butter and the chocolate cake and refrigerate until assembly. DAY 2: Remove the hazelnut butter from the refrigerator at least 2 hours before assembly so it can soften, making it easier to spread. While the hazelnut butter is softening, prepare the chocolate ganache. Remove the cake from the refrigerator and slice horizontally. Assemble the cake and refrigerate for 2 hours or partially freeze before slicing.

Use several toothpicks inserted in the sides of the cake as guides to accurately cut the cake horizontally.

For an extra touch, toast an additional ¹/₂ cup of hazelnuts, chop the nuts by hand or in a food processor until they are ¹/₈ inch in size, then press the chopped nuts into the icing on the sides of the assembled cake, coating evenly.

The full-blown Trellis presentation for Chocolate Phantasmagoria includes portioning 4 tablespoons of Mocha Anglaise (see page 17) onto each plate, highlighting the Anglaise with streaks of chocolate ganache, sprinkling golden sugar (see page 70) in a circle over the sauce near the outside edge of the plate, placing a slice of the cake in the center of each plate, and then finishing with a scoop of Double Mocha Ice Cream (see page 131), on each side of the cake (whew!). Serve immediately.

After assembly, you may keep this cake in the refrigerator for 2 to 3 days before serving. Bring the slices to room temperature for 30 to 40 minutes before serving.

# DOUBLE MOCHA MADNESS

**EQUIPMENT:**

*Measuring cup, measuring spoons, 2 baking sheets with sides, 2 large 100-percent-cotton towels, food processor with metal blade, 2 2 1/2-quart saucepans, whisk, metal spoon, 2 2-quart plastic containers with lids, double boiler, film wrap, electric mixer fitted with a paddle, rubber spatula, 2 stainless steel bowls (1 large), instant-read test thermometer, ice-cream freezer*

Preheat the oven to 325 degrees Fahrenheit.

Toast and skin the hazelnuts (see page 151), then allow the nuts to cool to room temperature.

In the bowl of a food processor fitted with a metal blade, chop the hazelnuts into pieces 1/8 inch in size. Spread the chopped hazelnuts onto a baking sheet with sides.

Combine 1/2 cup granulated sugar and the lemon juice in a 2 1/2-quart saucepan. Stir with a whisk to combine (the sugar will resemble moist sand). Caramelize the sugar for 4 1/2 to 5 minutes over medium-high heat, stirring constantly with a whisk to break up any lumps (the sugar will first turn clear as it liquefies, then light brown as it caramelizes). Pour the caramelized sugar over the chopped hazelnuts. Stir the mixture with a spoon, then spread it into an uneven mass, about 4 to 5 inches in diameter. Allow the pralines to cool to room temperature. Break the pralines into uneven pieces, then place in the bowl of a food processor fitted with a metal blade. Chop the pralines into 1/8-inch pieces. Transfer the chopped pralines to a plastic container with a lid. Freeze until needed.

To prepare the ice cream, heat 1 inch of water in the bottom half of a double boiler over medium-high heat. Place the semisweet and unsweetened chocolates, coffee, and instant espresso powder in the top half of the double boiler (see page 151). Tightly cover the top with film wrap. Heat for 6 to 8 minutes, then remove from the heat and stir until smooth. Set aside until needed.

Heat the heavy cream, half-and-half, and 1/2 cup granulated sugar in a 2 1/2-quart saucepan over medium-high heat. Stir to dissolve the sugar. Bring the cream to a boil.

While the cream is heating, place the egg yolks and the remaining 1/2 cup sugar in the bowl of an electric mixer fitted with a paddle. Beat the eggs on high for 2 to 2 1/2 minutes. Scrape down the sides of the bowl. Continue to beat on high until slightly thickened and lemon-colored, about 2 1/2 to 3 minutes. (At this point, the cream should be boiling. If not, adjust the mixer to low and continue to mix until the cream boils. If this is not done, the egg yolks will develop undesirable lumps.)

Pour the boiling cream into the beaten egg yolks and whisk to combine. Return to the saucepan and heat over medium-high heat, stirring constantly, until the cream reaches a temperature of 185 degrees Fahrenheit, 2 to 4 minutes. Remove from the heat and transfer to a stainless steel bowl. Add the melted chocolate mixture and whisk to combine. Cool the mixture in an ice-water bath (see page 150) to a temperature of 40 to 45 degrees Fahrenheit, about 20 minutes.

Freeze in an ice-cream freezer following the manufacturer's instructions.

Transfer the semifrozen ice cream to a plastic container. Using a rubber spatula, fold in the frozen, chopped pralines. Securely cover the container, then place in the freezer for several hours before serving. Serve within 3 days.

## HAZELNUT PRALINES

- 1/4 cup hazelnuts
- 1/2 cup granulated sugar
- 1/4 teaspoon lemon juice

## DOUBLE MOCHA ICE CREAM

- 8 ounces semisweet chocolate, broken into 1/2-ounce pieces
- 2 ounces unsweetened chocolate, broken into 1/2-ounce pieces
- 1/4 cup brewed coffee, full strength
- 2 tablespoons instant espresso powder
- 2 cups heavy cream
- 1 cup half-and-half
- 1 cup granulated sugar
- 5 egg yolks

### THE CHEF'S TOUCH

*I*t has been said that pastry chef John Twichell "is over the top" when it comes to his unrestrained enthusiasm for creating chocolate desserts. Illustrative of this penchant for lavish couplings is John's signature ice-cream dessert— Double Mocha Madness.

To deter crystallization, fresh lemon juice is added to the sugar before caramelization.

Be certain not to fold the chopped pralines into the ice cream until the semifrozen ice cream is transferred to the plastic container. If the pralines are added as the ice cream is being made, the pralines may melt.

We use Ferrara brand instant espresso powder at The Trellis.

# WHITE AND DARK CHOCOLATE DACQUOISE

SERVES 8 TO 12

## MERINGUE

- <sup>3</sup>/<sub>4</sub> cup confectioners' sugar
- 1 tablespoon cornstarch
- 8 egg whites
- <sup>1</sup>/<sub>4</sub> teaspoon cream of tartar
- <sup>1</sup>/<sub>8</sub> teaspoon salt
- 1 cup granulated sugar

## WHITE AND DARK CHOCOLATE BUTTERCREAM ICING

- 6 ounces semisweet chocolate, broken into <sup>1</sup>/<sub>2</sub>-ounce pieces
- 2 ounces unsweetened chocolate, broken into <sup>1</sup>/<sub>2</sub>-ounce pieces
- 8 ounces white chocolate, broken into <sup>1</sup>/<sub>2</sub>-ounce pieces
- 1 pound unsalted butter, cut into 8 pieces
- 8 egg whites
- <sup>3</sup>/<sub>4</sub> cup granulated sugar

## GANACHE

- <sup>3</sup>/<sub>4</sub> cup heavy cream
- 2 tablespoons unsalted butter
- 6 ounces semisweet chocolate, broken into <sup>1</sup>/<sub>2</sub>-ounce pieces

### EQUIPMENT

*Measuring cup, measuring spoons, 9-inch cardboard cake circle, parchment paper, sifter, wax paper, 3 baking sheets, electric mixer with balloon whip and paddle, rubber spatula, 3 stainless steel bowls, double boiler, film wrap, whisk, 2 pastry bags, 1<sup>1</sup>/<sub>2</sub>-quart saucepan, serrated knife, cake spatula, 2 medium star tips, 12-inch serrated slicer*

Using a 9-inch cake circle (or cake plate) as a guide, trace a circle on each of 3 sheets of parchment paper (cut to fit the baking sheets) with a pencil. Turn each sheet of parchment paper over and place with the trace mark down on a baking sheet.

Preheat the oven to 250 degrees Fahrenheit.

Sift together the confectioners' sugar and cornstarch onto the wax paper. Set aside.

Place 8 egg whites, the cream of tartar, and salt into the bowl of an electric mixer fitted with a balloon whip. Whisk on high until stiff but not dry, about 1<sup>1</sup>/<sub>2</sub> minutes. Gradually add 1 cup sugar while whisking on high for 1 additional minute. Remove the bowl from the mixer and use a rubber spatula to fold in the dry, sifted ingredients.

Fill a pastry bag with no tip with a third of the meringue. Fill a traced circle with meringue; start in the center and pipe a <sup>1</sup>/<sub>2</sub>-inch-wide spiral toward the outside of the circle. Repeat this procedure with each of the 2 remaining circles (each circle should be filled with about a third of the original amount of meringue). Place the meringues in the preheated oven and bake for 1 hour. Lower the oven temperature to 200 degrees Fahrenheit and bake for an additional 2 hours. Remove from the oven and allow to cool on the baking sheets for 30 minutes before handling.

To prepare the buttercream icing, heat 1 inch of water in the bottom half of a double boiler over medium heat. Place 6 ounces semisweet chocolate and 2 ounces unsweetened chocolate in the top portion of the double boiler (see page 151). Tightly cover the top with film wrap. Allow to heat for 8 minutes. Remove the chocolate from the heat and transfer to a stainless steel bowl. Use a whisk and stir until smooth. Repeat this procedure with the white chocolate. Set both melted chocolates aside and allow to cool to room temperature.

Place 1 pound of butter pieces in the bowl of an electric mixer fitted with a paddle. Beat the butter on low for 1 minute, then scrape down the paddle and the sides of the bowl. Beat on medium for 2 minutes, then scrape down the sides of the bowl and beat on high for an additional 5 minutes, until light and creamy. Evenly divide the butter into the 2 bowls of melted chocolate. Use a rubber spatula to thoroughly fold the butter into the chocolates. Set aside.

Place 8 egg whites in the bowl of an electric mixer fitted with a balloon whip. Whisk on high until stiff but not dry, about 1<sup>1</sup>/<sub>2</sub> minutes. Gradually add <sup>3</sup>/<sub>4</sub> cup sugar and whisk on high for 1<sup>1</sup>/<sub>2</sub> minutes. Remove the bowl from the mixer and fold half the amount into each bowl of combined chocolate and butter. Use a rubber spatula to vigorously and thoroughly combine. Separately reserve 2 cups dark chocolate icing and 2 cups white chocolate icing. Place the remainder of each of the icings in separate pastry bags with no tips. Set aside at room temperature until needed.

To prepare the ganache, heat the heavy cream and 2 tablespoons of butter in a 1<sup>1</sup>/<sub>2</sub>-quart saucepan over medium-high heat. Bring to a boil. Place 6 ounces semisweet chocolate in a stainless steel bowl. Pour the boiling cream over the chocolate and allow to stand for 3 to 4 minutes. Stir until smooth. Hold at room temperature until needed.

At the Lenotre Pastry School, I learned how to prepare the classic dacquoise. At The Trellis, I am a willing accomplice to doubling the layers of buttercream and covering the whole with ganache.

It is not a problem if the piped meringue slightly overlaps the drawn circle on the parchment paper. The excess can always be trimmed off after the meringue has baked. On the other hand, if the circles of meringue are too small, the sides of the cake will be unattractively uneven.

It is better to bake the three meringues on separate shelves. If the oven has only two shelves, place two baking sheets, slightly overlapping each other, on the same shelf. If this is done, it will be necessary to rotate the baking sheets once or twice while the meringues are baking in order to assure that they are uniformly baked.

Baked meringues may be prepared a day or two in advance of assembling the dacquoise. Store baked meringues in a closed container in a dry place at room temperature.

Baked meringues are brittle: Handle with care. A sharp serrated knife is the best tool to use to trim the meringues so they will fit exactly onto a 9-inch cake plate. Press the meringue layers down gently on the icing when assembling the dacquoise to avoid noticeable holes between the layers when sliced.

If a table-model electric mixer is not available, this recipe may also be prepared using a hand-held mixer (mixing time may increase slightly).

After assembly, you may keep this cake in the refrigerator for 24 hours before serving. Do not forget to hold the slices at room temperature for 10 to 15 minutes before serving.

Trim each meringue with a serrated knife so that it will fit perfectly on a 9-inch cake circle. Place a dab of dark chocolate icing in the center of a cardboard cake circle. Place a meringue, top side up, on the circle. Gently press down on the meringue so that the icing will hold it in place. Pipe a 1/2-inch-wide ring of dark chocolate icing along the outside edge of the meringue. Pipe a similar ring of white chocolate icing alongside the dark chocolate ring. Continue to pipe out alternating rings of icing until the surface of the meringue is covered.

Place a second meringue, top side up, onto the rings of icing and gently press down on the meringue; repeat the procedure of piping out alternate rings of icing until the second meringue is covered with icing.

Place the third meringue, bottom side up, onto the rings of icing, once again gently pressing down on the meringue. Using a cake spatula, spread 1 cup of the reserved dark chocolate icing in a smooth, even layer over the sides of the dacquoise. Put the dacquoise in the freezer for 20 minutes or in the refrigerator for 40 minutes.

Place the well-chilled dacquoise on a baking sheet, and pour the ganache on top. Use a cake spatula to spread the ganache evenly and smoothly over the top and sides of the dacquoise. Remove the dacquoise from the baking sheet and freeze for 10 minutes or refrigerate for 20 minutes.

Fill a pastry bag fitted with a medium-sized star tip with the remaining 1 cup dark chocolate icing. Fill another pastry bag fitted with a medium-sized star tip with the 2 cups reserved white chocolate icing. Pipe a circle of white chocolate stars (each star touching the other) along the outside edge of the top of the dacquoise. Pipe a similar circle of dark chocolate stars alongside the white chocolate stars. Finally, pipe another circle of white chocolate stars alongside the dark chocolate stars. Refrigerate the dacquoise for 4 hours before cutting and serving.

The dacquoise should not be cut unless it is very cold. If the 4 hours of refrigeration are not sufficient to chill the dacquoise properly, place in the freezer for an additional 30 minutes. Cut the dacquoise with a serrated slicer, heating the blade of the slicer under hot running water before making each slice. Allow the sliced dacquoise to come to room temperature for 10 to 15 minutes before serving.

# DEATH BY CHOCOLATE

SERVES 12

## EQUIPMENT

*Measuring cup, measuring spoons, sifter, 9-inch cardboard cake circle, parchment paper, 2 baking sheets, electric mixer with balloon whip, rubber spatula, pastry bag, double boiler, film wrap, 4 stainless steel bowls (1 large), 2 whisks, 9- by 1¹/₂-inch cake pan, 12-inch serrated slicer, 2¹/₂-quart saucepan, 9- by 3-inch springform pan, ladle, serrated knife, large metal spoon, cake spatula, large star tip*

Preheat the oven to 225 degrees Fahrenheit.

Using a 9-inch cake circle as a guide, trace a circle with a pencil on a sheet of parchment paper cut to fit a baking sheet. Turn the paper over and, with trace mark down, place on a baking sheet.

To prepare the cocoa meringue, place 4 egg whites, the cream of tartar, and salt in the bowl of an electric mixer fitted with a balloon whip. Whisk on high until soft peaks form, about 45 to 50 seconds. Gradually add 1 cup sugar while continuing to whisk on high. Whisk until stiff, about 1¹/₂ minutes. Remove the bowl from the mixer and use a rubber spatula to fold in and thoroughly combine the remaining ¹/₄ cup sugar, 2 tablespoons cocoa, and the cornstarch. Fill a pastry bag (with no tip) with the cocoa meringue. Fill the traced parchment circle with meringue: start in the center and pipe a ³/₄-inch-wide spiral towards the outside of the circle.

Place the meringue in the preheated oven and bake for 15 minutes. Lower the oven temperature to 200 degrees Fahrenheit and bake for 2 hours and 45 minutes. Remove from the oven and allow to cool for 45 minutes before handling. Raise the oven temperature to 325 degrees Fahrenheit.

While the meringue is baking, prepare the chocolate mousse. Heat 1 inch of water in the bottom half of a double boiler over medium heat. Place 6 ounces semisweet chocolate in the top half of the double boiler (see page 151). Tightly cover the top with film wrap. Allow the chocolate to melt slowly, about 9 to 10 minutes. Remove from the heat and stir until smooth. Keep at room temperature until needed.

Place 1¹/₂ cups heavy cream in the well-chilled bowl of an electric mixer fitted with a well-chilled balloon whip (see page 151). Whisk on high until peaks form, about 1 minute. Set aside .

Whisk 3 egg whites in a large stainless steel bowl, until soft peaks form, about 3 minutes. Add 2 tablespoons sugar and continue to whisk until stiff peaks form, about 2 to 2¹/₂ minutes. Add a quarter of the whipped cream to the chocolate and whisk quickly, vigorously, and thoroughly, then add to the egg whites. Now add the remaining whipped cream. Fold all together gently but thoroughly. Refrigerate the chocolate mousse until needed.

To prepare the chocolate brownie layer, coat a 9- by 1¹/₂-inch cake pan with 1 teaspoon of butter. Flour the pan with 1 teaspoon of flour, shaking out the excess. Pour the Simply The Best Brownie batter into the prepared cake pan, spreading evenly. Place the pan in the preheated oven and bake the brownie until a toothpick inserted in the center comes out clean, about 30 minutes.

Remove the brownie from the oven and allow to cool in the pan at room temperature for 5 minutes. Turn out onto a cake circle and refrigerate for 15 to 20 minutes. Remove the brownie from the refrigerator and cut in half horizontally. Keep the brownie at room temperature until needed.

To prepare the ganache, heat 1¹/₂ cups heavy cream and 3 tablespoons butter in a 2¹/₂-quart saucepan over medium-high heat. Bring to a boil. Place 22 ounces of semisweet chocolate in a

## COCOA MERINGUE

- 4 egg whites
- ¹/₈ teaspoon cream of tartar
- ¹/₈ teaspoon salt
- 1¹/₄ cups granulated sugar
- 2 tablespoons unsweetened cocoa, sifted
- 1 tablespoon cornstarch

## CHOCOLATE MOUSSE

- 6 ounces semisweet chocolate, broken into ¹/₂-ounce pieces
- 1¹/₂ cups heavy cream
- 3 egg whites
- 2 tablespoons granulated sugar

## CHOCOLATE BROWNIE LAYER

- 1 teaspoon unsalted butter
- 1 teaspoon all-purpose flour
- Simply The Best Chocolate Brownie (see page 42), uncooked

## CHOCOLATE GANACHE

- 1¹/₂ cups heavy cream
- 3 tablespoons unsalted butter
- 22 ounces semisweet chocolate, broken into ¹/₂-ounce pieces

## MOCHA MOUSSE

- 14 ounces semisweet chocolate, broken into ¹/₂-ounce pieces
- 4 ounces unsweetened chocolate, broken into ¹/₂-ounce pieces
- ¹/₂ cup water
- 4 tablespoons instant coffee
- 2 tablespoons cocoa, sifted
- 5 egg whites
- 2 tablespoons granulated sugar
- ³/₄ cup heavy cream

## MOCHA RUM SAUCE

Mocha Rum Sauce (see page 18)

stainless steel bowl. Pour the boiling cream over the chocolate and allow to stand for 5 minutes. Stir until smooth. Keep at room temperature until needed.

To prepare the mocha mousse, heat 1 inch of water in the bottom half of the double boiler over medium-high heat. Place 14 ounces semisweet chocolate, 4 ounces unsweetened chocolate, the water, instant coffee, and 2 tablespoons cocoa in the top half of the double boiler. Tightly cover the top with film wrap. Heat for 6 to 7 minutes, remove the film wrap, and stir the mixture until smooth. Keep at room temperature until needed.

Place 5 egg whites in the bowl of an electric mixer fitted with a balloon whip. Whisk on high until soft peaks form, about 1 minute. Continue to whisk while gradually adding 2 tablespoons sugar. Whisk until stiff, about 30 seconds.

Whip ³/₄ cup heavy cream in a well-chilled stainless steel bowl until stiff. Fold ¹/₄ of the egg whites into the melted chocolate mixture, then fold in the whipped cream. Now fold in the remaining egg whites. Keep the mocha mousse at room temperature.

To assemble Death By Chocolate, place a closed 9- by 3-inch springform pan on a baking sheet. Set the top half of the chocolate brownie inside the pan, top side up. Ladle 1¹/₂ cups of ganache into the pan over the chocolate brownie. Trim the cocoa meringue with a serrated knife so that it will fit tightly into the pan. Place the trimmed cocoa meringue, top side up, inside the pan on top of the ganache, pressing down gently on the cocoa meringue to eliminate air pockets.

Spoon the mocha mousse on top of the cocoa meringue, spreading evenly. Place the remaining chocolate brownie half, bottom side up, on top of the mocha mousse. Chill the cake in the freezer for 30 minutes or refrigerate for 1 hour.

Remove the cake from the freezer and cut around the edges to release from the springform pan. Pour the remaining ganache over the cake and use a cake spatula to spread the ganache evenly over the top and sides of the cake. Refrigerate the cake for 10 to 15 minutes to set the ganache.

Fill a pastry bag fitted with a large star tip with the chocolate mousse. Pipe a circle of stars (each touching the other) along the outside edge of the top of the cake. Continue to pipe out circles of stars until the top of the cake is covered. Refrigerate the Death By Chocolate for at least 4 hours, and preferably 12 hours, before cutting and serving.

Prepare the Mocha Rum Sauce (the sauce can be prepared just prior to service or several hours in advance). To serve, cut the Death By Chocolate into the desired number of servings. Heat the blade of a serrated slicer under hot running water before slicing into the cake. Repeat this procedure after cutting each slice. Before placing the cake slice on the 10-inch diameter plates, flood the base of each plate with 3 to 4 tablespoons Mocha Rum Sauce, then place a piece of Death By Chocolate in the center of each plate. Serve immediately.

*It is best to start work on this cake very early in the day if it is to be served that evening. Death By Chocolate may be held for 2 to 3 days under refrigeration, but it is at its best served within 24 hours of completion. The preparation of all the chocolate components for this cake might seem overwhelming, but if the production is spread out over a period of 3 days it is manageable. DAY 1: Prepare the chocolate brownie, and keep refrigerated until the cake assembly. DAY 2: Bake the cocoa meringue, and store in a dry place at room temperature (between 68 and 78 degrees Fahrenheit). Prepare the Mocha Rum Sauce, refrigerate until 2 hours before service, then bring to room temperature. DAY 3: Prepare the chocolate mousse (this mousse must be refrigerated for a minimum of 2 hours before assembling the cake), mocha mousse, and ganache. Assemble the cake.*

*Be certain that the meringue completely fills the traced circle. If the meringue is not large enough, the sides of the cake will be uneven. Do not be concerned if the meringue slightly overlaps the circle; any excess can be trimmed off after the meringue has been baked.*

*Baked meringues are very brittle: Handle with care. Use a very sharp serrated knife to trim the meringue; otherwise, the meringue will break apart.*

*If the ganache solidifies, place the bowl with the ganache in a pan of hot water and stir until the texture is correct for pouring.*

*Use several toothpicks inserted in the sides of the chocolate brownie as guides to accurately halve the brownie horizontally.*

*If you must have the bad news, I have saved it for last. Each slice of Death By Chocolate contains 1,354 calories.*

# THE "BIG DIG"

MAKES 6 INDIVIDUAL SERVINGS

## CHOCOLATE BLACKTOP CAKE

- 1/4 pound unsalted butter, cut into 1/4-ounce pieces, plus 2 teaspoons, melted
- 1 cup all-purpose flour
- 1 teaspoon baking powder
- 1/4 teaspoon salt
- 1 cup granulated sugar
- 4 eggs
- 8 ounces semisweet chocolate, coarsely chopped and melted (see page 150)

## TRIPLE CHOCOLATE BARRIER

- 6 ounces semisweet chocolate, coarsely chopped
- 2 ounces milk chocolate, coarsely chopped
- 2 ounces white chocolate, coarsely chopped

## DOUBLE CHOCOLATE PUDDING

- 10 ounces semisweet chocolate, coarsely chopped
- 2 cups half-and-half
- 1/3 cup granulated sugar
- 2 1/2 tablespoons corn starch
- 2 tablespoons water
- 6 ounces bittersweet chocolate, finely chopped

## WHIPPED CREAM TOPPER

- 1 1/2 cups heavy cream

### MAKE THE CHOCOLATE BLACKTOP CAKE

Preheat the oven to 325 degrees Fahrenheit. Lightly coat the insides of a 9- x 13- x 2-inch non-stick rectangular baking pan with some of the 2 teaspoons of melted butter. Line the bottom of the pan with parchment paper (or wax paper), then lightly coat the paper with more melted butter. Set aside.

In a sifter, combine the flour, baking powder, salt. Sift onto a large piece of parchment (or wax) paper and set aside until needed.

Place 1 cup sugar and 1/4 pound butter in the bowl of an electric mixer fitted with a paddle. Mix on low for 1 minute; then beat on medium for 2 minutes, until soft. Use a rubber spatula to scrape down the sides of the bowl. Add the eggs, one at a time, beating on medium for 30 seconds after each addition, and scraping down the sides of the bowl and the paddle once all the eggs have been incorporated. Now beat on medium for 1 more minute. Add 8 ounces melted semisweet chocolate and mix on medium for 1 minute, until incorporated. Scrape down the sides of the bowl and the paddle. Operate the mixer on low while gradually adding the sifted dry ingredients; mix until incorporated, about 45 seconds. Remove the bowl from the mixer and use a rubber spatula to finish mixing the ingredients until thoroughly combined. (This cake batter has the appearance of milk chocolate pudding; as much as you would like to, don't taste it. Because of the raw eggs in the batter, it may not be healthful to taste until the batter is baked.)

Transfer the cake batter into the prepared pan, spreading evenly to the edges (an offset spatula would work best). Bake the cake on the center rack of the preheated oven until a toothpick inserted into the center of the cake comes out clean, about 32 minutes. Remove the cake from the oven and cool in the pan at room temperature for 15 minutes. Invert the cake onto a clean, dry cutting board. Peel the paper away from the bottom of the cake. Use a 3 1/4-inch biscuit cutter to cut the cake into six 3 1/4-inch cake circles. As you will certainly notice and probably enjoy, there are lots of "scraps" of cake left over. Need I say more? Place the individual cake circles, baked side up, on a parchment (or wax) paper-lined baking sheet and refrigerate for 30 minutes before proceeding.

### MAKE THE TRIPLE CHOCOLATE BARRIER

Place six 12- x 4 1/2-inch strips of parchment paper on a clean, dry, and flat work surface. Making the barriers can get messy. I recommend plenty of counter space for this step. (After all, you are now in the construction phase of the "Big Dig," so make way.)

Separately melt 6 ounces chopped semisweet chocolate, the chopped milk chocolate, and the chopped white chocolate (see page 150). Keep in mind that, for this recipe, the chocolate needs to be kept fluid after being melted, so don't allow yourself to be distracted before moving on to the next step; otherwise, the chocolate will get too firm for piping.

Place the melted white chocolate and the melted milk chocolate in separate small Ziploc® bags. Snip about 1/8 inch of the tip from a bottom corner of each bag. Artfully pipe a looping circular pattern of white chocolate over the bottom 2/3 of each of the strips of parchment paper (the top 1/3 of the paper, lengthwise, should be free of chocolate). Then repeat with a like amount of milk chocolate. Now use a tablespoon to distribute a like amount of the melted bittersweet chocolate

over the white and milk chocolate, and across as much as possible of the bottom $2/3$ of each strip of the parchment paper. Use a small offset spatula to spread the melted chocolates evenly across each strip of paper to the short edges and across the entire bottom $2/3$, leaving approximately $1/3$ of each strip, lengthwise, not covered with the chocolate (the chocolate will now appear marbleized on the paper side, with dark chocolate on the top).

Remove the cold cakes (the cakes need to be cold in order for the chocolate barriers to adhere to them in the next step) from the refrigerator. One at a time, wrap a strip of chocolate paper (with the chocolate-smeared bottom edge of the paper encircling the bottom edge of the cake) around the cake, creating a cylinder effect. The chocolate on the paper will create a seal to hold the paper in place. It's a good idea to leave a small piece of the short edge of the paper sticking out a bit to facilitate the removal of the paper after the cylinders have been refrigerated. Repeat this process with the remaining 5 cakes. Incidentally, it's okay if your cylinders are not perfect; they actually look great even when a bit lopsided. Place the cylinders onto a baking sheet and refrigerate for at least 30 minutes.

### PREPARE THE DOUBLE CHOCOLATE PUDDING

Melt 10 ounces chopped semisweet chocolate in the top half of a double boiler or in a large glass bowl in a microwave oven (see pages 150-152), and stir until smooth. If the chocolate was melted utilizing the double-boiler method, transfer the chocolate to a large glass bowl. Set aside until needed.

Heat the half-and-half and $1/3$ cup granulated sugar in a medium saucepan over medium heat, stirring to dissolve the sugar. Bring to a boil, then reduce to a simmer. As soon as the cream is simmering, whisk together the cornstarch and water in a small bowl, until the cornstarch is dissolved and the mixture is smooth. Gradually drizzle the cornstarch-and-water mixture into the simmering cream mixture, stirring with a whisk until the cream has slightly thickened, about 20 seconds.

Reduce the heat to low and simmer for 2 minutes, stirring constantly with a rubber spatula. (Stirring with a rubber spatula will help prevent the thickened cream from sticking to the bottom of the saucepan and scorching.) Pour the thickened cream into the bowl of melted chocolate and whisk vigorously until thoroughly combined. Transfer the chocolate pudding to a baking sheet with sides, spreading evenly toward the inside edges; refrigerate until the pudding is cold, about 30 minutes. Remove the pudding from the refrigerator and transfer to the bowl of an electric mixer fitted with a balloon whip. Operate the mixer on medium for 1 minute to aerate the pudding. Add 4 ounces chopped bittersweet chocolate (the remaining 2 ounces will be utilized to garnish the tops of the "Big Digs") and whisk for 10 seconds on low to incorporate. Remove the bowl from the mixer. Use a rubber spatula to finish mixing the ingredients until thoroughly combined. Refrigerate until needed.

### MAKE THE WHIPPED CREAM TOPPER

Place the heavy cream in the bowl of an electric mixer fitted with a balloon whip. Whisk on medium-high for about 1 minute and 15 seconds, then whisk on medium-high until soft peaks form, about 1 minute. Refrigerate until needed.

## Assemble The "Big Digs"

Transfer the pudding and whipped cream to separate pastry bags fitted with large straight tips (#9 with a ³/₄-inch opening). Remove the cylinders from the refrigerator. Carefully remove the paper from each cylinder. Pipe an even layer of slightly more than ¹/₂ cup of the pudding on top of the cakes in each chocolate cylinder. Top the pudding in each cylinder with an even layer of about ¹/₂ cup of the Whipped Cream Topper. Sprinkle 2 ounces of chopped bittersweet chocolate, about 1 slightly heaping tablespoon for each serving, over the whipped cream in each cylinder. Refrigerate the "Big Digs" for 30 minutes before excavating.

## To Serve

Drizzle one or two, or even three, of your favorite fruit purées onto each serving plate. Place a "Big Dig" onto each plate. Serve immediately. Be certain to provide a long-handled spoon with each "Big Dig." There's a whole lot of digging ahead!

*A*t Ganache Hill, the conceptual phase of recipe creation occurs in the first year of a 3-year process of producing a cookbook. The "Big Dig" was an unlikely inspiration from two of Boston's omnipresent icons: Boston Cream Pie and construction. Like Boston's roads and its pie, the "Big Dig" layers different textures that combine to form a masterpiece, but crumble under the force of man and machine (or spoon).

Although I call for both semisweet and bittersweet chocolate in the Double Chocolate Pudding, you may use just semisweet chocolate without critically altering the recipe, but then it will simply be chocolate pudding rather than "double chocolate."

The "Big Dig" may be prepared over 2 days. DAY 1: Bake the Chocolate Blacktop Cake. After the baked cake has cooled for 15 minutes, cut it into six 3¹/₄-inch cake circles as described in the recipe. Refrigerate the cake circles until needed. Prepare the Double Chocolate Pudding as directed, then refrigerate until needed. DAY 2: Make the Triple Chocolate Barriers, then affix them to the cake circles. Refrigerate for 30 minutes. Prepare the Whipped Cream Topper. Assemble as directed in the recipe, then refrigerate for 30 minutes before serving.

As you might expect, a creamy but assertive Guinness Stout is perfect with the "Big Dig."

# Cowboy Syd's Sextuple Truffle Tart
## With Bittersweet Chocolate Whiskey Cream
## and Sensuously Sensational
## Chocolate Espresso Ice Cream

SERVES 8

### Sensuously Sensational Chocolate Espresso Ice Cream

- 3 ounces unsweetened chocolate, coarsely chopped
- 3/4 cup heavy cream
- 1 cup strong (robustly flavored) coffee, hot
- 3/4 cup (6 ounces) tightly packed light brown sugar
- 1/4 teaspoon salt

### "Sweetie Pie" Tart Shell Dough

- 1 1/4 cups all-purpose flour
- 1/4 cup almonds, toasted
- 1/4 teaspoon salt
- 3 ounces unsalted butter, cut into 1/2-ounce pieces
- 1/3 cup granulated sugar
- 2 egg yolks
- 1 tablespoon sour cream

### Sextuple Truffle Filling

- 2 ounces unsweetened chocolate, coarsely chopped
- 1 ounce semisweet chocolate, coarsely chopped
- 1/2 cup heavy cream
- 2 ounces unsalted butter, cut into 1/2-ounce pieces
- 2 eggs
- 1/2 cup granulated sugar
- 1 tablespoon whiskey (Cowboy Syd says "name your poison")

### Ultra-Sexy Ganache

- 4 ounces semisweet chocolate, coarsely chopped
- 1/2 cup heavy cream

### Prepare the Sensuously Sensational Chocolate Espresso Ice Cream

Place 3 ounces chopped, unsweetened chocolate in a medium stainless steel bowl. Heat 3/4 cup heavy cream in a small saucepan over medium heat. Bring to a boil. Pour the boiling cream over the chopped chocolate, then stir with a whisk until smooth. Set aside.

Place the hot coffee, light brown sugar, and 1/4 teaspoon salt in a small bowl and stir gently until the sugar is dissolved. Add the coffee mixture to the chocolate-and-cream mixture, and stir to incorporate. Cool in an ice-water bath to a temperature of 40 to 45 degrees Fahrenheit.

When the mixture is cold, freeze in an ice-cream machine according to the manufacturer's instructions. Transfer the semifrozen ice cream to a 2-quart plastic container. Cover the container securely, and place in the freezer for several hours before serving.

### Make the "Sweetie Pie" Tart Shell

Preheat the oven to 350 degrees Fahrenheit.

Place the flour, toasted almonds, and 1/4 teaspoon salt in the bowl of a food processor fitted with a metal blade. Process for 1 minute until thoroughly combined and fine in texture. Set aside.

Place 3 ounces butter and 1/3 cup sugar in the bowl of an electric mixer fitted with a paddle. Mix on low for 1 minute, then beat on medium for 3 minutes until soft and light in color. Use a rubber spatula to scrape down the sides of the bowl and the paddle. Add the egg yolks, one at a time, beating on medium for 30 seconds after each addition, and scraping down the sides of the bowl once both egg yolks have been incorporated. Operate the mixer on low while gradually adding the flour mixture; mix until incorporated, about 1 minute. Add the sour cream and mix on low for 15 seconds. Remove the dough (including any that has adhered to the sides of the bowl) from the mixer and form it into a smooth, round ball. Wrap in plastic wrap, and refrigerate for 15 minutes.

Remove the dough from the refrigerator, then remove and discard the plastic wrap. Wearing a pair of disposable vinyl (or latex) gloves, evenly press half the dough into the bottom of a 9- x 2 1/2-inch leakproof, nonstick springform pan (see The Chef's Touch with this recipe for information about this innovative pan), pressing the dough firmly from the center to the edges to a thickness of about 1/4-inch. Cut the remaining dough into 4 equal pieces, then roll each piece into about a 6-inch-long log. One at a time, place a log on one side of the pan and press it into the side to within 1/4 inch of the top edge of the pan and to a thickness of about 1/4 inch. When done with all 4 logs, the sides of the pan (excluding the 1/4-inch area from the top edge) should be covered with dough. Place onto a baking sheet (makes for easier handling of the pan) on the center rack of the preheated oven; bake for 12 minutes until lightly golden brown. Remove from the oven and cool at room temperature until needed.

## ALL-MIXED-UP MILK CHOCOLATE GANACHE

6 ounces milk chocolate, coarsely chopped
1 ounce white chocolate, coarsely chopped
$^1/_2$ cup heavy cream
1 tablespoon whole milk

## CHOCOLATE WHISKEY CREAM

4 ounces bittersweet chocolate, coarsely
    chopped
1 cup heavy cream
2 tablespoons whiskey

## THE CHEF'S TOUCH

*M*y friend Sydney Meers is the chef/owner of
Cowboy Syd's in Newport News, Virginia. The
Mississippian is, however, more than a superb chef.
Sydney is an artist (several of his works adorn the walls
at Ganache Hill), gifted teacher, impenitent wild man,
and certified bachelor. This dessert (or as Sydney
describes it, "dangerous weapon") should be served with
caution because, depending on the recipient, it may
have an effect that is contrary to maintaining the
so-called state of unwedded bliss.

While prowling the baking equipment aisle at a
Crate & Barrel store, I spotted a 9- x 2$^1/_2$-inch Noblesse
Kaiser leakproof springform pan
manufactured in Germany. Immediately what caught
my eye was the trough-like ridge of the bottom insert,
which protrudes $^1/_4$ inch away from the outside of the
clamped side piece. Reading from the label that this
atypically designed pan was leakproof, I decided to add
it to our Ganache Hill pan collection. While we have
yet to have a problem with a leaky springform pan (we
always recommend placing springform pans on a baking
sheet to capture occasional drips), this pan came in
particularly handy for baking the "Sweetie Pie" Tart
Shell due to its smooth (perfectly flat), nonstick-
surfaced bottom insert. All of our other springform

*pans at Ganache Hill have a corrugated bottom insert that proved to be nettlesome when trying to remove the baked Sextuple Truffle Tart from the pan.*

*The reason I specify a stainless steel bowl for the preparation of the chocolate espresso ice cream is that steel is a much better conductor of cold than glass or plastic, so when you set up the ice bath, the subsequent cooling of the ice-cream mixture will take less time.*

*Although Sydney may take exception to the following suggestion (he may be Cowboy Syd, but Dr. Chocolate rules in this book), I will nevertheless offer that you may substitute semisweet for the bittersweet chocolate specified in the Chocolate Whiskey Cream recipe.*

*After assembly, you may keep Cowboy Syd's Sextuple Truffle Tart in the refrigerator for 2 to 3 days before serving. To avoid permeating the tart with refrigerator odors, place the tart in a large, tightly sealed plastic container.*

*This dessert may be prepared over 3 days. DAY 1: Make and freeze the chocolate espresso ice cream. Prepare and bake the tart shell. Cool the tart shell to room temperature then place in a large, tightly sealed plastic container and keep at room temperature until needed. DAY 2: Make the truffle filling. Pour the filling into the baked tart shell; bake and cool as directed in the recipe. Make the ganache and pour on top of the truffle filling in the tart shell. Refrigerate as directed. Prepare the milk chocolate ganache, then pour on top of the ganache layer in the tart shell and refrigerate as directed. DAY 3: Make the chocolate whiskey cream and prepare to rock on!*

*Wishing to enhance his roisterous image, Cowboy Syd is an advocate of serving ancient whiskey with 4 cubes of ice as an enabler with his chocolate. What "rocks" subsequently is up to you.*

### PREPARE THE SEXTUPLE TRUFFLE FILLING

Preheat the oven to 325 degrees Fahrenheit.

Place 2 ounces chopped unsweetened chocolate and 1 ounce chopped semisweet chocolate in a medium bowl. Heat $1/2$ cup heavy cream and 2 ounces butter in a small saucepan over medium heat. Bring to a boil. Pour the boiling cream mixture over the chopped chocolate, then stir with a whisk until smooth. Set aside.

Place the eggs, $1/2$ cup granulated sugar, and the whiskey in the bowl of an electric mixer fitted with a balloon whip. Whisk on high for 3 minutes, until light in color and frothy. Add the chocolate-and-cream mixture and whisk on medium to incorporate, about 20 to 25 seconds. Remove the bowl from the mixer and use a rubber spatula to finish mixing the ingredients until thoroughly combined. Pour the filling into the baked tart shell and use an offset spatula (or a rubber spatula) to spread the filling to the edges. Place the pan onto a baking sheet on the center rack in the preheated oven and bake for 35 minutes, until the internal temperature of the filling reaches 160 degrees Fahrenheit. Remove the tart from the oven and cool at room temperature for 15 minutes, then place in the refrigerator for 45 minutes before making the Ultra Sexy-Ganache.

### MAKE THE ULTRA-SEXY GANACHE

Place 4 ounces chopped semisweet chocolate in a medium bowl. Heat $1/2$ cup heavy cream in a small saucepan over medium heat. Bring to a boil. Pour the boiling cream over the chopped chocolate, then stir with a whisk until smooth.

Remove the tart from the refrigerator. Pour the ganache on top of the filling and use an offset spatula (or a rubber spatula) to spread the ganache to the edges. Refrigerate for at least 1 hour, until the ganache is firm to the touch.

### MAKE THE ALL-MIXED-UP MILK CHOCOLATE GANACHE

Place 6 ounces chopped milk chocolate and 1 ounce chopped white chocolate in a medium bowl. Heat $1/2$ cup heavy cream and the milk in a small saucepan over medium heat. Bring to a boil. Pour the boiling cream over the chopped chocolate, then stir with a whisk until smooth. Pour the ganache onto a baking sheet with sides, spreading it evenly. Refrigerate for 10 minutes until cold to the touch. Transfer the milk chocolate ganache onto the firm layer of Ultra-Sexy Ganache, using an offset spatula (or a rubber spatula) to spread it evenly to the edges. Refrigerate the tart for at least 2 hours before cutting and serving.

### PREPARE THE CHOCOLATE WHISKEY CREAM

Place 4 ounces chopped bittersweet chocolate in a medium stainless steel bowl. Heat 1 cup heavy cream and 2 tablespoons whiskey in a small saucepan over medium heat. Bring to a boil. Pour the boiling cream mixture over the chopped chocolate, then stir with a whisk until smooth. Cool in an ice-water bath to a temperature of 40 to 45 degrees Fahrenheit.

When the mixture is cold, transfer to the bowl of an electric mixer fitted with a whisk. Whisk on medium-high for 15 seconds, until thickened. Cover with plastic wrap and refrigerate until ready to serve.

### TO SERVE

Heat the blade of a serrated slicer under hot running water and wipe the blade dry before making each slice. Serve each portion of tart accompanied by 2 heaping tablespoons (about $1^1/2$ ounces) of Chocolate Whiskey Cream and a scoop or two of the chocolate espresso ice cream and, in Cowboy Syd's words, prepare to rock on!

# Chocolate Applesauce Spice Cake
# With Jacked-Up Caramel Apple Sauce

### SERVES 16

**MAKE THE QUICK APPLESAUCE**

Place the apple juice, light brown sugar, and cinnamon in a medium saucepan and stir the mixture to partially dissolve the sugar. Wash and dry 3 Red Delicious apples. One at a time, peel, core, and quarter the apples. Cut the quarters in half widthwise; then immediately place the apple sections in the saucepan with the apple juice mixture. Stir to coat the apples with the apple juice. Cover the saucepan, then bring to a boil over medium heat; lower the heat and simmer for 20 minutes until the apples are cooked through and tender.

Remove from the heat and drain the apples in a colander that has been placed over a bowl. Place the apples along with 2 tablespoons of the cooking juice (discard the remaining juice) in a food processor fitted with a metal blade; process for 30 seconds until completely puréed. This should yield 1 cup of applesauce. Set aside.

**PREPARE THE CHOCOLATE APPLESAUCE SPICE CAKE**

Preheat the oven to 350 degrees Fahrenheit.

Lightly coat the inside of a 9½- x 3¼-inch nonstick fluted tube pan using the 2 teaspoons of melted butter. Set aside.

In a sifter, combine the flour, baking powder, baking soda, allspice, nutmeg, and salt. Sift onto a large piece of parchment (or wax) paper and set aside until needed.

Place ½ pound of butter and 1¼ cups granulated sugar in the bowl of an electric mixer fitted with a paddle. Mix on low for 1 minute, then beat on medium until soft, about 2 minutes. Scrape down the sides of the bowl and the paddle. Add the eggs, one at a time, beating on medium for 30 seconds after each addition, and scraping down the sides of the bowl once the eggs have been incorporated. Now beat on medium for 30 seconds. (Admittedly, at this point, the batter is not a pretty picture; it looks a bit like a curdled custard sauce. But through the marvel of chocolate, in just a few seconds it will look quite delicious.) Add the melted semisweet chocolate and mix on medium until incorporated, about 30 seconds. Operate the mixer on low while gradually adding about half of the sifted dry ingredients, followed by ½ cup of the Quick Applesauce. Once these ingredients have been incorporated, about 15 seconds following the addition of the applesauce, gradually add the remaining sifted dry ingredients, then the remaining applesauce. Mix until incorporated, about 15 seconds after adding the last of the applesauce. Add 2 tablespoons apple brandy and the vanilla extract; mix on low for 5 seconds, then beat on medium for 15 seconds until combined. Remove the bowl from the mixer and use a rubber spatula to finish mixing the ingredients until thoroughly combined. Transfer the batter to the prepared fluted tube pan, using a rubber spatula to spread evenly.

Bake on the center rack of the preheated oven until a toothpick inserted into the center of the cake comes out clean, about 1 hour and 5 minutes. Remove the cake from the oven and cool in the pan for 15 to 20 minutes at room temperature. Invert the cake onto a cake circle (or a cake plate). Set aside.

### QUICK APPLESAUCE

- ½ cup apple juice
- 2 tablespoons (1 ounce) tightly packed light brown sugar
- 1 teaspoon ground cinnamon
- 3 Red Delicious apples

### CHOCOLATE APPLESAUCE SPICE CAKE

- ½ pound unsalted butter, cut into ½-ounce pieces, plus 2 teaspoons melted
- 2½ cups all-purpose flour
- 1 teaspoon baking powder
- 1 teaspoon baking soda
- ½ teaspoon ground allspice
- ½ teaspoon freshly grated nutmeg
- ½ teaspoon salt
- 1¼ cups granulated sugar
- 4 eggs
- 6 ounces semisweet chocolate, coarsely chopped and melted (see page 150)
- 1 cup Quick Applesauce
- 2 tablespoons apple brandy
- 1 teaspoon pure vanilla extract

### JACKED-UP CARAMEL APPLE SAUCE

- 2 cups granulated sugar
- 1 teaspoon fresh lemon juice
- ¾ cup heavy cream
- 4 tablespoons unsalted butter
- 1½ cups walnuts, toasted (see page 151) and coarsely chopped by hand with a cook's knife
- 2 medium Red Delicious apples
- ¼ cup apple brandy

## MAKE THE JACKED-UP CARAMEL APPLE SAUCE

Place 2 cups granulated sugar and the lemon juice in a large saucepan. Stir with a long-handled metal kitchen spoon to combine. (The sugar will resemble moist sand.)

Caramelize the sugar for about 10 minutes over medium-high heat, stirring constantly with the spoon to break up any lumps. The sugar will first turn clear as it liquefies, then light brown as it caramelizes. Remove the saucepan from the heat. Slowly add the cream to the bubbling hot sugar, whisking vigorously with a 12-inch-long balloon whisk until the mixture stops bubbling. (Adding the cream to the sugar creates very hot steam, so be careful to avoid a steam burn on your whisking hand.) Add 4 tablespoons butter and whisk until incorporated. Add 1 1/2 cups hand-chopped, toasted walnuts and stir to distribute.

Wash and dry 2 Red Delicious apples. One at a time, core (do not peel), quarter, and then dice the apples into 1/4-inch pieces. Immediately place the diced apples into the caramel and walnut mixture. Stir to combine. Add 1/4 cup apple brandy and stir to incorporate. The sauce may be used immediately, held warm in a double boiler for up to 1 hour, or cooled and refrigerated until needed. Warm the refrigerated sauce in a double boiler before using.

## TO SERVE

Heat the blade of a serrated slicer under hot running water and wipe the blade dry before making each slice. Place each slice onto a serving plate. Spoon 3 tablespoons of warm Jacked-Up Caramel Apple Sauce over each piece of cake. Serve immediately.

*I* have never had apples at the top of my list of chocolate and fruit affinities. It isn't because I don't enjoy the sweet crunch of a fresh apple, but rather as a personal preference I have many other fruits that I think of almost by rote when devising chocolate recipes. Pears, bananas, raspberries, figs, and more seem to elbow apples aside. But hold on, in this recipe we give apples an opportunity to share the bill with chocolate, and it is quite a show.

Red Delicious apples are sweet and crisp and maintain their shape in most situations. But even Red Delicious apples lose their shape in applesauce —- I simply chose them because I like them! Feel free to use a variety of available sweet apples for this recipe.

Captain Apple Jack apple brandy, which is distilled in Virginia, was the brandy we used in testing this recipe. Other brandies distilled from apples are available, including the estimable Calvados from France which is actually categorized as an eau-de-vie (a colorless spirit). I would not hesitate to enjoy a dram or so of Calvados, but for my pocketbook the more ordinary apple brandies will do as an ingredient for this dessert.

I recommend chopping the walnuts by hand for this recipe versus chopping in a food processor. The hand-chopped walnuts maintain a more distinct shape and hand chopping also cuts down on fragmenting the nuts into tiny shards.

After assembly, you may keep the Chocolate Applesauce Spice Cake in a tightly sealed plastic container at room temperature for 2 to 3 days before serving. I prefer not to refrigerate this cake as doing so seems to adversely affect the crumb texture of the cake.

This dessert may be prepared over 2 days. DAY 1: Make the Quick Applesauce, then prepare the Chocolate Applesauce Spice Cake. Cool the baked cake to room temperature; then place in a large, tightly sealed plastic container and keep at room temperature until needed. DAY 2: Make the Jacked-Up Caramel Apple Sauce and serve with the cake as detailed in the recipe.

Apple brandy seems to be the natural choice as the beverage to accompany this dessert. Try an ounce or two of a preferred brandy heated with a cup of apple cider for each serving. Now all you need is a snowstorm.

## CARAMEL POPCORN

1 tablespoon vegetable oil

8 cups freshly popped popcorn (Orville Redenbacher's is recommended; see The Chef's Touch)

2 cups granulated sugar

1 teaspoon fresh lemon juice

1/4 cup heavy cream

## CHOCOLATE BROWN BUTTER GANACHE

8 ounces semisweet chocolate, coarsely chopped

4 ounces unsweetened chocolate, coarsely chopped

2 ounces unsalted butter, cut into 1/2-ounce pieces

3/4 cup heavy cream

### THE CHEF'S TOUCH

*In Betty Fussell's fascinating book, The Story of Corn, she tells us that popcorn "is a truly indigenous fast-finger food." Later on in the narrative, she says that "corn defined life for native Americans." I can relate to that. Corn in the form of popcorn has been a passion for me all my life (which is fortunate, because it's the only thing my wife Connie can cook). I could happily eat popcorn everyday. But add caramel and chocolate, and I could eat it every minute.*

*Simply put, Orville Redenbacher's has the best poppability. We used 1 tablespoon of vegetable oil and 1/2 cup Orville Redenbacher's Original Gourmet® Popping Corn, and yielded about 10 cups of popped corn. On the other hand, 1/2 cup of most popcorn yields about 4 cups of popped corn.*

*The Chocolate Caramel Popcorn Crunch will stay crunchingly good in a tightly sealed plastic container at room temperature for 1 to 2 days, or in the refrigerator for 4 to 5 days.*

*Native Americans believed that corn housed an angry demon that exploded when exposed to heat. Perhaps a late-night snifter of corn-based whiskey with the Chocolate Caramel Popcorn Crunch would hold those demons at bay.*

# CHOCOLATE CARAMEL POPCORN CRUNCH

YIELDS ALMOST 2 POUNDS

**MAKE THE CARAMEL POPCORN**

Lightly coat the insides of a 9- x 13- x 2-inch nonstick rectangular baking pan with some of the vegetable oil. Set aside. Lightly, but thoroughly, brush both sides of the blade of a rubber spatula and both sides of the flat-blade of a utility turner with the remaining oil (this will prevent the caramelized popcorn from sticking to the spatula and turner) and set aside.

Place the popcorn in an extra large bowl. Set aside.

Place the sugar and lemon juice in a large saucepan. Stir with a long-handled metal kitchen spoon to combine. (The sugar will resemble moist sand).

Caramelize the sugar for about 10 minutes over medium-high heat, stirring constantly with the spoon to break up any lumps. The sugar will first turn clear as it liquefies, then light brown as it caramelizes. Remove the saucepan from the heat. Slowly add 1/4 cup heavy cream to the bubbling hot sugar, whisking vigorously until smooth. (Adding the cream to the sugar creates very hot steam, so be careful to avoid a steam burn on your whisking hand.) Immediately pour the hot caramel over the popcorn. Use the oiled rubber spatula to combine the mixture until the popcorn is thoroughly coated with caramel. Immediately transfer the caramel-coated popcorn to the prepared pan.

Use the oiled utility turner to spread the caramel popcorn evenly in the pan, then press down on the popcorn with the turner creating as even a surface as possible (don't be timid about pressing hard). The caramel popcorn should be pressed down into the pan until it is about 1 inch thick. Set the caramel popcorn aside.

**MAKE THE CHOCOLATE BROWN BUTTER GANACHE**

Place the chopped semisweet chocolate and chopped unsweetened chocolate in a large bowl and set aside.

Heat a small nonstick sauté pan over high heat. When the pan is very hot, add the butter and brown evenly, about 45 to 60 seconds (be sure to stay with the pan, shaking it back and forth to promote even browning, or the butter will go from brown to burnt in seconds). Immediately transfer the brown butter to a small saucepan, using a rubber spatula to remove all of the butter including any brown particles adhering to the insides of the sauté pan. Add 3/4 cup heavy cream; use a hand-held whisk and stir to incorporate.

Heat the cream mixture over medium heat. Bring to a boil. Pour the boiling cream mixture over the chopped chocolates, then stir with a whisk until smooth. Pour the resulting ganache over as much of the top of the caramel popcorn as possible, then use a spatula (a small offset spatula would work best) to spread the ganache smoothly and evenly. Refrigerate for at least 1 hour before cutting and serving.

**TO SERVE**

Remove the pan of Chocolate Caramel Popcorn Crunch from the refrigerator. Using a thin-bladed paring knife, cut around the inside edges of the pan to release the hardened Chocolate Caramel Popcorn Crunch from the pan. Invert the Chocolate Caramel Popcorn Crunch onto a large sheet of parchment (or wax) paper, then turn over onto a clean, dry cutting board so the ganache-covered side is turned up. For the clean-cut look, use a sharp serrated knife to trim about 1/4 inch from each side, then cut into desired-size pieces. Serve immediately, or refrigerate until needed.

Photograph by Ron Manville

# TECHNIQUES AND EQUIPMENT

The following information on techniques and equipment provides insight on how we work with chocolate at The Trellis. By no means is this an exhaustive text on the subject; however, I feel confident that anyone who follows our recipes, utilizes these techniques, works with appropriate equipment, and, of course, uses good chocolate, will produce chocolate confections as spectacular and delicious as those prepared by our pastry chef in the wee hours of the night, year-round, at The Trellis.

## TECHNIQUES

### COOLING FOODS IN AN ICE-WATER BATH

Several of the recipes in this book note that you should "cool the mixture in an ice-water bath." The effect of cooling food in an ice-water bath is a quick and efficient lowering of temperature. Ice cream and sorbet bases need to be cooled before they are placed in an ice-cream freezer to facilitate the freezing process.

The simplest ice-water bath consists of a large stainless steel bowl partially filled with ice and water. There should be enough ice and water in the bowl so that the outside surface of the container to be cooled will be surrounded by ice and water. If the volume of the container to be cooled is larger than can be accommodated by your largest bowl, then consider using the kitchen sink.

### CHOCOLATE CURLS

Chocolate curls are one of the most effective and simplest chocolate decorations to prepare. Large, flowing, ribbonlike curls can be easily fashioned with only one inexpensive tool: a vegetable peeler. The only catch is that you must have a sizeable block of warmed chocolate. I have found that an 8-ounce block of white or dark chocolate is perfect. The chocolate block needs to be placed in a warm (not hot) area so that it will soften slightly. During the testing of the White Chocolate Cheesecake (see page 104) we placed an 8-ounce block of chocolate on a plate and positioned the plate in between the heating elements on the range top. The block was occasionally turned over so that it would not get too warm. After about 3 hours the block was of a perfect texture to fashion curls. We then used the vegetable peeler and peeled 5 ounces of elegant curls from the block. The cheesecake recipe specified 2 ounces of curls, so we placed the remaining 3 ounces in a plastic container with a lid and froze them for a later date (they will keep for several weeks). The remaining 3-ounce portion of the block was not suitable for curls; it was wrapped and saved for another recipe.

### MELTING CHOCOLATE

In part due to the popularity of this book, we continue to melt hundred of pounds of chocolate every week at The Trellis. As I reported in the original edition, at The Trellis we melt chocolate in stainless steel bowls floating on hot water in an open hot-water bath. A bathtub or a double boiler can also be employed (see page 151). But by far the most efficient and quickest method of melting small amounts of chocolate is in a microwave oven (see page 151). Place finely chopped chocolate in a glass bowl on the medium setting in the microwave for $1^{1}/_{2}$ minutes to melt 1 to 3 ounces; 2 to $2^{1}/_{2}$ minutes for 4 to 8 ounces; and $2^{1}/_{2}$ to 3 minutes for 9 to 16 ounces. After removing the chocolate from the microwave, use a rubber spatula to stir until smooth.

Whatever method you choose to melt chocolate, be sure to prevent moisture from coming in contact with the chocolate. Just a few drops of water can stiffen a few ounces of chocolate.

### TEMPERING CHOCOLATE

Tempering is a heating and cooling technique for stabilizing chocolate so that it will harden and have a high gloss as well as an extended shelf life. Virtually all manufactured chocolate has been tempered so that it can be stored at air-conditioned room temperature for several months. When store-bought chocolate is melted, it will lose its sheen, so it must be tempered again if it is to be used in candy.

At The Trellis, however, we have developed recipes and techniques to create beautiful and professional desserts, confections, ice creams, and some candies that do not require tempering.

### TOASTING AND SKINNING HAZELNUTS

Toast the hazelnuts on a baking sheet at 325 degrees Fahrenheit for 20 to 25 minutes. Remove them from the oven and immediately cover with a damp 100-percent-cotton towel. Invert another baking sheet over the first one to hold in the steam (this makes the nuts easier to skin). After 5 minutes, remove the skins from the nuts by placing small quantities inside a folded dry kitchen towel and rubbing vigorously. If skinned hazelnuts are purchased, simply toast as directed above, then allow the nuts to cool before chopping or processing.

### WHIPPING HEAVY CREAM

The most time-efficient method for whipping heavy cream is to use well-chilled equipment. Whether using an electric mixer or a hand-held whisk, it is advisable to place both the bowl and the whisking instrument (balloon whip or whisk) in the freezer for several minutes before using. If space is not available, the bowl and whisk may also be chilled by filling the bowl with ice water (also place the whisk in the ice water). Be certain to thoroughly dry the bowl and whisk before adding and whisking the cream. All of the recipes in this book calling for whipped cream have noted to whisk the cream in a well-chilled bowl; ergo, the time noted is very short in comparison to the amount of time needed to whip cream utilizing room-temperature equipment.

## EQUIPMENT

### BAKING SHEETS AND CAKE PANS

All of the baking sheets and cake pans used to test the recipes in this book were purchased at a grocery store. Many of them were manufactured by Ekco Housewares, Inc. I found the quality of the Baker's Secret brand items manufactured by Ekco to be of good quality. I especially liked the nonstick (and very easy to clean)

baking sheets and pans. One note of caution regarding baking sheets: there are different gauge steel baking sheets; consequently, the baking times and toasting times for different products can vary by several minutes.

### DOUBLE BOILER

The purpose of a double boiler is to provide slow, even heat. In this book, it is frequently recommended as the piece of equipment necessary for melting chocolate. An authentic double boiler is a double pot with a lower section that holds water and an upper section that holds the food to be heated.

As mentioned above, we use an open *bain-marie* for melting chocolate at The Trellis. I recommend, however, that in home kitchens a two-sectioned double boiler be utilized. If a traditional double boiler is not available, I recommend that you fashion your own double boiler using a medium-size stainless steel bowl (3 quart) as the top section and a 2½-quart saucepan as the bottom section. The bowl should cover the circumference of the top of the saucepan and also should not touch the recommended 1 inch of water in the bottom of the pan.

### ELECTRIC MIXER

As far as I am concerned, a table-model electric mixer is indispensable for most of the recipes in this book. Mixing by hand or using a hand-held electric mixer is suitable for a few recipes, and I have noted that in the Chef's Touch section of those recipes. Using a table-model mixer insures that your mixing, whisking, or beating will be done in the most efficient manner, as well as produce the desired volume and the most consistent and high-quality end product possible. For our recipe testing, we used a KitchenAid Model 5SS. This mixer is dependable, and although it is primarily marketed to the serious amateur, it can, in fact, be found in many professional kitchens.

### ICE-CREAM FREEZER

Through the 1980s and 1990s, and now into

the 21st century, dessert sales at The Trellis have never waned. We have noted the rise and fall of quiche, the rise and fall and rise again of the hamburger, and the vicissitudes of seafood. We do sell more or less of certain foods, depending upon yesterday's "recent findings have proven that. . . ." Happily, the popularity of ice cream continues unabated by headlines or lifestyle changes.

Our Italian batch-freezer, which produces 24 quarts of ice cream at a time, is still running strong (and more often) after 23 years. People simply love ice cream, and for those who also enjoy preparing it at home, I suggest a Gelataio ice-cream freezer manufactured by the Simac Appliance Corporation. All of the ice-cream recipes in this book were tested using a Gelataio 1600, which produces 1½ to 2 quarts of ice cream or sorbet per batch.

Pastry chef John Twichell swears by his compact Donvier ice-cream maker. John (young eligible bachelor that he is) claims it is the quickest way to a woman's heart.

### FILM WRAP

I am sold on the benefits of using film wrap (a.k.a. plastic wrap). Using film wrap helps eliminate the dissipation of flavor, the loss of moisture, the transfer of odors, and cross contamination. It's all very alimentary, my dear Watson!

### MICROWAVE OVEN

For many years I found humor in disparaging the microwave oven. I was arrogant in my disdain for what I later discovered was a great boon to the chocolatier. I capitulated at home after many years of exhortations from my wife, Connie (although at home Connie cooks vegetables, not chocolate, in the microwave). I finally relented at my test kitchen, Ganache Hill, and purchased a microwave for testing recipes for my eighth cookbook, *Death by Chocolate Cakes*. There I discovered what people had been telling me for many years: the microwave has no peers when it comes to melting small quantities of chocolate.

The settings and the wattage on microwave

ovens vary widely, so I suggest erring on the side of caution. Use a lower setting and a few seconds less than suggested until you get a feel for the power of your equipment.

## OVENS AND RANGES

Every recipe in this book was tested at least twice. The first test was done at The Trellis using a Maytag model LCNE2O electric range. The second testing was done at my home using a General Electric model JBP22. I am not making a plug for electric ranges. The point of giving this information is to illustrate the type of standard home equipment that was utilized.

It is also worth mentioning that there are temperature variables both in the oven and on the range top from one piece of equipment to the other, regardless of their energy sources. Oven calibrations seem to be the bane of many a fledgling baker. My advice is to check temperature accuracy frequently, as it is not uncommon to have 10 to 20 degree Fahrenheit differences between the setting and the actual temperature. As for the range top, one must factor in the size of the element and understand that time needed to bring a 2½-quart saucepan of water to the boil on high heat will vary depending on the size of the element that is used.

## RUBBER SPATULA

This seems to be a crossover item; that is, I believe that for some time rubber spatulas were more often found in a home kitchen than in a professional kitchen. I am not sure when rubber spatulas came on the scene in professional food service. I know we were not issued one in our knife and equipment kit when I registered for my first year at the Culinary Institute back in September 1963, and I do not remember using them at any of the operations where I worked during the 1960s and 1970s. So why do we use them now at The Trellis and why are they included in virtually every recipe in this book? The reason is that every ounce of cake batter, every precious ounce of melted chocolate, and anything else that needs to be quickly and efficiently and entirely removed from a saucepan, stainless steel bowl, or mixing bowl can be best

removed using a rubber spatula. A rubber spatula is also the tool recommended for scraping down the sides of mixing bowls, and it is the right piece of equipment to fold certain batters.

## WHISK

Whenever I look at a whisk, I see energy, movement, and grace. Perhaps I have whisked too many egg yolks into hollandaise (in my early days in New York) and quite enough eggs into sabayon (again in my earlier days), that I cannot look at a whisk without knowing that lots of movement will take place once placed in the palm of my hand. The whisk is an essential tool in many of the recipes of this book; and although I have not specified the gauge of steel nor the flexibility of the tines, it is important to know that specific whisks are needed for different tasks. Generally speaking, light and very flexible whisks are needed for very light batters and for a task such as whisking egg whites into meringue. Heavier gauge and stiffer whisks should be used for stirring and whisking thick batters, sauces, ganache, and custards.

## STAINLESS STEEL BOWL

My fondness for recommending the usage of stainless steel bowls in most of the recipes in this book does not stem from any proprietary interest in a stainless steel manufacturer. Rather, I believe it is the most sanitary and safest container you can use wherever it is specified. Although it is not essential in some of the recipes, I nevertheless recommend it across the board because of its resistance to corrosion. For me, knowing that bacteria will not be lurking in any unnoticed pores, as can occur with plastic and other metals such as aluminum, makes stainless steel bowls well worth the investment.

Unless listed otherwise, the stainless steel bowls used in the recipes in this book should be 3-quart bowls. When a large bowl is specified, I suggest a minimum size of 5 quarts.

## THERMOMETERS

*Oven Thermometer* I mention this thermometer first because I think that accurate oven temperatures are a prerequisite to successful baking. It

is rare to find an oven temperature that is perfectly in sync with the dial on the range.

*Instant-Read Test Thermometers* For my money, the Taylor brand thermometers are a solid investment for accurate results. For testing the temperature of melted chocolate, cheese cakes, chocolate pecan pie, and other recipes, I recommend a Taylor thermometer with a range of 0 to 220 degrees Fahrenheit; this is a good general-use thermometer. For deep frying, I suggest the Taylor bi-therm thermometer with a range from 50 to 550 degrees Fahrenheit.

*Candy Thermometer* A good inexpensive candy thermometer is manufactured by Ekco Housewares, Inc. It has a range of temperatures in 5-degree increments. This thermometer can be found in many grocery stores and is quite inexpensive.

# BIBLIOGRAPHY

Amendola, Joseph. *The Bakers Manual for Quantity Baking and Pastry Making*. New York: Ahrens Publishing Company, Inc., 1960.

Asquith, Pamella. *Truffles and Other Chocolate Confections*. New York: Holt, Rinehart and Winston, 1984.

Beranchon, Maurice and Jean-Jacques. *A Passion for Chocolate*. New York: William Morrow and Company, Inc., 1989.

Beranbaum, Rose Levy. *Rose's Christmas Cookies*. New York: William Morrow and Company, Inc., 1990.

Beranbaum, Rose Levy. *The Cake Bible*. New York: William Morrow and Company, Inc., 1988.

Bilheux, Roland, and Alain Escoffier. *Petit Fours, Chocolate, Frozen Desserts, and Sugar Work*. New York: Van Nostrand Reinhold, 1988.

Brody, Lora. *Growing Up on the Chocolate Diet—A Memoir with Recipes*. New York: Henry Holt and Company, 1986.

Goodbody, Mary. *Glorious Chocolate—The Ultimate Chocolate Cookbook*. New York: Simon and Schuster, 1989.

Heatter, Maida. *Maida Heatter's Book of Great Chocolate Desserts*. New York: Alfred A. Knopf, 1980.

Lenotre, Gaston. *Lenotre's Desserts and Pastries*. New York: Barron's, 1977.

Levy, Faye. *Chocolate Sensations*. Tuscon, Arizona: HP Books, 1986.

Medrich, Alice. *Cocolat—Extraordinary Chocolate Desserts*. New York: Warner Books, 1990.

Mimifie, Bernard W. *Chocolate, Cocoa, and Confectionary—Science and Technology*. New York: Van Nostrand Reinhold, 1989.

Morton, Marcia and Frederic. *Chocolate—The Illustrative History*. New York: Crown Publishers, 1986.

Olney, Judith. *The Joy of Chocolate*. New York: Barron's Woodbury, 1982.

Robbins, Carol T., and Herbert Wolff. *The Very Best Ice Cream and Where to Find it*. New York: Warner Books, 1985.

Smith, Beverly Sutherland. *The Book of Chocolates and Petit Fours*. Los Angeles: HP Books, 1986.

# SOURCES

*Mocha Java blend coffee*

FIRST COLONY COFFEE & TEA COMPANY
P.O. Box 11005
Norfolk, Virginia 23517
www.firstcolonycoffee.com

*Unsalted Virginia peanuts*

PEANUT SHOP OF WILLIAMSBURG
P.O. Box GN
Williamsburg, Virginia 23187
www.thepeanutshop.com

*General baking equipment and ingredients*

DEAN & DELUCA
560 Broadway
New York, New York 10012
www.deandeluca.com

*Instant-read test thermometers*

WILLIAMS SONOMA
"the place for cooks"
at a mall near you
www.williams-sonoma.com

All the Chocolate News That's Fit to Print, *published bimonthly*

CHOCOLATIER MAGAZINE
45 West 34th Street
New York, New York 10001

*Outrageously chocolaty cookies*

DESSERTS TO DIE FOR
403 Duke of Gloucester Street
Williamsburg, Virginia 23185
www.dessertstodiefor.com

# ABOUT THE AUTHOR

## MARCEL DESAULNIERS

Perhaps it is fitting that Marcel, who as a young boy wished to be a mortician, grew up to write *Death By Chocolate*. He recognized his culinary calling at age 15, when he filled in as short-order cook at the restaurant where he washed dishes on weekends. Henceforth preferring kitchens to funeral parlors, he eventually went to the Culinary Institute of America, from which he graduated in 1965.

After working in New York City at The Colony Club and the Hotel Pierre, Marcel moved to Virginia and worked for the Colonial Williamsburg Foundation from 1970 to 1974. For the next six years, he co-owned a food brokerage. Then in 1980, Marcel returned to his beloved kitchen, when he opened The Trellis restaurant, along with partner John Curtis.

Since then, Marcel and The Trellis have received numerous accolades and awards, including *Food and Wine* magazine's honor roll of American chefs, and *Restaurants and Institutions* magazine's coveted Ivy Award.

In 1988, Marcel's first cookbook, *The Trellis Cookbook*, was published by Weidenfeld & Nicolson.

The James Beard Foundation conferred on Marcel the Best Chef: Mid-Atlantic States Award in 1993, and in 1999, the Outstanding Pastry Chef in America Award

# ABOUT THE PASTRY CHEFS

## KELLY BAILEY
### (1995 - PRESENT)

A 1994 graduate of the Culinary Institute of America, Kelly Bailey has maintained the sweet perfection of her predecessors. Her outstanding pastry skills helped propel chocolate decadence at The Trellis into the twenty-first century.

## JOHN TWICHELL
### (1988 - 1994)

Like his predecessor, John Twichell began at The Trellis in the pantry and progressed to several stations in the kitchen.

A 1986 graduate of the Culinary Institute of America, "Twich" found baking and pastry making his preferred endeavor — citing the early morning hours and the creative freedom as prime benefits.

Becoming pastry chef in 1988 at the age of 22, Twich developed dozens of different ice cream and dessert recipes. He served as the chief recipe tester for this book.

## ANDREW O'CONNELL
### (1983 - 1987)

Andrew O'Connell was born into the restaurant business. The son of a well-known Williamsburg restaurateur, he worked odd jobs at a variety of local eateries before joining The Trellis staff in 1980, at the age of 19.

His first job was in The Trellis's pantry making sandwiches and salads for lunch. Andrew's endless energy and desire to learn propelled him to the position of lead sauté. He was, however, entranced by large bowls of melting chocolate and lured into pastry production, in time to succeed Don Mack in 1983.

## DONALD MACK
### (1981 - 1982)

Don Mack was the originator of The Trellis's wildly popular Death By Chocolate dessert.

Don's first job at The Trellis was as a rounds cook, but he clearly found his niche when he shifted to the nocturnal pastry department. Don is now an instructor in food service technology at Puget Sound Community College in Olympia, Washington.

We gratefully acknowledge the assistance of the following manufacturers and merchants in providing us with the props and accessories used in this book.

ABC   ABC CARPET & HOME
    888 Broadway
    New York, NY 10003

D   DERUTA OF ITALY
    225 Fifth Avenue
    New York, NY 10010

FF   FITZ & FLOYD, INC.
    225 Fifth Avenue
    New York, NY 10010

JT   JABARA/TABLESCENES
    70 West 40th Street
    New York, NY 10018

LJJ   LALIQUE/JACQUES
    JUGEAT, INC.
    225 Fifth Avenue
    New York, NY 10010

MC   MARK CROSS
    645 Fifth Avenue
    New York, NY 10022

M   MIKASA
    28 West 23rd Street
    New York, NY 10011

MR   MILLER ROGASKA INC.
    225 Fifth Avenue
    New York, NY 10010

PLG   PHYLLIS LUCAS GALLERY
    981 Second Avenue
    New York, NY 10022

P   PLATYPUS
    126 Spring Street
    New York, NY 10012

PB   POTTERY BARN
    700 Broadway
    New York, NY 10003

R   ROSENTHAL
    41 Madison Avenue
    New York, NY 10010

S   SASAKI
    41 Madison Avenue
    New York, NY 10010

LS   THE L S COLLECTION
    765 Madison Avenue
    New York, NY 10021

WS   WILLIAMS-SONOMA
    20 East 60th Street
    New York, NY 10022

WGG   WOLFMAN GOLD & GOOD
    COMPANY
    116 Greene Street
    New York, NY 10012

Z   ZONA
    97 Greene STreet
    New York, NY 10012

**22:** plate–M, napkin–J;
**25:** platter–Z;
**26:** glasses–LJJ;
**29:** plate & bowl–PB;
**30:** plate & leaf-handled glass bowls–LJJ;
**31:** box–Zona;
**33:** cup & plates–R;
**34:** plate–FF;
**35:** champagne flute–WGG;
**36:** plates–ABC;
**39:** plates–Z, vase–M;
**40:** marble chess & tic-tac-toe boards–LS;
**43:** silver tray–LS;
**44:** lace doily–JT;
**45:** glass bowl–LJJ;
**48:** plates & candlestick–FF, flatware–P;
**50:** spoon–P;
**51:** plate and bowl–PB;
**54:** plate–P, flatware–S;
**57:** gold-and-glass banana–D, double-stemmed glass–R;
**58:** plate–P;
**60:** plate–PB, glass–D, clay relief–ABC;
**61:** plate and napkin–P;
**62:** footed cake plate–M, cake server–LS;
**65:** plate–LJJ;
**69:** glass pear and cordial glass–LJJ, serving utensil–M, original pear etching–PLG, plate–D;
**71:** dinnerware–M;
**73:** silver bowls–P; spoon–LS;
**75:** plate and rose-colored tablecloth–ABC, vase–LJJ, floral tablecloth–JT;
**76:** plates–WGG;
**79:** cup and saucer–R, spoon–WGG;
**81:** plates–WGG, fork–M;
**83:** stemmed glass–LJJ;
**84:** champagne flute–MR, plate–D/WGG,
**87:** star and moon napkin rings–LS, gold tray–Z;
**89:** stemmed glass–LS;
**91:** plates–Z;
**96:** plate–M;
**100:** plate and tea service–R, napkin–LS;
**103:** plate–FF;
**105:** plate–M, tea set and flatware–R;
**109:** plate–FF;
**110:** stemware–M;
**114:** plate–Z;
**117:** plate–FF;
**124:** plates–D/WGG;
**125:** desk set–MC, stemmed glass–D, pen–Z, plates–FF;
**129:** plates–FF; napkin–LS, champagne flute–MR;
**130:** goblet–WGG;
**132:** plate–LJJ, serving utensil and napkins–LS;
**136:** plate and glass–LJJ.